SCHOOL DISCIPLINE

School Discipline

A SOCIALLY LITERATE SOLUTION

Alfred S. Alschuler

McGRAW-HILL BOOK COMPANY

New York St. Louis San Francisco
Auckland Bogotá Hamburg Johannesburg London Madrid
Mexico Montreal New Delhi Panama Paris São Paulo
Singapore Sydney Tokyo Toronto

Thomas H. Quinn, Michael Hennelly, and Karen Seriguchi were the editors of
this book. Christopher Simon was the designer. Sally Fliess supervised the
production. This book was set in Times Roman by Haddon Craftsman, Inc. and
was printed and bound by R. R. Donnelley and Sons.

Library of Congress Cataloging in Publication Data

Alschuler, Alfred S
  School discipline.

  Bibliography: p.
  1. School discipline. 2. Freire, Paulo 3. Education—Philosophy. I. Title.
LB3012.A47   371.5   79–26621
ISBN 0–001127–3

1 2 3 4 5 6 7 8 9 R R D R R D 8 0 6 5 4 3 2 1 0

For Lisa, Britt and Alfie
whose capacity to love and learn
inspired this book

Contents

Preface   ix

Part I   SOCIALLY LITERATE GOALS

Chapter **1**   SCHOOLS IN WHICH IT IS EASIER TO LOVE   3

Classroom discipline in the Ecuadorian mountains
Freire's philosophy of education
Social literacy

Chapter **2**   LIBERATING PEOPLE FROM CONFLICT   23

Naming the central conflict: the discipline problem
Analyzing the problem: war games
Resolving conflicts through social literacy

Chapter **3**   REBELLION OR PEACE IN OUR NATION'S
SCHOOLS   47

Waging war
Winning peace

Part II   SOCIALLY LITERATE METHODS

Chapter **4**   RESOLVING DISCIPLINE CONFLICTS THROUGH
DIALOGUE   63

Anti-dialogue
Dialogue
Learning how to resolve discipline conflicts

Chapter **5**   SPEAKING TRUE WORDS ABOUT CENTRAL CON-
FLICTS   71

True words
Central conflicts
Speaking about central conflicts and true words

Chapter **6**   RAISING CONSCIOUSNESS   83

Developing consciousness of oppression
Consciousness in context
Consciousness-raising exercises

Chapter **7**   CREATING GUIDES FOR SURVIVAL AND LIBERA-
TION   97

Chapter **8**   THE NUCLEAR PROBLEM-SOLVING PROCESS   107

The process
Evaluating Socially Literate problem solving
Reporting Socially Literate solutions

Chapter **9**   MAINSTREAMING AND MINIMUM COMPETEN-
CIES   121

Chapter **10**   CONQUERING BURN OUT, BATTLE FATIGUE,
AND FRENZY   131

Naming problematic patterns of stress
Finding the systemic causes
Planning the battle against stress

Chapter **11**   PROBLEM SOLVING IN THE CLASSROOM   147

The steps and the results
Problem-posing education

Chapter **12**   PROBLEM SOLVING IN A STREET GANG   157

Joining up
Solving problems
The facilitator role

APPENDICES

1. How to start, lead, and participate in a Social Literacy group   167
2. The discipline game manual   177

Bibliography   205
Index   209

Preface

Several years ago an assistant superintendent of a public school district told us, "Teachers won't come to your summer in-service workshop because you're not paying them." In fact, teachers did come to our workshop, stayed late, and worked over the weekends. Several teachers even took a second, similar workshop we offered through the University of Massachusetts later in the summer, that time *paying* for it. Again, the response was enthusiastic commitment beyond our expectations. Over two-thirds of the teachers continued to meet regularly over the course of the year and started Social Literacy support groups in their own schools.

We asked teachers what had involved them so intensely. Reasons were varied.

It works. Finally, I'm hopeful again that we can reduce discipline problems.

Most approaches to discipline problems are remedial and situation-specific. Social Literacy focuses on primary prevention. By analogy, this is the difference between treating individual cases of malaria, and the primary prevention of malaria through a campaign to get rid of malarial mosquitoes. Teachers know that any approach to discipline problems that requires one-to-one contact in each conflict situation, no matter how effective, is impractical. There are too many incidents every day. Solutions are needed that prevent the primary causes of discipline conflict and reduce the overall level of conflict.

It's relevant. We name the worst stresses on our lives, create guides for survival and liberation, pinpoint what people really want and work out solutions together.

Following the principles of Social Literacy, teachers have created techniques for collaboratively resolving interpersonal, classroom, and school-wide conflicts. This book will detail many of the specific solutions, but more importantly, it also provides instructions for using the problem-solving techniques to devise your own effective solutions.

I appreciate having a challenging philosophy. It brought out my old idealism.

Our approach is based on the philosophy of Paulo Freire, a Brazilian educator living in exile in Switzerland. He taught basic literacy to slum dwellers in Recife, Brazil, to prepare them for full democratic participation in the governance of Brazil. We are teaching Social Literacy to increase the democratic participation of teachers, students, and administrators in the governance of schools. Our goals are to raise consciousness of oppression and liberation in schools; to decrease dehumanization, violence, and victimization; to stop blaming each other for problems; and to start working collaboratively in solving them.

Frankly, it's the contact with other teachers, just getting together and talking about common educational problems. Usually, about the only things teachers do together is bitch and complain or drink and bowl.

For many reasons, teachers rarely get together to search for constructive solutions to common problems, or to discuss educational ideas, or even to get to know each other more deeply as persons. When teachers make time for these activities, the intrinsic, the immediate satisfactions often keep Social Literacy groups meeting voluntarily over long periods of time.

It's about the only approach that was developed originally in junior high schools.

For many people junior high schools are neither "primary" nor "secondary" education. Yet, obviously, these vital years of rapid growth for children are not "tertiary" in any sense. Although the principles and techniques of Social Literacy are effective in all educational settings, many junior high school teachers appreciated that their locale, for once, was an initial setting.

After our one-line, small-print offers at the end of the articles, "The Discipline Game: Playing Without Losers" (*Learning Magazine,* September 1974), and "Social Literacy, a school discipline game without losers" (*Phi Delta Kappan,* April 1977), we were overwhelmed by more than a thousand requests for further information. The size of this demand made us cautious. We were not confident enough to disseminate these methods so widely until we had completed our research evaluation of Social Literacy in the Hartford, Connecticut, and Springfield, Massachusetts, secondary schools. We are now convinced that it is time to make this approach available as efficiently as possible.

This book has been written as an elaborate manual. No training in certification workshops is necessary. Getting started is easy and fun. Although each chapter presents concepts, techniques, and exercises that build on previous chapters, the book can be read meaningfully starting with Chapter 12 and working back to Chapter 1. Individual chapters also can be useful reading. You should have enough background and written guidance to work with other educators or your students in devising socially literate solutions to troublesome discipline problems. If you are interested in starting a Social Literacy group with a few of your peers, you will find complete suggestions for how to proceed in the Appendix. Also, the National Education Association distributes a set of eight audio tape cassettes, *Resolving Classroom Conflicts: A Socially Literate Approach.* Based on chapters in this book, these tapes provide verbal guidance for eight Social Literacy group meetings.

All the techniques and solutions described on the following pages have been created and tested by teachers. They have been given appreciative credit at the appropriate places in the book. Several individuals have provided ongoing support and deserve recognition here. Paulo Freire's writings constantly challenged us to act and to reflect and then to act again. Superintendents John Deady and Edyth Gaines gave us the places to work and firm support from the top. The Social Literacy group at Van Sickle Junior High School, and John Shea, the principal, were the major creators and testers of techniques. They also suffered most from our mistakes. We have received financial support from institutions and moral support from individuals: Robert Van Wart, director of the Community Council of Greater Springfield; Theodore Parker, Region I, U.S. Office of Education; Oliver Moles, National Institute of Education. Coworkers and friends at the University of Massachusetts School of Education who made major contributions to this effort were R. Bruce Irons, Michelle Moran-Zide, James Dacus, Solmon Atkins, Nellie Santiago-Wolpow, Ronald McMullen, and Sally Habana-Hafner. In my dialogues and problem solving with teachers I have accumulated a comparative wealth of material. Their successes challenged me to write a book affirming their efforts. The responsibility for these affirming statements is, of course, mine.

ALFRED ALSCHULER

SCHOOL DISCIPLINE

PART I

SOCIALLY LITERATE GOALS

ONE

Schools in Which It Is Easier to Love

Classroom Discipline in the Ecuadorian Mountains

"If you really want to see the project, you can ride my motorcycle. It has no headlights, but . . . ." Patricio Barriga's smile meant either, "You're welcome" or "You'd be crazy." He was the project director and driver of the small, green, vintage pickup truck. It held three people and was full.

"Sure. I love motorcycles. I used to have a Honda 350."

"This one's a mother to ride, an old Triumph 700." Patricio's slang did not seem to be affected. He spoke fluent English with Americans and was equally at ease with all classes of Ecuadorians, a true multicultural person.

When I was seated on the rumbling, vibrating, 600-pound machine, it felt like a palsied monster on a tight leash. In addition to the absent headlight, the gear shift worked differently, the front brakes were shot, and the gas gauge, tachometer, and speedometer were permanently at rest. I thought about going back to my room and reading a good book. But, as a gringo in the land of macho, I knew how that would be seen. I hoped to earn a few points if I could ride the two hours from Quito to the small town near Mount Chimborazzo and not look like an obvious fool. I had known Patricio only three days and wanted his respect as a person, not just as "the expert on achievement motivation." One of my books on motivating adolescents had been translated into Spanish, had come to Patricio's attention, and he had persuaded the Quito branch of the Agency for International Development to pay for my trip. Patricio thought the methods would be useful for members of the project staff.

The nonformal education project was attempting to teach "functional literacy," basic competence with numbers and essential problem-solving skills. Fifty percent of Ecuadorians drop out of school by the end of the second grade because what they are learning is less useful than their labor in the fields. Yet, basic intellectual competencies are increasingly needed for survival by these former students as they come into adulthood. The cost of building enough schools, and training and supplying enough teachers was prohibitively expensive, even with Ecuador's new oil discoveries. Thus, this simple, radical idea was adopted: teach basic skills fast, without schools, without teachers, and without texts. I wanted to see this magic trick.

Next to Patricio in the cab of the truck was Jim Hoxeng, Patricio's U.S. counterpart, a soft-spoken, self-effacing man in spite of his photographic memory and the fluent Spanish he had "picked up" by ear. Somewhat later I found out from Patricio that Jim suffered continual pain from an arthritic condition. (He must have mentioned it to Patricio.)

Enrique Tasiguano, the third project member in the cab, was a full-blooded Quechua Indian, field coordinator of the project and the only natural genius I have ever met. His older brother had begun to organize *campesinos* (local farmers) into a trucking cooperative. The *hacendados* (local landlords and large land holders) expressed their attitude toward the cooperative by knocking him down in front of his peers and backing a truck over him twice. In Ecuador, as in the United States, political murders get scant attention in the papers where motives are obscured, and [then] the case fades from public attention. Enrique led the fight to prosecute the *hacendados* and managed to get the case before the Ecuadorian Supreme Court, an accomplishment comparable to the same feat in the U.S. He also carried on his brother's work in organizing the trucking cooperative and starred in a popular photo-novella version of his brother's story (a type of adult comic book with photographs), sold at the country's newsstands. As a national celebrity, he was invited to attend a meeting in Paris sponsored by the U.N. where he, like Jim, "picked up" conversational French in two weeks. As a member of one of Ecuador's severely oppressed minority groups, Enrique lacked an extensive formal education, but had a reputation for teaching others survival skills in profoundly meaningful ways. I wanted to see him in action as much as I looked forward to watching any superstar.

The two-hour ride from Quito was deceptively beautiful. A series of rugged mountain ranges running as high as 14,000 feet divide the land into several rich valleys. Each valley is surrounded by hundreds of multicolored, patchwork plots. But this visual magnificence belies an oppressive inheritance of landownership that gives the rich valleys to a small percentage of the ruling population. The vast majority of rural poor cling to mountainsides on plots smaller than one acre, fight the constant erosion of slopes as steep as 40 degrees, and harvest so little that they are forced either to work for the *hacendados* or migrate to the cities and work as *cargadores* (carriers of heavy loads).

The Andean cold at more than 9,000 feet, intensified by the wind chill factor, numbed my hands and caused deep body tremors. So much for my ignorant assumption that Ecuador, named because it rests on the equator, is hot. As it became dark, I had to ride ahead of the truck to see by its lights. Outside of Quito there are no street lights because electricity is scarce and expensive. At one point, when the "road" became a dried river bed, then a rock-filled, dry cascade, the Triumph got away from me, and I fell. Three of us got it up and walked it down the "road." Then came the dogs. The high-pitched whine of the motorcycle had made them mad. In the pitch-blackness I never saw them, but I heard the yelping and growling get closer. To avoid what I imagined to be long, drooling fangs, I would jam the accelerator, but the sudden burst of speed caused the Triumph to skid in the deep talcum-dust road, several times nearly upending me. Waging this battle with the Triumph required complete concentration, and I was only vaguely aware of shadowy figures walking along the road. They were simply more hazards to avoid.

We stopped in an open field of packed clay where the local soccer games were held. To the left of the field was a bungalow with a corrugated tin roof, no lights, no glass in the windows, no doors in place. Our meeting was to be held there, in the center of the community. Three men, standing quietly in their ponchos, were waiting for us. As we began to unload the materials from the truck, one of the men walked up with a kerosene lamp (fondly called a "petro"), and introduced himself as Marco. As the community had no electricity, the ownership of a petro, which may cost as much as a third of what a man earns in a year, signified relative wealth. After the required series of greetings, we were told that the others would be along any minute. Because no one in a rural Ecuadorian community has a watch, the expression "any minute" must be understood metaphorically.

As people began to arrive, I realized that, while I had been silently congratulating myself, these were the people I had passed on the motorcycle. Patricio told me they usually went to sleep at sundown and got up at dawn. Nonetheless, attendance at these sessions had grown to 60 people, ranging, as I could see, from the village elders to mothers with their infants wrapped in colorful slings across their backs, like diagonal papooses.

While I waited, I thought about my school and workplace, the University of Massachusetts in Amherst. The high-rise dormitories and grey, concrete, campus buildings look like an oasis in reverse, a concentrated urban blight set in a beautiful rural farming community. But even "slum" schools I had seen in the United States were castles in comparison to the empty shell where the class was to be held that night. In spite of the opportunities back home, many students from junior high school to senior year in college were bored with the lectures, reading assignments, homework, papers, and exams. The brightest students were cynics. Other students, from ten years old and up, were joining the heavy traffic in hard drugs. Students' low interest in learning seemed like a national epidemic of motivational anemia. In contrast, the villagers' motivation to learn was a continent away in place and degree. Witnessing an entire community trek miles in pitch-dark night cold, tired from a day of stoop labor, carrying infants, and supporting the elderly in order to learn, made my "statistically significant" research results seem miniature. I wondered what I had to offer as a consultant and what was so compelling about this classroom.

Within an hour, the community members had arrived. Enrique took charge of the session. He tried to explain what we were doing there and to dispel expectations that the gringo would be distributing gifts at the end of the session.

We had brought along *Hacienda* (roughly translated, "plantation"), a game that looks something like Monopoly but that focuses on the daily lives of rural Ecuadorians rather than the process of capital accumulation in nineteenth-century North America. The game board was spread out on the dirt floor. It was getting colder outside and the wind blew through the empty windows and door at will. But inside, physical closeness and emotional investment in the game (which became a series of free-form role plays reenacting events in the *campesinos'* lives) made the cold little more than a passing annoyance.

The faces of the players were alive with excitement, especially those who had volunteered to be the lawyer, or the priest, or the hacienda owner. Few of the men could read; those who could, did so with so much painstaking effort that it took on a magical quality—a power to translate those colorful, but meaningless cards into high-powered emotional events. "You have been accused of stealing a sheep from the *hacendado's* land, go to jail or seek out a lawyer." "Your child has been elected queen of the school pageant, pay two-hundred *sucres* for a new dress." "You were found drunk, pay a fine and go to jail." Everything was new about the game. Rolling the dice was a new experience for hands more accustomed to plowing land or cutting wood. Moving a colored button five places on the board meant you had to be able to count to five. Competition was irrelevant. The goal was not to beat your neighbor, but to help him understand this experience. *Campesinos* called it "the game of life."

The role plays dealt with how the *campesinos* relate to the hacienda owner, the local priest, the local police officer, or the lawyer. While the role plays themselves were suggested by the construction of the game, the nature of the relationship came entirely as a projection of the *campesino's* own experience. If the *campesino* who played the police officer took bribes in the game, it was because he had seen, or heard of police officers who took bribes in real life.

The game was arbitrarily stopped at about 9:30 P.M. so that there would be time for a discussion. The role players joined the others, who were sitting on wooden benches in a large circle with enough room behind for the elderly men and women and nursing mothers to stand listening. When everyone was settled and quiet, Enrique, who was sitting on a bench, too, got to the point without a wasted word. Apparently, his brilliance was not in lecturing, an activity that occupied most of the time in most of the classes I had attended or observed since first grade. In contrast with this community simulation game, lecturing, even at its best, seemed like beautiful arias without music, without action or consequence, just exquisitely constructed points of view to be appreciated in and of themselves.

"In real life, why does the *hacendado* have a large house, huge land holdings, a car, and whatever he wants?" asked Enrique.

Jim provided me with a simultaneous, whispered translation, but I thought I heard bitterness in Enrique's tone, as though his question were an answer: "It is absolutely unfair, the result of an unjust, inhuman, oppressive system." Other *campesinos* had their own explanations.

"Because the *hacendado* works. God has given each person his own work."

"Yes, and *we* work like slaves on the hacienda. It is wrong that we should be forced to work there. We should be free to work where they pay best, or where they are fairest."

"That may be the way things should be," Enrique commented, "but *why* are things the way they are? Why aren't we free and treated fairly?"

An older *campesino* adjusted his poncho and answered bluntly, as if he knew the obvious answer.

"Indians can't organize. We don't think. We just act. We are bad businessmen, women chasers, and drinkers. If the *hacendado* gives a party, we have to have a bigger one. And what happens if God gives us a better harvest? We go drinking with our friends, give a party, or find another woman until all our money is gone."

No one said anything. Enrique did not comment or smile. Apparently, he never criticized a peer, no matter how pessimistic, passive, or self-critical. A younger man, who had been active in several role plays and still seemed excited, broke the silence.

"You saw what happened tonight. When the *hacendado* hears that we are going to buy land, he runs quick and buys it all. We should know by now that he wants to keep us like slaves. He doesn't want us to be free to work on our own land or anybody else's land."

The strategy of oppression behind the *hacendado's* actions had been discovered. Here was a perfect chance for Enrique's charismatic leadership. I waited for him to be brilliant, to summarize disparate points of view, to arouse them to concerted action with a passionate speech. Enrique, however, looked ill.

"O.K. That's the way things are. What can we do about it?"

"We need the *hacendado*," a young man protested. "What would happen to us if the *hacendado* went away? Where would we go if the *hacendado* didn't give us work and we didn't work for him?"

Another *campesino* reacted loudly to these scared, defeatist questions.

"One day *we* will say, 'O.K., this is the road to go, and not wait for someone to tell us what to do, or give us work, or buy the land before we can get organized. Until now, we've acted like goats. We never questioned what others told us to do. We never say, 'Is this good?' or 'Is this bad?' We just listen to people because they give us a drink or because they have pretty blue eyes or because they come with an orchestra."

The right to question authority was a discovery and became a more widely shared belief as the *campesinos* kept thinking of other previously unquestioned practices. "Why does the priest charge us money to do a special Mass?" "Why do the electric power lines only go as far as the *hacendado's* house?" "Why don't we have a bus that comes to our village?" "Why don't we own our own trucks to take our produce to market?" Within these questions there was a second discovery: things might be different.

It was 10:30 P.M., very cold, and I agreed without protest to Patricio's suggestion that he ride his motorcycle back to Quito. I pretended to sleep in the crowded cab of the truck, but kept thinking about what had happened. That half-finished house did not contain a single item that would tempt a vandal. There was nothing to take, break, steal, or deface: no desks, no chairs, no equipment, no windows, not even books. Nor would equipment have increased learning. Would a glossy game board have helped? There was no visible curriculum, no need to get to the civil war by the end of the semester, chapter by chapter, traveling a prescribed path of tasks laid down like walking stones in texts whose weightiness was measured in pounds. The "game of life" was its own curriculum. What social studies, history, literature, or "core" curriculum could have improved the *campesinos'* collaborative study of their social life, their personalized assessment of their history, their functional literacy in reading the game cards leading to so much communication?

Tests? Yes, there were tests, but life tests, not assessments of academic skills that are *supposed* to predict life success, but do not. Without a flicker of concern, the *campesinos* by-passed the cul-de-sac of final exams and nationally normed standardized achievement tests that mean so much in the United States only because they exist in such force and give access to the next higher set of tests unrelated to competence in living. Achievement testing is an unnatural act. Unencumbered and undistracted by such bogus goals, the *campesinos* were free to exercise their intelligence naturally, to see the obvious, to ask "why," and to do something about it if they chose. For me *campesinos,* snap quizzes consisted of combining clear thoughts into a sound plan of action, of solving tactical problems of group cooperation, and of sustaining their efforts until their goals, not their grades, were achieved. Poverty tested them and racism tested them, not in a tightly packed examination room for a strictly limited period of time, but every day in their cold, tired, hungry, sometimes beaten and murdered flesh. No master teachers certified by the system were needed to grade them. Their "exams" were truly "final."

I had looked in the wrong time and place for Enrique's superstar teaching. He propelled people indirectly by conducting the Hacienda Game and by gently posing questions. He never bombarded "students" with information about distant issues. Enrique created options for action by "modelling" new behavior. The *campesinos* discovered that all human beings have the right to ask questions, like Enrique: Why is the situation this way? What can be done about it? These were not academic questions posed by teachers you could recognize by dress, age, formal degree, and location in the classroom. Enrique, the "teacher," was a student of the situation, just as everyone else in the circle questioned and answered and taught and learned. He had the same stake in what happened as all of the *campesinos.*

Then, suddenly, I realized something had been missing, something that has been an integral part of education for centuries, maybe for millenia— the discipline problem. There was no visible restlessness, boredom, or lack of motivation, nor any disobedience, disrespect, or defiance. Instead, there was full community involvement in learning about common problems, energetic role playing, and shared laughter within a sequence of serious discussions. Education without a discipline problem is like a society without crime. Was this possible on a continuing basis?

I had witnessed radically simple answers to perennial questions. What is necessary for education to occur? Very little. Certainly not expensive buildings and fancy equipment. What should the curriculum be? Shared problems in living. How should success be measured? By the effectiveness of solutions. Who should be students? Everyone, regardless of age. What is the teacher's role? To lead by modelling new behavior. How should education be conducted? Through reflection, discussion, and collaborative action to solve central problems.

All I said to Patricio, Enrique, and Jim that night in Quito before we went to bed was, "That's an incredible project." I fell asleep asking more questions. Could this type of education be exported and adapted to schools in the United States? Could junior and senior high school students be so intensely motivated and involved? Could students and teachers work together as smoothly? Would it be possible to develop basic skills through solving shared problems effectively?

The next morning I asked Jim, "Where did this project come from? Is there some training manual?"

"Here, read this," he said, handing me a copy of Paulo Freire's book, *Pedagogy of the Oppressed.* Jim told me that Freire, poor and hungry as a child in Brazil, had devoted his adult life to helping poor people overcome their problems. By the early 1960s he had developed a method for teaching basic literacy to Brazilian adults in just thirty hours. In becoming "functionally" literate in words describing central problems in their lives (e.g., *slums, work, health*) these Brazilians understood the "functioning" of slums, work, health, and began to "function" more effectively as concerned citizens. Freire's program was supported by the U.S. Agency for International Development and by the Brazilian government until a right-wing military junta took its stand against democratic participation by citizens. Freire was placed under arrest, then allowed to go into exile.

From Freire's book I expected to learn the practical details of teaching reading and citizenship. Instead, he presented his philosophy of education in such continuous cosmic abstractions that it caused psychological whiplash. For instance, Freire offers this plausible but remote description of the Hacienda Game.

[The teacher and students are] cointent on reality, . . . not only in the task of unveiling that reality and thereby coming to know it critically, but in the task of recreating that reality. As they attain this knowledge of reality through common reflection and action, they discover themselves as its permanent recreators. (Freire, 1972 p. 56)

After reading this book twice within two days, I wondered what I—a loyal member of the Democratic party, a clinical psychologist by training, originally from an affluent suburb of Chicago—was doing in a Latin American capital high in the Andes mountains avidly studying a tract by a Brazilian Marxist living in exile. I had no interest whatsoever in fomenting revolution of any kind. As a clinical psychologist, I was devoted to the resolution of inner conflict. As a humanist educator I wanted to reduce interpersonal conflict and to promote human development through education.

That was seven years ago. Today I still am not a Marxist and am equally uninterested in fomenting revolution. However, I am convinced that some of Freire's ideas lead to practices that embody our country's publicly stated ideals more fully than many current procedures in our nation's classrooms. I am also convinced that his ideas are powerful tools for "unveiling" the "reality" of schools, for "recreating that reality through common reflection and action," for reducing conflict, and for promoting human development. To make Freire's ideas more accessible I will summarize his philosophy in the remainder of this chapter, then illustrate its potential power by describing in the next two chapters how we used his ideas to "unveil" the discipline problem, to examine it "critically" and to "recreate" positive discipline.

Freire's Philosophy of Education

Three convictions form the core of Freire's philosophy:
(1)   People can and should create "a world in which it is easier to love."
(2)   People develop the ability to create their world.
(3)   Problem-posing education facilitates this development.
Everything else Freire says either amplifies these axioms or traces their implications for education.

1. Creating a world . . .

Freire does not justify love as the ultimate goal of his work. He simply confesses that, "From these pages I hope at least the following will endure: my trust in the people and my faith in human beings and in the creation of a world in which it will be easier to love" (Freire, 1972, p. 24). He concentrates instead on oppressive conditions in the world that make it difficult for people to love each other. These conditions are what need to be unveiled, analyzed critically, and recreated.

An act is oppressive when it prevents individuals from becoming more fully human (ibid., p. 42).

"Becoming more fully human" involves both economic development and psychosocial development.

Any situation in which A objectively exploits B or hinders the pursuit of self-affirmation as a responsible person is one of oppression (ibid., p. 40).

"Objective exploitation" includes economic blocks to development in which one person, class, race, or nation gets a disproportionate amount of material or labor for what they give to the other person, class, race, or nation. "Hindering the pursuit of self-affirmation as a responsible person" refers to actions like the murder of Enrique's brother for organizing a trucking co-op, and discriminatory hiring, housing, and educational practices. Clues to the existence of an oppressive situation are strong feelings, often expressed in such words as, "That's not fair," or "That's really undemocratic," or "It's really frustrating that I'm not allowed to do that." Then the situation must be examined critically. Is there objective exploitation? Does it interfere with responsible human development?

It is oppression when the *hacendado* buys all the available land to keep *campesinos* dependent exclusively on the *hacendado* for work at ridiculously low wages. When the *hacendado* exploits in this way, it is more difficult for the *campesinos* to pursue self-affirmation as responsible human beings. This exploitation also makes a loving relationship between them difficult.

Similarly, it is oppression when educators control all the available school resources (grades and other rewards and punishments) that keep students dependent exclusively on them for determining the content, sequence, pace, and style of their school work. (Presumably, what students learn constitutes their wages.) This oppressive situation makes it more difficult for students to pursue self-affirmation as responsible persons, and to develop an open giving, loving relationship with teachers.

According to Freire, "[an oppressive] situation in itself constitutes violence because it interferes with human beings' ontological and historical vocation to be more fully human. . . ." (ibid., p. 41). When individuals' natural right to grow, to create, and to venture forth responsibly is blocked, that right is violated. "Violence is initiated by those who oppress, who exploit, who fail to recognize others as persons—not by those who are oppressed, exploited, and unrecognized" (ibid., p. 41). It may be easier to understand these statements by translating them to a school situation.

Discipline conflicts (the most prevalent form of school violence) are initiated by teachers who oppress, who exploit, who fail to recognize students as persons, not by students who are oppressed, exploited, and unrecognized. Teachers are not inherently evil, however. From Freire's perspective, it is the "unjust order that engenders violence in the oppressors, which in turn dehumanizes the oppressed" (ibid., p. 28).

Freire trusts that people can create "just orders," situations in which it is easier to love. The nonoppressive, nonexploitative evening of education in the Ecuadorian mountains exemplifies the participants' growth of self-affirmation as responsible persons. If "love," in the broadest sense, was not present, there was at least communion in the community. And, there were no discipline conflicts.

2. Developing the ability . . .

The ability to create a world in which it is easier to love develops in stages. Or, more to the point, the ability to create an educational situation without oppression, violence, or discipline conflict develops in stages. In the first, *magical-conforming* stage, people do not recognize their situation as oppressive and passively play their role. They conform to the situation. In the second, *naive-reforming* stage, people assume that problems lie in individuals who are not sufficiently good, intelligent, competent, or law-abiding as defined by the system. These individuals need to be reformed in order for the situation to improve. In the third, *critical-transforming* stage, people realize that they all are victimized by a conflict-producing system. They criticize the crucial aspects of the system that cause conflictful situations and collaborate to transform the system. As people develop through these stages, their problem solving becomes more active, comprehensive, and effective. They move from being pessimistic, passive victims in an oppressive situation to being optimistic, active recreators of victimless situations in which it is easier to love and to pursue self-affirmation as responsible persons.

Each stage in this sequence is a coherent style of solving problems with its characteristic way of *naming* the problem, *analyzing* the causes, and *resolving* conflicts. The magical-conforming way of naming problems is to see difficulties as inevitable, unchangeable "facts of existence." "There will always be a few bad kids." "The curriculum is fixed by the school board and the state." "There will never be enough supplies, enough time, enough support, or enough money." The analysis of these "facts" is magical in the sense that their causes seem to go beyond logical explanation, like a magic trick: historical inevitabilities, for example ("It's the times," "That's the way things have always been") or gross external forces like fate, luck, or God. The first response to Enrique's question about why the *hacendado* has so much was a magical-conforming explanation: "Because the *hacendado* works. God has given each person his own work." When a situation is seen as a fixed fact caused by uncontrollable, external forces, the idea of change causes fear: "We need the *hacendado*. What would happen to us if the *hacendado* went away? Where would we go if the *hacendado* didn't give us work and we didn't work for him?" Educators and students in the magical stage also have fears of change: fears of trying something new and not succeeding; fears of feeling stupid or incompetent; fears of exposing one's problems to others; fears of what others may say or think without saying; fears of being let down if one starts a collaborative effort; fears that it will take too much time to change; fears that the results will not justify the efforts; fears of someone else's dependence on oneself; fears of believing something is important, then falling short of the ideal; fears that once one learns to be different one will feel obligated to be that way all the time; fears of failing sometimes and then feeling guilty and inadequate; fears that advocating anything will be doomed because others, especially administrators, always win. These fears are neither new nor unique to education. They do constitute, for many people, a gut-level, instinctive "no" in response to even the most gently stated, simple, plausible invitations to change. Because of these fears, little action is taken. Resignation, accommodation, conforming, and a sense of hopelessness characterize action at this stage of problem-solving. "Why bother? Nothing can be done. You'll just get frustrated or hurt." This inaction is a form of passive collusion, though unconscious and unintentional, to maintain oppressive, conflict-laden situations.

In the naive-reforming stage, specific problems are seen to lie in individuals who deviate from the system's idealized rules, roles, standards, and expectations. "Indians can't organize. We don't think, we just act. We're bad businessmen, women chasers, and drinkers." "I was kicked out of school because I broke some rules." "I didn't get tenure because I couldn't control my classes." "If we had a better school disciplinarian, everything would be better." At this stage individuals either blame themselves for their problems, which causes feelings of inferiority, incompetence, guilt, and other forms of self-deprecation, or others are blamed, which leads to resentment, anger, and hostility. As a result, individuals try to improve themselves or change others. This is the pervasive mind-set of both educators and students toward discipline conflicts. According to Freire, the implicit, naive assumption is that, when individuals reform and act properly, then the system will function perfectly and oppressive, conflictful situations will not exist. Because of their belief in the intrinsic soundness of the system, individuals at the naive-reforming stage actively "play host" to the rules, roles, expectations, and standards of the system, just as we play host to guests at parties. Love and criticism exchange places. The system is loved and individuals are criticized.

In the third, critical-transforming stage, people exercise their intellectual skills in naming the critical (in the sense of "crucial") rules and roles of the system that create unequal power, responsibility, and freedom; that place them in conflict; and that exploit, oppress, or hinder their human development. Groups of individuals analyze the ways they have naively played host to the oppressive aspects of the economic, political, social, school, or classroom system. They come to understand how they have victimized themselves and others by their active collusion in supporting the conflict-producing rules and roles. Together, they act to transform those aspects of the system.

The dawning of this orientation to problem solving was evident in Enrique's group: "Until now we've acted like goats. We've never questioned what others told us to do." Here are some "critical" questions about "the discipline problem": Is it caused by students, teachers, and administrators who deviate from prescribed rules and roles? Or do oppressive aspects of the educational system place people in conflict? As students, teachers, or administrators are we playing host to those oppressive conditions most when we are trying hardest to do "what others have told us to do?" If this is so, what can be done?

Ultimately, this type of critical questioning is

characterized by depth in the interpretation of problems; by the substitution of causal principles for magical explanations; by the testing of one's "findings" and by openness to revision; by the attempt to avoid distortion when perceiving problems and to avoid preconceived notions when analyzing them; by refusing to transfer responsibility; by soundness of argumentation; by the practice of dialogue rather than polemics; by receptivity to the new for reasons beyond mere novelty and by the good sense not to reject the old just because it is old—by accepting what is valid in both old and new (Freire, 1973. p. 18).

Freire could be describing a collaborative research team investigating a scientific problem requiring careful analysis, hypothesized logical causes, testing of the hypothesis, being open to positive or negative results, and revising the hypothesis to fit the data. This critical-transforming approach to problem solving "is characteristic of authentically democratic regimes and corresponds to highly permeable, interrogative, restless and dialogical forms of life" (Freire, 1974, pp. 18–19).

FIG. 1

Stages of Problem Solving

	Magical-Conforming	Naive-Reforming	Critical-Transforming
NAMING THE PROBLEM	The situation is seen either as not problematic or as an unchangeable fact of existence.	The problem is in individuals who deviate from the rules and roles of the system.	The problem is in conflict-producing, oppressive rules and roles of the system that victimize many individuals.
ANALYSIS OF THE CAUSES	Magical thinking places the causes beyond logical explanation: e.g., historical inevitabilities and uncontrollable external forces. This leads to basic fears of change.	Belief in the goodness of the system and the the badness of individuals leads to conclusions and feelings of inferiority, incompetence, guilt, anger, resentment and hostility. The system is loved and people are criticized.	A group of individuals investigates common problems, common causes and sees clearly how they have actively played host to the system, thus perpetuating the problem. People are loved and the system is criticized.
TYPES OF ACTION TAKEN	Individuals passively play host to the system by resigning themselves to the situation, accommodating, adjusting, waiting, and conforming. Little or no action is taken.	Individuals actively play host to the system by trying to change themselves and to reform or remove others so the system will work well.	Collaboratively, the group acts to change the oppressive rules and roles in ways that do not victimize anyone and do promote human development.

NOTE: William Smith and Alfred Alschuler have developed an objective measure of these stages of problem solving for a wide variety of situations. It is available from the authors at 456 Hills South, University of Massachusetts, Amherst, MA, 01003.

3. Problem-posing education

Paulo Freire was a professor of the history and philosophy of education at the University of Recife, Brazil, until 1964. As early as 1947 he had been interested in the education of illiterate adults. Naturally, he was familiar with the standard methods for teaching people to read, but was dissatisfied with them for four reasons: (1) The primers used the same material for adults as for children. (2) The language and situations in the primers were characteristic of the urban middle class, not the rural poor he was trying to teach.

> It required practice, indeed, after the hardships of a day's work (or of a day without work), to tolerate lessons dealing with "wing," ("Johnny saw the wing." "The wing is on the bird.") or lessons talking of Graces and grapes to people who never knew a Grace and never ate a grape ("Grace saw the grape.")
>
> (Freire, 1973, p. 43).

(3) The normal teacher-student relationships were paternalistic, thus intensifying the adults' feelings of subordination and worthlessness. (4) The materials taught a magical-conformist or naive-reformist ideology.

> We wished to design a project in which we would attempt to move from naiveté to a critical attitude at the same time we taught reading. We wanted a literacy program which would be an introduction to the democratization of culture, a program with people as its subjects rather than as patient recipients, a program which would be an act of creation, capable of releasing other creative arts, one in which students would develop the impatience and vivacity which characterize search and invention (ibid.).

The method Freire developed uses language and situations familiar to adults and teaches reading using a critical, problem-solving process.

In 1963 the Brazilian Ministry of Education committed itself to a national literacy campaign using Freire's method. Within eight months, training courses for "coordinators" (the new term for those leading the learning sessions) were established in nearly every Brazilian state. Six thousand people, many of whom were students, volunteered in the state of Guanabara alone. It was anticipated that in 1964, 20,000 "circles of culture" (the new term for the literacy group) would be underway, teaching two million people in the thirty-hour, three-month course, so that the problem of illiteracy of 40 million Brazilians would be eliminated within a few years.

A simple law forbidding illiterates to vote had cut the potential electorate in half. Freire's quick and effective training was a powerful vehicle for moving from limited to universal participation in Brazilian politics. This imminent democratization threatened many people. The influential Rio de Janeiro daily, *O Globo,* regularly accused Freire's method of stirring up the people with ideas about change and of being subversive. On April 1, 1964, the military leaders of Brazil took control of the government at all levels. Freire was placed under house arrest until June, when he finally sought refuge in Chile. After a year in Santiago, where he helped launch a national literacy campaign, he went to Geneva, Switzerland, to work for the World Council of Churches. Since 1965 he has written, taught, and helped develop literacy and democratization campaigns in other Latin American and African countries.

Freire's method consists of a series of problems to be solved, from the creation of the curriculum to the coordination of a culture circle. From start to finish it is a collaborative process of critical problem solving, in contrast with the typical "banking" methods of education that require teachers to deposit prepackaged knowledge into the impoverished minds of students. "Knowledge emerges only through invention and re-invention, through the restless, impatient, continuing, hopeful inquiry people pursue in the world, with the world and with each other" (Freire, 1972, p. 58). The sequence of problems posed by Freire led to the invention of the education-out-of-schools project I observed in Ecuador and to our own critical-transforming approach for solving discipline problems in the United States.

Problem 1: Name the important conflicts in the situation

A team of adults including teachers, a psychologist, sociologist, and local leaders "coinvestigate" the community in which the training is to occur. This involves interviewing a diverse cross-section of people and observing them at church, at work, in meetings of local associations, in homes, in leisure games and sports. Through team discussions of these investigations eventually as few as seventeen "generative words" are chosen to represent familiar conflict situations. Here are three partial lists from an urban area in Brazil, a rural area in Chile, and a prison:

favela (slum)	casa (house)	salida (getting out)
terreno (plot of land)	camino (road)	visita (visit)
comida (food)	radio (radio)	abogado (lawyer)
salario (salary)	trabajo (work)	libertad (freedom)
profissão (profession)	fábrica (factory)	
riqueza (wealth)	pueblo (people)	

These words are "generative" in the sense that the coordinator can generate an energetic discussion by posing questions about the familiar situation depicted by the word; for example, *casa* (house), "Do all Chileans have adequate houses? Where and why do they lack houses? Is the system of savings and loans sufficient for acquiring a house?" The words are also "generative" in the sense that students are able to generate solutions to this problem posed by the coordinator: "Can you make some other words by rearranging the parts and by using other vowels?" "Cosa," "saco," "casi," "seco," etc. Because the list contains the basic sounds in Spanish or Portuguese, creatively recombining the syllables in short lists of words generates a large vocabulary.

Problem 2: Analyze the system causes of conflict

Behind the "generative words" are a few "generative themes." These themes are central conflicts and have at least three characteristics: (1) they involve central roles of unequal power, (2) the conflicts are central to a wide variety of specific conflicts, and (3) they reflect the central conflict of our times, "the fundamental theme of our epoch . . . domination, which implies its opposite, the theme of liberation" (Freire, 1972, p. 93). "Development" is one such generative theme frequently used in Freire's training because of the several interconnected meanings of development, i.e., psychological, social, political, economic, and national. Discussions about housing, slums, plots of land, food, salaries, roads, work, factories, all relate to aspects of this generative theme. Through reflection on these familiar, specific problems and conflict situations, designated by these words, the larger permeating generative theme is eventually unveiled. Students come to see that their personal, political, economic, and national development, or lack of it, are related to the domination of one group by another group of unequal power, status, or wealth. These the larger system causes.

Problem 3: Encourage collaborative action to resolve conflicts

By collaboratively naming and analyzing problems, instead of merely "depositing" information, Freire's method encourages students to solve problems. Enrique asked why the *hacendado* had so much, and how things should be. In that session the *campesinos* began to develop a critical, questioning attitude.

Students, as they are posed with problems relating to themselves in the world and with the world, will feel increasingly challenged and obliged to respond to that challenge. . . . Their response to the challenge evokes new challenges, followed by new understandings, and gradually the students come to regard themselves as committed (ibid., pp. 68–69).

In a subsequent session, according to Jim, Enrique had focused on a role play involving men getting drunk at the local bar. At first there were "magical" answers to his question, "Why do we drink so much and get drunk?" "Because that's the way we are. We've always done it." Then naive-reforming responses began to emerge. "We spend all our money there and have nothing left over. We shouldn't drink so much." By the end of the evening the group realized that a pattern existed in the community. Men would drink more than they could afford, then go into debt with the local bar owner, also a *campesino*. Money earned by the *campesinos* flowed out of the community as beer flowed in, enriching the people who manufactured beer and impoverishing the *campesinos*. This system was stopped by the bar owner, with the community's encouragement. He no longer stocked beer and served soft drinks only to the limit of what the men could pay: no more debts. This critical-transforming solution changed a small part of the economic, social, and psychological system. It transformed the bartender's role and invented a new informal rule that altered the flow of money and the quality of consciousness of the men on payday. Enrique's questioning encouraged the *campesinos* to move from drunkenness as a fact of existence, to drinking debts as a solvable problem, to an actual, limited solution.

Enrique was committed to a process of authentic dialogue among equals trying to find or create answers to problems in living. In the inauthentic dialogue characteristic of banking education, teachers question students to see if they can produce information preestablished as correct. Because authentic dialogue is at the heart of problem-posing education, rather than specific techniques, any techniques that facilitate this type of communication are acceptable. Such techniques have included discussions of ambiguous pictures of familiar scenes containing the generative words and themes; charts of the words broken down into syllables in all their variations with different vowels; the Hacienda Game depicting their familiar institutions and conflict situations; dramatizations of typical dilemmas; newspaper editorials; and even lectures, provided they occur in the context of dialogue. Freire's method does not exist in these or any techniques, but in a collaborative, critical, problem-solving orientation to the world.

Problem-posing education bases itself on creativity and stimulates true reflection and action upon reality, thereby responding to the vocation of humans as beings who are authentic only when engaged in inquiry and creative transformation (ibid., p. 71).

Problem-solving education engages people in the critical, creative transformation of their world into a place where it is easier to love, where there is less oppression and greater self-affirmation as responsible persons. And, problem-posing education itself is a process of loving development.

Social Literacy

Literacy is more than simply learning to read and write the conventional idiom. It is a much broader problem-solving process involving *naming* problems, *analyzing* the causes, and acting to *solve* these problems. For instance, quantity is a fundamental aspect of reality. In math classes students learn the *names* for different quantities (numbers) and how to *analyze* basic relationships between these quantities (more than, less than, included in). They also learn ways of *solving* problems, (multiplication, division, subtraction, addition, raising to a power, solving equations, etc.). Not only can students play with numbers divorced from reality, they can apply these names, analytic methods and problem-solving methods to reality. They are literate with numbers every time they *name* the reality of their bank account balance, *analyze* the upcoming additions and subtractions and *solve* a financial problem by either saving or spending. Without this basic numeracy (being literate with numbers) we would be less powerful in solving all kinds of problems from carpentry to planning more adequate transportation facilities using census data. Numeracy is powerful. So is chemical, biological, legal, and political literacy. All types of literacy give people more power to name, analyze, and solve certain types of problems.

From this perspective most of us in schools are socially illiterate. We do not have a precise and shared vocabulary as we do in mathematics, chemistry, or the law. People involved in school problems each have their own words to describe what happens. There are few widely accepted methods for analyzing or for resolving social conflicts. It is wishful thinking to hope that Social Literacy will reach quickly the same precision of language, procedural elegance, and clarity of results as mathematics. It should be possible, however, to move a step or two toward critical-transformist Social Literacy. By posing questions with others about important conflicts in schools, it should be possible to name the conflict-producing rules and roles. By searching for the "generative themes" (the central conflicts), it should be possible to understand how the system victimizes us, in part by our actively playing host to it. Through energetic democratic action and a commitment to dialogue, it should be possible to change the system, liberate people from conflict, and make schools an easier place in which to love. This is the hope of becoming socially literate.

TWO

Liberating People from Conflict

"Making schools an easier place in which to love" is high rhetoric and a utopian goal. It may even be desirable, but these statements are likely to leave classroom teachers, students, and administrators unmoved. A natural and appropriate question is, "So, what do I do? I've got thirty-five kids six times a day, hundreds more in the hallways, meetings, paperwork, and a life outside of school to live. The goals of liberation and love are a wee bit vague and rather ambitious, don't you think?"

Yes. That's why a group from the University of Massachusetts School of Education worked with educators in the Springfield, Massachusetts, and Hartford, Connecticut, public school systems over a six-year period to translate this large perspective into practical action.

We[1] began work in Springfield because it was the largest urban desegregated school system close to the University of Massachusetts. They allowed us to work in their schools in spite of our being from "the university," whose School of Education was seen as an asylum for radicals who knew nothing about running safe schools. This disdain was returned in equal measure by numerous professors who believed the

[1]"We" initially consisted of R. Bruce Irons, Michele Moran Zide, and myself. Later we were joined by Solomon Atkins, James Dacus, Nellie Santiago-Wolpow, Ronald McMullen, and Sally Habana-Hafner.

Springfield system was beyond conservative, actually preservative, like formaldehyde. A minimum of truth resided in both views. Many professors had worked in troubled schools across the nation making educational innovations work. These professors did not "believe" changes were possible, they knew it. And the Springfield school system *had* changed, reluctantly but irreversibly. They fought the desegregation order to the state supreme court, lost, then chose to desegregate rather than secede from the union. This was accomplished with less violence and disruption than in any city of its size in the country.

We entered the Springfield school system in 1971 with the blessings of the superintendent, Dr. John Deady, after a sequence of meetings with school administrators who assessed our sanity and intentions. We promised to take as much time as was necessary to identify a central conflict of common concern. We chose to work with Dr. John Shea, a junior high school principal. He was reported to be the most innovative in the system, a former Marine drill sergeant who had managed the first junior high school desegregation process in Springfield, in which the black student population rose from 4 to 30 percent in his school, when a new wing was under construction and the teacher turn-over rate was 60 percent. He was able to maintain a safe environment in spite of this flux due to his intense energy and willingness to try anything that promised a reasonable chance of being effective.

Members of the social studies department agreed to meet with us on a weekly basis to assist in the search for the school's central conflict. The teachers met with us regularly because we cost nothing, spent time in their workplace, and because we wanted to do something relevant together. Our points of departure were rather different, however. Their concept of a relevant curriculum began with geography in the seventh grade. One must first know the nature of the earth on which social life occurs. One must then learn the world's history of social life and conflict in eighth grade, and then specialize in U.S. history during the ninth grade. With these solid perspectives, daily social and political events can be appreciated in perspective. We thought that understanding the central social conflicts experienced by everyone each hour of every day could be the experiential bases for understanding other conflicts in the school, the community, the country, and the world. We believed that seeing up close the dynamics of domination, collusion, resistance, negotiations, compromises, contracts, and trade-offs would allow meaningful generalization to events far removed in time and place. Much of the time I felt we were being indulged like canaries in Alaska, a fascinating novelty, harmless and doomed.

Naming the Central Conflict: The Discipline Problem

We went everywhere looking for the central conflict. We rode on the buses to school. Other days we were with the assistant principals greeting students as they got off the buses, the first place to diagnose trouble and often resolve it on the spot; for example, a scared seventh grader in tears because his lunch money has been taken is noticed, questioned, and the culprit caught. Some days we sat in classrooms. Other days we followed a group from class to class as the day evolved. We stood beside teachers in the hallways as rush hour traffic erupted for 5 minutes every hour. We watched students at lunch voluntarily segregate themselves by race and sex. We spent time in the locker rooms, on the playing fields, and the two places where you can find out fast what is happening: the bathrooms and the office of the two "assistant principals in charge of curriculum and instruction." That is their official title. Picked because of their outstanding teaching record and consistent classroom control, they spent most of their time punishing children, over one thousand per semester in 1971 and 1972, according to their records. I cannot imagine that they enjoyed this paradoxical reward for excellence in teaching: We spent ten days watching them. Each week for almost two years we met with the social studies teachers to discuss our observations and to decide on "the central conflict." Often it is hardest to see what is most obvious. We all earned a prize for patience if not for rapid, dazzling insight.

There are two basic agenda in school. Educators want students to master the subject matter. Students focus on other matters, anything and everything except the official curriculum. In class, students usually paid attention when asked, but only as long as necessary and only to the minimal degree. Then they would get back to their conversation with friends about other friends, movies, records, what was happening after school. The dead matters discussed officially in class were perfect opposites of the lively topics that mattered to students: basic biology versus basic sex in general and Mary Lee's pregnancy in particular; inequitable distribution of the world's resources versus "dress" in general and Fred's shoes which were outrageous. Images come to my mind, . . . of a young beauty queen wearing a tight sweater and a skirt that could only be described as a maxi-belt, followed by four young men walking behind appreciatively watching every wiggle and commenting on her "style." I remember sitting in the back of a class as two students passed a reefer eight inches in front of my nose. And I remember numerous short young men who had not yet experienced their growth spurts, constantly looking out of the corners of their eyes at the bigger students, envious and vulnerable. And I heard the constant rumors of an impending fight or a locker search, or a dope bust, or who was about to be suspended for what, or who was now going out with someone's ex-boyfriend. This stuff of students' social lives was precisely the subject matter banned from formal discussions in school. There was learning and then there was living.

We decided that the central conflict was the battle for students' attention. On the one hand, adults control all external forces designed to focus students' attention artificially on the instructional material: buses (students must be in attendance before their attention can be captured); truant officers, bells, hall passes, and monitors; the creation and enforcement of rules; decisions about what, when, and how the students will learn; the command of classrooms; coaxing, cajoling, pleading, threatening and, when that fails, detention or referral to the front office for disciplining. In opposition to these external forces are all those inner interests that command students' attention: friends, enemies, "face," pride, esteem, contact, music, money, sports, and, especially, "doin' nothin'."

The battle for students' attention is central in several respects. Obviously, students must be paying attention before they can learn anything. Even Pavlov knew that. He remarked in his scientific diary that his dogs would not learn to salivate to the bell when they were not paying attention, i.e., when they had "bored," flopped-down ears. Students' attention is a prerequisite for teaching. If teachers are consistently unable to obtain a minimal level of students' attention (if their classes are out of control), their job or tenure or promotion or merit pay increment may be in danger. Not only is attention necessary for learning and teaching (the central purpose of schools), but this battle subsumes most of the other conflicts in school. If one were able to identify *all* of the opposing forces in this battle, most of the forces in other school conflicts would be known as well.

If this battle were substantially reduced, a significant improvement would be made in other problems: stress, referrals, suspensions, dehumanizing labeling, lost learning time, intruders, vandalism, violence, subsequent juvenile delinquency. If the consequences of this battle alone are treated, for example, "reducing suspension," then the "cure" of a symptom could actually intensify the central conflict. For instance, executive or legal fiat could reduce suspensions by simply prohibiting them for anything other than "dangerous offenses." (In Springfield, "assaults" accounted for only 14 percent of all long-term suspensions in 1974–75. The remainder involved nonviolent interpersonal conflicts and violations of school rules.) While this would reduce the suspension symptom, just as aspirin reduces the temperature accompanying disease, it would increase the stress and conflict within schools by removing one option available to administrators for cooling off hot situations. Ultimately, the need for suspensions must be reduced by reducing the number of referrals. This in turn requires a reduction in the amount of conflict in the classroom.

This battle also has the characteristics of a true central conflict, according to Freire. One powerful group dominates a less powerful group: "the generative theme of our epoch."

We decided to call this battle for students' attention, "the discipline problem," because it reflects essential difficulties in several types of discipline. Self-discipline involves the personal control of one's own attention. Acquiring a subject matter discipline requires attention to a field of inquiry. "Disciples" are those who pay attention to their teachers. Military discipline involves subordinates who do what they are told. When these types of discipline break down into a battle for attention, students are sent out of class for "disciplinary" purposes. As a quality of consciousness, a powerful tool for action, and a characteristic of cooperative life in organizations, discipline is both a means for learning and a goal of education.

Analyzing the problem: war games

If the heart of the discipline problem is the battle for students' attention, it is reasonable to ask, "Who is winning?" We attempted to find an answer by measuring the amount of Mutually Agreed-upon Learning Time, or, as we now happily call this measure, the MALT. To get a MALT score we observed ten students in a classroom every 4 minutes to see if they were attending to instructional material. In a typical 43-minute period ten sets of observations of ten students created a potential range of scores from 0 to 100.[2] Sometimes during class no instructional material is presented—during roll taking, time out for discipline lectures, or preparation time for racing to the next class, for example. Such activities often take 8 to 10 minutes per period, or over 25 percent of class time. While instructional material is presented, not all students pay attention. Their eyes are the best clues. Are they looking at the books or out the window, at the teacher lecturing or at a friend whispering? This index of attention is fallible, however, as it is not possible to determine whether a student gazing at a teacher, unblinking, is in a state of rapt attention or semicomatose withdrawal. We gave such behavior the benefit of the doubt, scored it as evidence of MALT and accepted the fact that the total MALT score for classrooms

[2]Copies of this measuring instrument are available from Alfred Alschuler, 456 Hills South, University of Massachusetts, Amherst, MA., 01003.

was probably artificially high. Nonetheless, in the dozens of classrooms we observed, few had MALT scores of over 50. At best, the classroom battle for students' attention was a standoff.

These classrooms are "orderly." Teachers say they are in control while these constant, quiet rebellions continue. Students passively resist the teacher, the instructional style, and the subject matter by simply not paying attention and by not causing too much trouble. While it would be a crisis for over 50 percent of a business work force to strike or to cut work speed in half, this appears to be the daily, accepted fact of existence in classrooms. Our measure does not even take into account noninstructional time, e.g., between classes, homeroom, and lunch, or for those who are late, absent, or suspended. When these factors are considered, perhaps less than a third of a school day is spent attending to instructional material.

This situation provides a certain grim optimism. If students across the country learn a year's work, as measured by standardized tests, in the ten months of school by working less than 50 percent of the available class time, then most increments of work time would produce major gains. For instance, suppose students are paying attention 20 minutes out of every 40-minute class period. To increase their learning by 25 percent would mean getting a mere 5 minutes more of attention per period. An average gain of 25 percent in learning would make most teachers, administrators, and parents happy. And, it would mean an additional 25 percent of *mutually* agreed-upon learning time, and that much less passive resistance, since ultimately only students can focus their attention on the instructional material.

1. War games, tactics and strategy

We asked the next logical questions: If students are paying attention less than 50 percent of the time in class, what else are they doing? If attention is a prerequisite for learning, what do educational psychology books say about getting it or what students do with it? We discovered that the experts have said virtually nothing about this fundamental and scandalous problem.[3] The experts assume teachers have the students' attention and recommend ways to coordinate, and aim it. Teachers know that the first and continuous problem of teachers is getting and maintaining attention. We decided to take an inventory. What do teachers and students do during

---

[3] A notable exception is Jacob Kounin's classic book, *Discipline and Group Management in the Classroom,* Holt, Rinehart and Winston, N.Y., 1970

non-MALT periods? What are the battle tactics each side uses? Our lists are neither definitive, lengthy, nor suprising.

BASIC STUDENT TACTICS

1. Communicating with other students about subjects unrelated to lesson: whispering, talking, lip reading, passing notes.

2. Verbally abusing other students: teasing, threatening, playing the dozens, "ranking."

3. Putting down the teacher (verbally, semiverbally, nonverbally): asking "why" to any rule-enforcing direction, mumbling, shrugging, grimacing in response to a teacher.

4. Complaining about orders: defending self by insisting someone else did it, or in response to a teacher's order to stop, saying "I didn't do anything."

5. Making physical contact with other students: brushing, touching, pushing, hitting, throwing an object at another student.

6. Moving around: Getting up, changing seats, stretching, getting materials, walking to friends, meandering.

7. Making noise: tapping feet, drumming on desk, playing imaginary harmonica, snapping cigarette lighter open and shut, giggling, snapping gum, crumpling paper, banging teeth with a pencil.

8. Solitary escape: ignoring the teacher, daydreaming, combing hair, pretending to work, sleeping.

9. Intruding: coming in late, making funny faces through window in door.

10. Declaration of independence: categorically refusing to do what the teacher asks.

BASIC TEACHER TACTICS

1. Starting class: taking role, giving initial instructions.

2. Building: starting lesson based on comments from students, building on a personal example. ·

3. Bantering: joking to cool off a potentially disruptive situation.

4. Using body language: pointing, gesturing, waiting, staring.

5. Applying tunnel vision: ignoring or not seeing disruptions.

6. Using sounds: modulating tone of voice, yelling, making loud noises, clapping hands, snapping fingers, slapping ruler.

7. Implementing rules: ordering students.

8. Invoking sarcasm: "Do you think you can remember if I say it a fifth time?"

9. Threatening: "If you don't. . . . , I'll. . . ."

10. Minilectures on good and bad behavior and its consequences: "She wouldn't be bothering you if you didn't turn around in your seat."

11. Implementing threats: referring a student to front office for discipline, giving detentions, calling parents, assigning extra work.

12. Making physical contact: touching, grabbing, hitting.

13. Denying requests: for hallpasses, bathroom passes, changing seats or plans for the day.

14. Come backs: any response to a student's put-down of the teacher.

These tactics are the ABCs of social interaction in the classrooms. Typically, they are combined into sequences of moves or games that most teachers and students will recognize: "Passing out" (getting a pass out of class anywhere), "target shooting" (throwing objects at people or into things), the "pencil sharpener game," the "secret message game" (students exchanging messages during class undetected), the game of "I forgot it today" (a pencil, the book, my assignment, etc.), the "missing objects" game (usually something the teacher needs for the lesson). We identified about thirty-five regularly occurring games made up of these tactics. Classroom games are characterized by informal rules, implicit scoring systems, obstacles that must be overcome to score, and a method of decision making.[4] Here is an analysis of a frequently played game.

The bell rings.

Students group around the teacher with questions and comments "I forgot my homework." "Can I get a drink of water?" A few students talk in the corner of the room.

[4]The analysis of behavior as a function of games has been applied to individual linguistic behavior (Segal and Stacey, 1975), neurotic and psychotic interpersonal relationships (Berne, 1964), children's behavior (Roberts and Sutton-Smith, 1962), students' behavior (Ernst, 1972), behavior in the classroom and cultural patterning of behavior (Alschuler, 1973), and juvenile delinquency (Empey, 1971).

The *teacher* asks each student individually to sit down.

Other *students* come up who didn't hear or pretend not to have heard the teacher's request.

The *teacher's* voice rises so that the whole class can hear the command, "All right! Everybody sit down. C'mon."

Students move ever so slowly to their seats as if only an intermission warning bell had sounded. They chat leisurely as they move.

The *teacher* becomes impatient since it is difficult to take attendance. Often a threat occurs here.

Still some *students* get up, this time to sharpen pencils or deliver a note.

The *teacher* stops, stares, warns, or gives a detention notice, depending on the situation.

This "milling game" happens so regularly teachers would think something were wrong if one day all students were quiet, in their seats, eager to begin the lesson when the bell rang. The purpose of the "milling game" is to delay the opening of class (i.e., decrease attention to learning). If we were to create a rulebook for new teachers and new students on "How to participate in the milling game," it would be short and simple.

To new teachers:

1. Answer as many requests as possible within reason.
2. Beware of questions about your favorite topic that have nothing to do with the course.
3. Anger is O.K. to a degree, but you lose points if the students get to you.
4. Don't get hooked and turn your back on the class.

To new students:

1. Always ask questions as if you really wanted to know the answers.
2. Provoke the teacher, but not enough to get punished. You get points for how close you come to the cliff without getting shoved off.
3. Never move farther or faster than you absolutely have to.
4. Never, ever mill alone!

What is the payoff? Why do teachers and students play the milling game in almost every class? There must be some powerful gratifications, or big "points," to continue our analogy. As best as we could determine, students became part of a team, enjoyed beating the system, and received attention from both their peers and the teacher, though for different reasons. Teachers want to be responsive, to feel competent, to have students' respect and most of all, they want to help students get what students want.

After analyzing several such games we realized that there were characteristics of these classroom war games that implied strategies for winning peace.

2. Characteristics of war games

WAR GAMES HAVE WIN-LOSE SCORING SYSTEMS

Almost all needs of students and teachers satisfied in war games are legitimate in and of themselves, virtuous, and innately human (being part of a team, getting attention, being responsive, feeling competent, getting respect). But, when the milling game, or war games in general, are the means for satisfaction, the needs of teachers and students are mutually antagonistic. Either the teachers win and students lose, or students win and teachers lose. Winning peace involves figuring out mutually agreeable methods to satisfy these needs in cooperative, win-win learning games.

THE RULES OF WAR GAMES CAUSE CONFLICT

Just as the rules of football "cause" certain types of behavior on the field while prohibiting and penalizing other types of behavior, so too do the rules of war games "cause" classroom conflict. If these rules can be collaboratively named and changed, conflicts can be resolved, and peace won. This is not as pollyanna-like as it may sound. Students' behavior in school, for the most part, is rule-governed. Dramatic behavior changes occur many times every day, contrary to the pessimistic opinion of most psychologists, teachers, and parents that it is very hard to change adolescents' behavior. For example, a bell rings, students sit more or less quietly, not eating, running, or throwing. The bell rings and everyone is running, talking, touching for 5 minutes. The bell rings again and now some students in new uniforms are running and throwing things, legitimately—baseballs, footballs, soccer balls, basketballs, volleyballs, etc. Other students are making noise, legitimately "singing" or playing instruments. The bell rings again, and students race to their next period where many are now eating. Each period brings instantaneous mass behavior change.

The point is that the rules defining the "do's and don'ts during a period of time in a designated space determine behavior and behavior changes far more extensively than personality, IQ, social class, or ethnic background."

If you want to predict what students will be doing at 10 o'clock on Wednesday, which would you rather know: their Rorschach test results, their SAT scores, their family backgrounds, or the class they are in plus the formal rules of learning and informal rules of the war games? In a milling game, as in other classroom war games, the rules *cause* conflict: "Provoke the teacher . . . ," "Never move farther or faster . . . ," "Anger is O.K. . . ."

Of course, individuals differ in their responses to each period's game (the classroom game, the hallway game, the gym game, the cafeteria game, the study hall game, and so on). But the differences between games is far greater than the individual differences within games. This became obvious to us when we followed groups of students from classroom to classroom during the day. In one class the teacher presided over an incipient rebellion. Students ignored the teacher's requests, voiced muffled insults, and played the milling game all period. The two or three "pet" students were as noticeable as the two or three rebel leaders. The next period the same group of students spent the majority of the period on the edge of their seats in total attention as they worked on diagramming sentences! Within this orderly learning environment the same rebel leaders stood out, and the same pet students could be identified. The transformation from a killer class to a model class in 5 minutes was far more impressive than the differences between the rebels and pets. Even the rebels were "decent," tolerable learners in the model class.

This phenomenon is observable to anyone who can follow a group of students through the day. Unfortunately, this excludes virtually all practicing teachers who must spend all day in their own classroom. Teachers only see the variations in student behavior. Over lunch, or in the teachers' lounge, they confirm their identification of the rebels and the pets and reinforce their conviction that the problems lie in the rebels rather than in the rules and roles.

Students see the extreme variation from class to class and simplistically conclude that there are good teachers and bad teachers. We believe that both views are incomplete and that the essential differences among classrooms are the formal learning games and the informal war games. These games can be changed.

IN WAR GAMES PLAYERS ARE UNJUSTLY BLAMED FOR THE CONFLICT

A teacher has had a long day of war games. It is June, hot, and the last period of the day. A student returns from the pencil sharpener for the fourth time that period entertaining everyone with a magnificently stylish "slow walk." The teacher barks: "Out! Get out!" writes a referral slip, and sends the student to the front office. The student continues to slow walk to the door of the classroom and exits to the appreciative applause of the class. The teacher massages her aching head as another student with a "broken" pencil heads slowly toward the sharpener.

Players in war games rotate through the roles. Punishing players does not change the games or reduce conflict any more than putting a high-sticking hockey player in the penalty box reduces the level of violence on the ice. The game is to blame, not the players. The rules and roles need to be changed if the level of conflict and the number of war games is to be reduced.

This characteristic points to an obvious injustice. To the degree that the game causes conflict, then to that degree are students treated unjustly. While the vast majority of specific discipline war games involve both a teacher and a student, only students are punished, referred, paddled, detained, suspended, expelled, or excluded. Typically, in desegregated schools the punishment of students is also racist. Our data from Springfield in 1971–1973 are consistent with the national norms reported by the Children's Defense Fund (1975). The percentage of black students on the suspension rolls is usually about twice the percentage of the black population in the school. This is evidence of the double domination of them as "students" and as black Americans.

What is done about this problem depends to a great degree on what people believe to be the causes. "Blacks can't get along. They come from poor and broken homes where they are not taught proper discipline and respect. They aren't as bright, as a group. Consequently, they don't learn to read as well or as quickly. This leads to conflict in the classroom. They'd rather fight than admit they can't read." This stereotyped and racist explanation blames the victims and generates efforts to change them. An alternative explanation is, "White teachers are racist. Some, in particular, are killer teachers who account for a disproportionate number of referrals. If only they could be reformed or terminated, the situation would improve tremendously." This explanation, like the first, blames victims, for it is a rare teacher who enjoys conflicts and expulsions. Most often referrals to the front office are painful, last-resort acts taken after all else has failed. In contrast, blaming the war game focuses on the regular mismatch of learning-teaching styles, systematically misunderstood interaction patterns, or errors of omission within the system (e.g., personnel composition, textbooks, posters, or cafeteria food that does not adequately accommodate diverse ethnic tastes). This way of naming and understanding the problem focuses our energies on the systemic factors that place people in conflict, victimize them, and waste human resources.

Punishing players is inefficient as well as unjust. If punishing players were a solution, the number of suspensions would decrease from year to year. During a seven-year period of desegregation in the Springfield school system the number of short-term suspensions increased by 747 percent. Even though more and more students were suspended, the classroom war games continued, the ranks of the armies of the streets were swelled, and the numbers of intruders increased, along with vandalism and violence. Teachers, then administrators, simply pushed the problem along, relocating it rather than resolving it.

Perhaps our tendency to blame persons rather than systems stems from our formal and informal education. From toilet training to lectures in the assistant principal's office, from merit badges to diplomas, from the Declaration of Independence ("Every individual has the right to pursue . . .") to marriage contracts, from mass media that display our magnificent array of choices to courts that hold us accountable for our poor choices, we have been taught to believe that we determine our own behavior. And we have a pervasive, gut-level, unnamed conviction that the schools in which we work are basically democratic, unoppressive, and sound.

Often social scientists collude in blaming the players instead of the game. Many studies ask questions like, "What are the characteristics of problem students?" We asked that question and our data "proved" that such students are more often boys than girls, proportionately more of them are in ninth than the eighth or the seventh grade, they have lower IQ's and lower reading scores, and they are disproportionately black (Irons, 1975). What do such results mean? Obviously, we could decrease the number of referrals to the front office by mass anticipatory protective expulsions of black, low IQ, ninth grade males at the beginning of the school year.

We also asked, "What are the characteristics of teachers who have more discipline problems?" The answer, in brief, is: young, first-year teachers without tenure. And in most schools usually fewer than 10 percent of the teachers, "killer teachers," account for well over 50 percent of all front office disciplinary referrals. The solution: Don't hire young first-year teachers and fire the killers.

Obviously, both solutions are absurd, because the *questions* are biased. They blame individuals and dictate the answers. We can only find individual characteristics if that is all we look for.

We believe that an overemphasis on blaming individual students, teachers, or administrators not only prevents us from seeing more fundamental causes in the classroom and school, but *creates* a cycle of adversary relationships based on uncharitable assumptions. Although it is appropriate to feel upset about the pain inflicted on all victims, it is not appropriate to direct our anger naively at those individuals who appear to be inflicting the damage. Most people are doing their jobs the best they know how and believe their efforts will promote the common good.

IN WAR GAMES TEACHERS RULE STUDENTS

Teachers make decisions about what students should do, when, how, how fast, where, and why. Students react, respond, resist, and rebel. If a teacher unilaterally changes the rules of the class to be "better," "fairer," "more humanistic," "more individualized," "more efficient," that teacher will have perpetuated this characteristic of war games. Teachers need to make decisions *with* students, not for them, if peace is to be won.

Some teachers who have seen the light at a weekend retreat return to class on Monday, ready and eager to love instead of punish. Imagine what would happen if a reformed hockey coach came to practice one day ready to lead the team on a nature hike? He wouldn't coach for long. Yet that is the well-intentioned strategy of some teachers. They believe that if they are nicer, gentler, more loving, allowing, open, direct, honest, empathetic, and respectful, then the problems of the classroom will melt away. These human characteristics are valuable—and insufficient. Teachers, with students, need to name, analyze, and transform the formal and informal rules governing behavior in the classroom, define what is desirable and what the rewards will be for good performance. Some names for this process are: collaboration, cooperation, the democratic way, liberation, Social Literacy.

WAR GAMES EXIST AT SEVERAL LEVELS IN SCHOOLS

Educators tend to think about problems as if they were caused by individuals even when classroom and school-wide war games are obvious. For instance, several seventh grade students failed a course at the end of the first semester. In fact, 183 of 450 seventh graders failed one or more courses that semester. This was twice the rate of the previous year. Yet their scores on the Iowa Test of Basic Skills were 10 percent higher than those of the previous year. The principal was concerned and asked the guidance counselor to investigate the problem—no, not by looking for changes in the school-wide war game—(get-tough grading policies, new textbooks, new norms among teachers, increases in student loads, etc.) but by talking with each of those 183 students individually. The principal's request was well intentioned, and he may even have seen the possibility of a school-wide war game causing so many learning casualties. But no matter what he had in mind, when a student is called down to the guidance office and asked, "Why did you fail?", the student is likely to take it personally. The school-wide cause remained hidden while the students' self-esteem was battered twice, first when they were failed, and second when they were asked to name their inadequacy. As difficult as it is to focus on the classroom game instead of blaming the players, it appears to be even more difficult to see and act to change school-wide war games.

Test yourself on this actual situation. How would you name, analyze, and solve this problem? You teach in a desegregated urban junior high school. Every day the same student arrives late to your class without a pass. The daily doorway scene reminds you of Tom Sawyer's attempts to persuade Aunt Polly that his tardiness was caused by unavoidable and highly virtuous rescue missions. Whether or not you believe these excuses, the discussion always steals precious learning time from the whole class. The interruptions bother you and the other students.

What would you do? Try to change the student? Coax him? Threaten him? Send him to the front office? Enlist other students to exert peer pressure? Meet with him after class to negotiate a better "contract?"

All of these solutions assume that the cause of the problem is *in* the student. In the school where these doorway debates took place, we discovered that teachers had made 121 referrals to the front office over the course of a year because these "con jobs" had broken down into angry confrontations. Approximately one-third of these students were expelled from school —paradoxically, a punishment quite similar to the "crime." In a school of 1,200 students, this was a problem of epidemic proportions. No matter what an individual teacher did with an individual student, "the problem" would remain.

In this school, the principal changed a rule. The next year all students late to class went immediately to the front office for a free pass, up to three times. A fourth "lateness" was considered a chronic personal problem and led to a serious discussion. This simple system change resulted in a 75 percent reduction in this type of referral to the front office, fewer classroom conflicts and interruptions, and more learning time. In retrospect, the success of this solution indicates that the cause of the problem was in the rules that forced students and teachers into conflict. Also in retrospect, numerous students had been suspended unnecessarily *because* the assistant principals were doing their job the best they knew how, enforcing the rules and attempting to get compliance, instead of changing the conflict-causing rules.

The assistant principals in this school had denied that they were a part of the problem. During a district-wide "Suspension Committee" study of the problem, its causes and cures, we discovered that over one of every five long-term suspensions in the entire district of forty-three schools came from this one junior high school. By contrast, another junior high school in the same district had virtually no long-term suspensions, although it was similar in size and ethnic composition of students and faculty. After a brief discussion, the significant difference appeared to be the rules governing the assistant principals' roles. In the killer school both assistant principals spent nearly full time in the front office disciplining students. In the other junior high school, one of the assistant principals was in the front office and the other was in classrooms, particularly those of teachers with high referral rates, helping them revise their procedures to reduce classroom conflict, and thus reduce the necessity for referrals. This deescalated the level of conflict and short-circuited the cycle of school violence. The assistant principals in the killer school believed they were doing a good job, and they were. The job was wrong. They waged war on the students, who, needless to say, were always provided with a rationale for their suspension and legal due process as they were victimized. The rules governing the assistant principals' role in the killer school needed to be changed to stop the cycle of violence and to start winning peace in classrooms.

This analysis of "the discipline problem" can be summarized quickly. Battles for students' attention often consume more than half of the school day. These battles comprise a variety of war games. The rules of war games force educators and students into conflicts in which the satisfaction of legitimate human needs comes at the expense of the other side. It is difficult to see that oppressive classroom war games are to blame and should be changed, not the warriors (teachers or students). It is even more difficult to see and blame school-wide war games for these systemic conflicts.

The next operational questions are these: How do you democratically name, blame, and change war games? How do you create mutually satisfying rules? How do you transform warrior roles into peaceful educational roles? In short, how do you liberate people from conflict and win peace in school? The stakes are high. The battle for students' attention can be decreased. The discipline problem can be reduced.

Resolving Conflicts Through Social Literacy

The goals of Social Literacy training are to change oppressive roles, not the role inhabitants; oppressive goals, not those who advocate them; oppressive rules, not the rule enforcers; oppressive practices, not the practitioners; oppressive policies, not the policy makers; oppressive norms, not the normal people who act them out. We believe that it is both more humane and usually more effective to see these distinctions clearly and to cherish all persons while acting collaboratively to change oppressive war games, the rules of school wars, and the warrior roles.

This is an idealistic and difficult aim, particularly for teachers whose total day is consumed by literally hundreds of brief encounters with specific individuals. One way to start counteracting the strong pressure to see, name, and blame individuals only, is to make several assumptions when conflict is experienced. Try saying to yourself:

1. My needs are legitimate. Other people's needs are legitimate too, even though we are in conflict and even though I may not be sure what their needs really are.

2. This conflict is not unique. I am sure other people are having similar problems. There is a pattern in these conflicts, though I may not see it now.

3. We can find a way for all of our needs to be met without conflict, though I may not know that solution now.

4. We are playing a war game and *it* is to blame for the conflict. We need to change the rules and roles, not the players.

5. As an individual, I cannot figure this out and solve it alone. I need to talk with other teachers or students or administrators to name the game, the rules, the roles, the needs. I need the cooperation of others to resolve this pattern of conflict and to play a new game in which we all can win.

A Machiavellian social architect could not have invented a more effective system than the one we have for discouraging teachers from getting together to name, understand, and solve common problems. For the better part of each working day, teachers are isolated from other adults, a working condition suffered in few other professions. Almost never do a significant number of teachers have simultaneous free time for discussion, planning, and collaborative action. The minimal free time available must be spent in preparation or recuperation. Some schools have strong informal norms against serious discussion of educational issues in the lunchroom and teachers' lounge, where cards and gossip are useful diversions. Shortly after the final bell, many teachers leave school as if shot from a cannon, too tired to spend an extra hour thinking about school. Teachers' meetings are more often times when administrators inform, announce, or decree than a time for open discussion of school-wide problems. Teachers know that if they say anything they are likely to be put on another committee and, in any case, they will have delayed the close of the meeting. Teachers who are isolated and preoccupied in these ways remain unaware of problems common to most teachers and often assume that difficulties they experience are caused by personal incompetence. Survival in the classroom takes precedence over attempts to innovate or change the war games, since any change risks the loss of classroom control.

By contrast, when a Social Literacy group meets, it develops camaraderie and an awareness of common interests, provides support, reduces risks, and increases the power to solve problems. Social Literacy groups need not be large. As Saul Alinsky observed, about 4 percent of an organization's membership run it. The rest remain in a state of acquiescence. Because the Machiavellian characteristics of most schools so effectively disorganize teachers, even as few as four teachers in a faculty of sixty can be a mutually beneficial, politically powerful force. Having three other adults you know you can count on for help, can make the difference between a fulfilling and frustrating year.

A Social Literacy group is radical in at least three senses. As in mathematics, where a radical is an essential quantity of a larger quantity, Social Literacy groups try to name the essential systemic causes of widespread problems. In botany, a radical is that which grows out of a root. As teachers become socially literate, radical explanations grow out of naming the root systemic causes. In politics, being a radical means to advocate basic social change in the same way that the Social Literacy group focuses on the transformation of troublesome rules and roles rather than on the rule enforcers and role occupants. For instance, we are more interested in negotiating simple changes in the school's tardiness rules than in training all teachers in better doorway tactics. We are more interested in radical solutions to the problem of students racing for the exits after school (e.g., changing the bus schedule) than in coaxing other teachers to patrol the hallways. We are more interested in changing the assistant principal's role than in kicking more kids out of school.

Here are some of the socially literate solutions that emerged from the first groups to meet in Springfield.

. "No referrals" became the motto in one group. But there were times when conflict with a student had to be stopped quickly for everyone's sanity before an underlying pattern was identified and analyzed and a change in the rules or roles was implemented. Several Social Literacy teachers made a "mutual aid agreement." Explosive situations were defused either by sending the student to the other teacher's class or by immediate mediation by the second teacher. This solution did not work perfectly, but did cut the number of referrals to the front office to one quarter of what it had been the previous year.

▪ Three teachers in a Social Literacy group discovered that they shared a common frustration with the way geography was being taught. They managed to arrange their schedule to get the same period free each day to develop more relevant subject matter and methods.

▪ A shy teacher in a Social Literacy group realized that her frustrated desire to get supervisory experience was complemented by the pressing need of two first-year teachers for help in devising exciting lesson plans.

▪ A new state law in Massachusetts required that students with special needs be "mainstreamed." No preparatory training was provided for teachers. One Social Literacy group collaborated with the Special Education teachers, who held classes in their school to plan, publicize, and conduct a district-wide workshop. In the process they also discovered new methods for individualizing and humanizing instruction. What student doesn't want to be considered special?

▪ In one junior high school students travel in the same group from class to class all day. This decreases the range course options available to students, limits instruction in the student body, and tended to fix them in a narrow social role. The Social Literacy group learned the necessary computer technology from a university professor who donated his time, and led the effort to install flexible scheduling.

▪ While visiting each others' classes to diagnose what was happening during the time students were not attending to instructional material, Social Literacy teachers discovered a common pattern. Every time the P.A. system blurted out, there was a disruption period averaging four minutes in most classes. Past individual attempts to cope included talking back to the box, installing off-on switches in the wires or simply cutting the wires (on the correct assumption that it wouldn't be fixed for a year and that crucial messages would be hand-delivered anyway). Realizing that a union contract provision was being violated by using the P.A. between the first and last 5 minutes of the period, the Social Literacy group presented the situation to the principal. He had not realized that school-wide disruption was being caused and agreed to abide by the contract.

▪ In one school, teachers set up a "care room." Each teacher who donated a period of time to staff the care room was entitled to refer students there at any time for any purpose—special help, cooling off, etc.

▪ Women teachers in one school discovered that they were being treated in a sexist way and were colluding in playing stereotyped, feminine teacher roles. They formed a consciousness-raising group to work on this problem in detail.

These examples illustrate several unique characteristics of socially literate methods of reducing the discipline problem: (1) Socially literate solutions do not blame individuals. Individuals cooperate to change the rules and roles of the system. (2) Social Literacy leads to multileveled solutions that win peace in interpersonal, classroom, and school-wide war games. (3) Socially Literate solutions yield a broad range of outcomes related to better discipline—fewer classroom conflicts, more learning of the subject matter discipline, greater disciple-ship and increased personal discipline.

During the first five years of our collaboration with teachers in the Springfield school system, we had come to understand Paulo Freire's philosophy by translating it into practice in one urban school district. As we worked with teachers in three of the six junior high schools on specific daily problems, we also invented a number of more generally useful collaborative problem-solving procedures. During this period, research on the Springfield school system's discipline procedures and on Freire's theory was completed in five doctoral dissertations. Through articles in national magazines and a national radio interview, workshops in fourteen states and responses to over one thousand direct requests for information from across the country, over 200,000 educators received information about Social Literacy. Informal estimates of the dollar cost to obtain this amount of research and development approximate $500,000. In fact, during the first two years we needed only $48 to buy some books for teachers. In the next three years we stretched a two-year, $32,000 grant[5] to pay partial living expenses of several doctoral students working on the project. During this five-year period, most of the time, energy, space, and materials were donated.

In contrast with these accomplishments and our many heart-warming anecdotes, we had little hard data that discipline problems were significantly reduced. We decided to train a critical mass of educators in the secondary schools of Springfield, Massachusetts, and Hartford, Connecticut, and conduct a sophisticated research evaluation of the effects on discipline. We obtained funding from the U.S. Office of Education for a Title IV Civil Rights Act Desegregation Training Institute.[6] During the summer of 1976 we trained 100 teachers from ten schools in an intensive three-week

[5]We express our gratitude to the Community Council of Greater Springfield and to its director, Mr. Robert Van Wart, for their generous support.
[6]Increased discipline conflict and inequitable exclusion of ethnic minority students frequently occur with desegregation. We were given funds to help reduce these unfortunate and unjust consequences.

workshop. Those who continued in the Social Literacy project during the school year recruited and trained an additional 93 of their peers. By the end of the year, the total group had reported 293 socially literate solutions to interpersonal problems (21 percent), classroom problems (40 percent), and school-wide problems (31 percent).[7] Over half of the teachers endorsed all of the following fifteen items in describing the effects of Social Literacy in their lives:

Effects of Socially Literate Problem Solving	Percentage of teachers endorsing this item
I have adapted Social Literacy techniques for handling problems with students	82%
I feel I am better equipped to handle discipline problems	86%
The way I handle discipline conflicts has improved	81%
I have fewer disruptions because of discipline conflicts	65%
I am more understanding of students' views	65%
There is a positive change in my behavior with students	73%
I am more satisfied with my behavior with students	75%
I share more of my experiences with other staff members than I used to	74%
Interpersonal relationships around staff members have improved	75%
I have adopted socially literate techniques for handling problems with administrators	65%
This is a change for the better in the rapport between staff and administrators	57%
The workshop training had a beneficial impact on my professional style	83%
My attitude about school is more positive	61%
I am able to apply this training in my personal life	77%
I have personally benefitted from the project training	83%

[7]Eight percent were unclassifiable.

We also intensively studied pairs of classes taught by twelve different teachers, with one experimental class and one comparison class in each pair. The comparison class did not go through any Social Literacy problem solving with the teacher. In brief, students in the experimental classes reported significantly more democratic participation in decision making and more orderly classes, and they learned significantly more as measured by the objective portions of their final exams. Decreased conflict in the classroom was reflected in the rate Social Literacy teachers referred students to the front office for disciplining. On the average, other teachers in the same school not trained in Social Literacy methods sent more than three times as many students out of the classroom for disciplining. Interestingly, the impact of Social Literacy training was not reflected in decreased suspension rates. Stabbings of two teachers in the school system led to a system-wide crackdown. This took the form of suspending more students more quickly, even though there may have been fewer total referrals to the front office. It appears that the major effects of Social Literacy are in the classroom and in the quality of interpersonal relationships in the school.[8]

During the last six years the Social Literacy project has demonstrated that it is possible to overcome the obstacles to collaborative problem solving and to develop workable solutions to daily conflicts. Oppression and the victimization of students decreased. Democratic classroom management, order, learning, and collaborative relationships increased. How was this done? The standard answer is both accurate and *un*informative. We began small, with a two-year entry process guided by Freire's beacon philosophy. We diagnosed the central conflict, analyzed the causes, invented ways of resolving those conflicts, then taught those problem-solving methods to others. Over time, with the success of the problem-solving methods and specific solutions, we gradually accrued some positive publicity. This became a lever to recruit new educators, new schools, and eventually, sizable federal support. Slowly, each specific success eroded (but never conquered completely) teachers' conviction that conflict and stress are "facts" of their existence, professional hazards that come with their chosen vocation. While these institutional and personal obstacles were being reduced, we explicitly taught an alternative mind-set. Democratic problem solving is a goal of education; dialogue is a means, and system blaming rather than person blaming is a guiding principle.

While this summary explanation is crudely accurate, it misses the heart

---

[8]A complete presentation of our research is contained in A.S. Alschuler's "School discipline through Social Literacy", in *Education for Values,* D.C. McClelland (Ed.), Irvington Press, N.Y., 1980.

of the matter. We began with a commitment to one school, in one school system, to solve some mutually determined problems and to continue that process so long, and only so long, as it was mutually beneficial. The *sine qua non* was this commitment to actualizing an ideal of humane relationships among people in schools. All else was secondary and followed from this first and abiding commitment.

We do not believe there are standard answers or final solutions to conflicts in school. Consultants peddling solutions in slick multimedia packages raise justifiable questions in experienced educators' minds about the motives of the purveyor, about the "workableness" of the product and about their own, often dehumanized roles as passive consumers of magical answers. Often teachers immediately and instinctively reject these modern circuit riders selling patent medicine for school ills. We believe that it is important for each group of teachers to engage in the socially literate problem-solving *processes* of naming basic conflicts, reflecting on the causes, and cooperatively changing the system. We believe that making collaborative problem solving a reality in schools begins with the commitment to democratic processes as an ideal.

THREE

Rebellion or Peace in Our Nation's Schools

On a sunny spring afternoon I opened the door of a junior high school library where I was to meet with several teachers. Instead, the entire faculty was sitting silently, listening to an assistant principal. I was hidden from general view by a tall bookshelf near the door.

"You failed," he shouted. "It's unprofessional. It's in your contract. It's a rule that you *must* be by the door of your room when school closes to monitor the hallways. If you'd been doing what you were supposed to, we wouldn't have had the assault this afternoon. Do I have to patrol the halls checking on you? Do I have to treat you like children?"

No one answered. My fists were clenched and slightly shaking as each sentence clubbed the teachers. After the 25-minute tirade was over, the teachers sat in silence. Then one teacher raised his hand slowly.

"The 'assault' started because two students ran into each other, right? Maybe they were running because of the buses. They only have 4 minutes before the buses leave. Couldn't the buses leave a little later?"

"No! The buses have to get to the next stop."

After a brief pause the principal dismissed the faculty. While waiting for my meeting to begin, I thought about the teacher's suggestion. It was simple and plausible, although only a partial solution. Why was it instantly rejected? The assistant principal seemed so determined to blame the teachers solely, to keep them on the spot and not allow them any excuses. Yet, I was sure he didn't detest them. I imagined him dealing with hundreds of conflicts each week—petty burglaries, shake downs, extortion in the bathrooms, grudge fights, insolence, disobedience, and disrespect. While life in school is not constantly dangerous, all he saw every day, all day, were examples of conflict, hate, and brutishness. As he tried to cope with this tide of violence, perhaps his own frustration rose past the breaking point with that fight that afternoon. He had to get the help of teachers; the two assistant principals could not resolve all discipline conflicts themselves. To ensure the physical safety of students, he righteously demanded that teachers do their jobs as defined in their contracts. Yes, I could understand his position and even grant that his intentions were noble. But it was equally clear that his dictatorial style was insulting and his lack of sympathy angered his professional peers.

The next day I observed classes at the same school. At the close of school I was in the front office sitting at a vacant secretarial desk making notes, when a teacher pulled a stumbling student in by the collar, yelling "Sit down!"

The student hung his head but remained standing.

"Sit down!!" he repeated as if the student were a disobedient dog.

"Better watch yourself," the student mumbled.

"I'll watch myself when you're this tall," snapped back the teacher, indicating the height of a basketball center. "What's your name?" Silence. "What's your name?!"

The principal, standing nearby filling out a pass, calmly said to the teacher, "That's OK, I'll handle it. What's the problem?"

"This student was running in the halls."

The principal witnessed the teacher's zeal, excused him, and politely asked the student to sit on the long, blond oak bench in front of the office.

It was easy to feel sympathy for the student who was dragged in and verbally brutalized in public. My first reaction was to silently condemn the teacher. Then I realized the teacher was doing exactly what he had been told to do, with a vengeance. This was a well-meaning teacher under stress, forced into conflict with a student by a contractual obligation and an explicit command from his superior.

Within twenty-four hours I saw violence spread like a contagious disease. A fight in the hallway led to an angry confrontation in the library which led to cuffing a student. I wondered how the student would abide by the informal code of honor that demanded revenge. Would he take it out on an innocent student with a random punch in the stomach to prove that his "machismo" was intact, and thus start another circle of violence with another assault? Would he shake down a seventh grader in the bathroom, or defiantly smoke dope behind the corner of the gym? Or would one of his teachers encounter surliness the next day or discover a grade book stolen, or a tire slashed, or a window broken? Or would the student simply feel more deeply disaffected, resentful, and angry? I wondered where, not whether, this chain of hate would continue. I watched good people pass on their anger. All played their prescribed roles in this ongoing drama of conflict. Freire's "trust in the people" and faith that they can create "a world in which it will be easier to love" seemed as remote as the rings around Saturn.

This specific cycle of violence illustrates several characteristics of violence in schools. Acts of violence are not isolated, random events. They are understandable reactions in a chain of events that cause everyone to suffer —administrators, teachers, and particularly students, who are oppressed by governance of the adults, by the adults, for everyone. The lack of participation by students in determining the rules governing even the most trivial aspects of their lives in school is a nationwide phenomenon and one cause of nationwide violence in schools. Liberation from this conflict first requires a critical analysis: How extensive is the oppression of students? What is the range of students' reactions and the response of educators?

Waging War

Oppression of students

All experiences hath shown that mankind are more disposed to suffer, while evils are sufferable, than to right themselves by abolishing the forms [of governance] to which they are accustomed. But when a long train of abuses and usurpations pursuing invariably the same object evinces a design to reduce them under absolute despotism, it is their right, it is their duty to throw off such government and to provide new guards for their future security.

Declaration of Independence

Are schools designed to reduce students under absolute despotism? If so, is this evil sufferable? In 1971, the prestigious Association for Supervision and Curriculum commissioned a national survey to answer these questions. A total of 10,731 students in grades four through twelve in 140 representative school districts across the country were asked about 255 oppressive school practices: Did these practices exist and, if so, did they bother students? (Frymier, Bills, Russell, and Finch, 1974).

In general, students do perceive schools as despotic: 80.5 percent said they did not have a chance to write the rules and regulations. This despotism appears to be nearly absolute: 73.1 percent said that everyone has to do the same thing at the same time and 71.2 percent claimed they needed permission to do anything. Students reported that teachers make the decisions about what students should learn (85.7 percent) and even where they should sit in class (64.0 percent). What students say is important to them is *not* studied (64.0 percent). Students have neither a chance to decide how much work they should do in a class (82.0 percent) nor what the learning activities should be (63.4 percent). Content, process, and pace are prescribed. One hallmark of a democracy is the existence of mechanisms for getting a fair hearing. A whopping 80.4 percent of the students said they cannot change the things they do not like. Even when they think a teacher's decision is not fair, 71.5 percent said they cannot get the decision changed.[1]

Do students suffer from these evils? Yes. In the Frymier et al. study, on the average three-fourths of those saying an oppressive practice existed also said they were bothered by it. Three other national surveys found equally pervasive student dissatisfaction with oppressive school practices. Of the students responding to a Harris Poll (*Life,* 1969), 88 percent said that student participation in policy making was important and 58 percent wanted more participation, particularly in the area of rule making (66 percent) and curriculum (63 percent). Eighty-three percent of the students in a 1970 Gallup Poll said they wanted a greater voice in making the rules and 77 percent wanted similar participation in determining the curriculum.

DeCecco and Richards (1974, p. 16) interviewed approximately 7,000 urban and suburban elementary, junior, and senior high school students from the East Coast and 1,500 from the West Coast to identify "democratic dilemmas" students face in school. They concluded that, "Of all the injustices students felt . . . the most frequent was their exclusion from the decision-making process in their own schools—their subjections to rules they could not help to form, change or enforce." Over 80 percent of the students said they had no say in how these conflicts were resolved. Social scientists who have studied single schools intensively (see Jackson, 1968; Rhea, 1968) concur that students see themselves as "conscripts," taken without permission into a system over which they have no control. Haney

---

[1]After analyzing the pattern of responses the authors concluded that students generally like their teachers as individuals but not the schools programs and policies. Further, boys tend to indicate greater oppression in these areas than girls, nonwhites more than whites, and older students more than younger students. These differences among students are minor, however, compared to the extent of oppression bothering all students in all grade levels, of both sexes, and all races in every part of the country.

and Zimbardo (1973) even go so far as to describe detailed similarities between schools and prisons.[2]

In principle, it is unacceptable that schools in a democracy should resemble medieval serfdoms with teacher-lords exacting learning-tithes from student-vassals. And there are pernicious consequences in practice. Certainly, some students find these oppressive practices insufferable and rebel. The connection between oppression and rebellion is explicit in the National Institute of Education's study of safe and violent schools (1978).

The violent students are more likely to be those who have given up on school, do not care about grades, find courses irrelevant and feel that nothing they do makes any difference. . . . Students need to feel that their courses are relevant and that they have some control over what happens to them. Otherwise, their feelings of frustration can erupt in violence" (p. 5).

These students need not be a majority to cause a crisis in schools. During our Revolutionary War the rebels were never a majority among the colonists. Nationwide oppression in schools and students' responses form a cycle of violence that has the mark and scope of a national school rebellion.

Cries and complaints

Men who injure and oppress the people under their administration provoke them to cry out and complain; and then make that very complaint the foundation for new oppression and prosecutions.

Alexander Hamilton

When classes are oppressive, dull, and irrelevant, students are provoked to cry out and complain. They passively resist in class, harass the teachers, boycott classes and school, and retaliate against persons and property in a set of tactics amounting to guerrilla warfare. Educators then make these cries and complaints the foundation for new oppression and prosecutions.

Distractions, defiance, and insubordination in classrooms are not newsworthy, but they consistently disrupt the educational process, drastically reduce learning time, and harass teachers. This daily, hourly, ongoing retaliation is a sniper war. Tactics consist of talking, whispering, lip reading, passing notes, insulting the teacher or other students, complaining about requests or instructions, pushing, brushing, touching, shoving or hitting other students, throwing things (peas, paper clips, pencils, split balls, gum,

[2] I am indebted to James Block and Robert Elmore for their review of this literature.

etc.), walking around to visit or to sharpen pencils or to stretch excessively, requesting passes to the toilets or lockers, making a veritable symphony of noises (tapping feet, drumming the desk top, humming, playing imaginary harmonicas, whistling, giggling, cracking gum, banging teeth with a pencil, snapping shut cigarette lighters). As many as thirty to sixty incidents take place per class period. Virtually all students snipe, sooner or later, more or less.

Another favorite revolutionary tactic is massive passive resistance in the form of boycotting. In a survey of 100 high school administrators in New York and California (Duke, 1978) the three top problems from urban and suburban communities were "skipping class," "truancy," and "lateness to class." [Statistically,] How extensive is this boycotting? Dr. Owen B. Kiernam, the executive secretary of the National Association of Secondary School Principals, testified before the Senate subcommittee investigating juvenile delinquency:

We have many cities where the absentee rates are 30 percent. There are some cities in fact where faculty members would be delighted to claim better than 50 percent attendance on a given day (Bayh, 1977 p. 23).

These figures do not include absenteeism created by the school in the form of suspensions and expulsions. Senator Bayh, chairman of the Senate subcommittee, traces a chain of consequences. Many truants and suspended students become "intruders [who] account for a surprisingly large percentage of the violence inflicted on teachers and students within our schools." It also has been estimated that up to 70 percent of the vandalism is done by "truants" and "class cutters." One further effect of violence and vandalism is to increase the boycotting. "Some students stay away from school because they are simply afraid to go" (Bayh, 1977, pp. 22–24).

A minority of students actively retaliate against the school. Attacks on property ("thefts," "vandalism," "malicious mischief," and "arson") cost as much as $590 million yearly. This sum exceeds the total amount spent on textbooks in 1972. It would be equivalent to a vandalism tax of $13 levied on every public school student. These funds are diverted from the direct support of education to meet the rising costs of assuring the schools' physical survival (increased insurance premiums, preventive security measures, and the expense of repairs). During a period of level school funding when other costs are rising (salaries and heating, for example), a few angry students can quickly bring a system to its financial knees. Arson by four boys of a senior high school learning resource center in one town cost $1 million, including damage to the building, loss of 40,000 volumes, 10,000 periodicals, and $50,000 in audiovisual equipment (ibid., p. 14). By far the most common sorts of sabotage, arson and window breakage (which cost 65 cents of every vandalism dollar), can leave schools looking like victims of a bombing raid.

The human toll from this guerrilla warfare is staggering. Each year over 52,000 (5 percent) of the nation's one million secondary school teachers are attacked, 10,000 of whom require medical treatment. Sixty thousand teachers (6 percent) are robbed each year and 120,000 (12 percent) have something stolen *each month* (National Institute of Education, 1978). Naturally enough, these types of student retaliation create a climate of fear in schools. According to a 1976 survey by *Instructor Magazine* (Sylvester, 1977), the number one health problem of teachers is stress. After interviewing 243 "battered teachers," Alfred Block, a Los Angeles psychiatrist, concluded that the syndrome of their symptoms was classic "battle fatigue" (Block, n.d.).

One index of guerrilla activity is the number of weapons in schools. Between 1970 and 1973 the number of the weapons seized in our nation's schools increased by 54.4 percent; many were capable of lethal force: knives, Saturday night specials, karate sticks (Bayh, 1977).

New oppressions and prosecutions

Why does this national cycle of violence continue? The answer is ultimately speculative. We can, however, describe some of the ways we collude by doing nothing about it.

TACTICS OF PASSIVE COLLUSION

DENY THE FACTS In 1977 The National Institute of Education surveyed 6,700 elementary and secondary school principals, asking them to assess the seriousness of vandalism, personal attacks, and thefts in their school. Only a minuscule 2 percent of these administrators said that this was a serious problem (National Institute of Education, 1978, p. 2). It was as though physicians claimed that cancer is not a serious problem because it kills only one in every twenty persons. If the official authorities in schools do not see a problem and admit it exists, there is little chance of initiating constructive solutions.

SUPPRESS THE FACTS Many incidents of violence, vandalism, thefts, and conflict in school are not reported. Estimates of the degree of underreporting vary, but not the fact of underreporting. The reasons for this "hush-up" are varied. Some schools lack effective record-keeping procedures. Some administrators pressure teachers not to report incidents that would reflect poorly on their ability to run the school. Some parents pressure teachers and administrators not to get their children into trouble by telling the police. Some school boards pressure educators not to tarnish the school system's public image for fear of losing the next bond issue or tax levy. Some teachers avoid or ignore problems because of the hassles that result from reporting. Some students do not report shake downs, extortions, thefts, or beatings for fear of retaliation. Some observers believe that only 10 percent of these rebellious acts in school buildings are reported (*The Reform of Secondary Education,* 1973, p. 117). If the true dimensions of the problem were known, the shock itself might be enough to force the public to recognize the rebellion and do something about it.

ISOLATE THE FACTS Those reporting the facts are often like blind people touching different parts of an elephant. Oppressive school practices are widely documented. The facts of vandalism, violence, and conflict have been disseminated nationally. Rampant absenteeism, truancy, declining test scores are well known. Detention, suspension, and expulsion rates are high, particularly in junior high schools. In isolation, these seem like magical phenomena from out of nowhere, like rabbits emerging from an empty hat. These facts need to be accepted, accurately estimated, and seen as *connected* in a cycle of violence to causes and effects.

BLAME IT ON IRRESISTIBLE FORCES Typical explanations for school violence include: rising violence in the larger society, the aftermath of a war that taught people how to be violent, the lack of full and satisfying employment opportunities for youths, the lack of adequate recreational facilities, the impact of TV violence, the availability of deadly weapons, the breakdown of family life, the growing acceptance of drugs and alcohol, and a recent favorite, hyperactivity caused by eating too much junk food. From this perspective, schools and teachers are innocent victims of irresistible forces in the outside social system. By this reasoning, individual educators must learn to cope with, but cannot cure, the problem in their schools.

DIVERT ATTENTION The cry, "Let us get back to the basics," is reminiscent of former President Nixon's plea on national TV at the height of the unfolding Watergate conspiracy. "Let us now put Watergate behind us and get on with the business of the nation." We could not get back to the normal business of government until the conspiracy was excised. Indeed, let us get back to basic democratic principles in schools, to basic operation in the teaching-learning enterprise, and to the acquisition of basic skills. But this will be difficult so long as basic oppression continues to provoke basic student rebelliousness, basic conflicts in the classroom, and basic diversion of funds to security, protection, and repair. If "getting back to the basics" means intensifying the rigid control of adults and getting rid of fashionable, "relevant" curricula, then the solution is likely to intensify the basic problem.

The tactics of passive collusion are the elements of what Freire terms "magical consciousness." When the existence of a problem is denied or suppressed, little action is taken. When the analysis of a problem consists of looking at isolated, unconnected facts, or of simplistic explanations blaming the problem on uncontrollable larger forces, then little action is likely to be taken. "Action" in a passive collusion consists of fatalistic resignation, pessimism that one can have any impact, and waiting for someone, some event, or something magically to solve the dimly recognized problem. Cycles of violence are passively allowed to continue.

The Tactics of Active Collusion

The essence of active collusion in maintaining cycles of violence is believing innocent educators are under attack. During the Vietnam war the Department of Defense coined a phrase that reflects this mentality: "anticipatory protective reaction." Translated into action this meant, "bomb the hell out of them before they have a chance to attack you." Put simply, the Department of *War* decided to strike first. To many observers this was action more than reaction, provocation more than protection. No one doubted, however, that these were acts of war, not acts of peace. The tactics of active collusion wage war on students in the name of securing peace.

BLAME THE STUDENTS A junior high school assistant principal expressed the essence of the killer philosophy one afternoon in the Board of Education meeting room. He listened with veiled impatience along with other administrators as we explained our approach. Finally, he interrupted angrily.

"Look, we all know that 5% of the kids are RATS. If we got rid of them at the beginning of school, most of our discipline problems would be solved." His colleagues nodded in agreement; apparently we were the only ones who did not know this. Only rarely have I heard teachers talk about students as "killers," "rats," or "assassins." Usually milder terms are used to place the problem of rebelliousness "in them," for example, "You know, there really *are* some bad kids." Often a single pejorative word is used to describe a complex, developing human being with a unique life history and environment in interaction with a specific teacher in a specific situation: "He is resistant." This is said as if "resistance" were a characteristic of the student, like the electrical property of a wire or a chemical property preventing rust, rather than a characteristic of a relationship. Students are "resistant" not because they are not inherently stubborn or impermeable; they are resisting someone or something. Teachers who kick students out of class because they are "resistant," "defiant," or "insubordinate" are implementing the killer philosophy. By using such words, teachers trick themselves into believing that they are innocent and under attack by "bad" students. Teachers perpetuate the cycle of violence when they kick out students out of class.

EXILE THE STUDENTS Some of these students are also kicked out of school. They are "suspended." Educationally, this is like being suspended by the neck with a rope. "Suspension rates" are more accurately termed educational "kill ratios." In the nation as a whole, one in every twelve secondary students is suspended at least once during the year (Children's Defense Fund, 1975). What makes this kill ratio sinister is the fact that the overwhelming majority of suspensions—63.4 percent in the Children's Defense Fund national survey—were for nondangerous offenses. "In schools in very different places, with very different student populations, the major reasons for suspension are for nonattendance, insubordination, or other minor infraction of school rules which could have been dealt with in ways other than exclusion" (ibid., p. 37). This prosecution merely exacerbates the problem. It increases the amount of school work missed, encourages permanently leaving school, creates self-fulfilling expectations in others about these "troublesome" students, denies students help, encourages juvenile delinquency by placing unsupervised youth on the street who become available recruits for street armies or who retaliate with vandalism and violence in school. "Kill ratios," like "anticipatory protective reactions," provoke war in the name of protecting the peace. Suspensions perpetuate, rather than reduce, the cycle of violence.

The war is waged in creative variations of this philosophy.

Several teachers in a school district in the upper mid-west, for example, adopted the practice of locking troublesome youngsters in a coffin type box for up to ten minutes at a time. The School Board and superintendent were apparently unaware of this procedure and immediately ordered it stopped when a parent complained that her son, who suffered from asthma, had been locked in the box (Bayh, 1977, p. 27).

This practice should not be surprising. In wars, both sides commit occasional atrocities.

CONVERT THE HEATHEN A natural way to implement the killer philosophy is to convert the rebels or, in other words, the heathen. Beginning with the unquestioned assumption that school rules and adult authority are unoppressive and legitimate, teachers and administrators try to convince students that their *mis*behavior is their fault and that they should reform. Students are taught tunnel vision, to look only at one link in the chain of violence—"their" actions—and to see themselves at fault, i.e., as faulty. The oppressive causes of action are not admissible evidence. The following three examples of attempted conversion are fictionalized composites of events in a disciplinarian's office.[3]

Baseball season had begun. By 2 P.M. it was 90°. The art teacher had chosen papier-mâché as the medium to be explored. She told everyone to sculpt a head. Daniel didn't hate art. He just wanted gym for his last period instead, so he could warm up for practice after school. Several students, including Daniel, had exercised their one option and made papier-mâché "heads" that looked and worked like baseballs.

The following morning the secretary ushered in Daniel and his father to the assistant principal's office. The assistant principal shook hands with Daniel's father, pointed to the chairs near his desk and began quietly.

"Daniel seems to have gone too far this time. He hasn't done this kind of thing before. We need to nip it in the bud." Then, turning to Daniel, he continued, "Do you think you can attend your classes now without endangering other students?"

Daniel nodded, looking down at the floor as his father added to the lecture.

"I'd better not have to come down here again. You're here to learn and behave, or I'll make you wish you did."

"We appreciate your coming in with your son. So many parents don't take the time."

Daniel's father got up, glared at his son, and began moving to the door.

"I have to get to work. I'm docked an hour already. I'll see *you* tonight."

"OK, Dan, I guess you know what's expected of you now, huh?"

Daniel began to cry, nodded, and left, still looking at the floor.

* * * * * * *

James was finally learning to read and liked the reading lab. He did not want to leave, when, without warning or explanation, he was informed that his schedule had been changed. The reading instructor was present the next

---

[3] I am indebted to R. Bruce Irons for much of the material on which these composites are based.

day in the assistant principal's office to discuss his protest. She began the discussion:

"James wouldn't leave the reading lab when he was told his schedule was changed. And he talked quite rudely."

The assistant principal interrupted.

"James, why do you have to be such a sourpuss? You're the one who's in trouble."

James looked up and down without saying anything.

Then, raising the ante, the assistant principal continued.

"The funny thing is that you're not a failure, but look at your report card. You told me you were going to try, but what happened? People aren't going to judge you by the color of your skin, but by your actions. We can't blame the teacher, can we? *You* got your*self* into trouble."

"With me, James has a big mouth, but in here he says nothing. I think he should be sent home for a vacation."

After a long pause for James to consider this possibility, he said, "I'm going to give you *one* more try."

* * * * * * *

"What's your story?"

"If you're not going to listen to my side of the story, I'm not going to say nothin'. (Pause) I was just goin' to the library. I had a pass. Is it a crime to be at my locker?"

"So you'll decide what's a crime. Last time you left your tray in the cafeteria, you thought that was OK."

"I paid for that."

"But you thought it was OK. You're mixed up about what's right and wrong. (Pause) Hey, look at me when I'm talking to you. You took advantage of that pass, didn't you? You were 10 minutes overdue."

The student nodded his assent.

"Good. Now you've admitted something. You've got an hour's detention today."

The oppressive context of students' reactions and the destructive consequences of educators' responses are rarely considered during these attempts at reform. Thus it is not surprising that the rate of referrals to the disciplinarian's office and the kill ratios remain high despite these "just" punishments.

ARM THE FORTRESS Blame students. Exile them. Convert them. Arm the fortress. This war tactic aims at increasing the physical security of schools by hiring plainclothes policemen (now present in half the junior highs and two-thirds of the senior highs in large cities [National Institute of Education, 1978, p. 71), creating a full-time custodial force, strategically placing a trailer home on school property, alerting neighbors to watch for intruders, installing sophisticated electronic surveillance systems, or remodeling schools into vandal-proof buildings. These measures do tend to cut the costs of vandalism and can reduce school violence, but not always. For instance, Senator Bayh has warned, "The use of police in this manner does not address the root of these problems and may not only fail to rectify the situation but in fact escalate tension to a higher level" (Bayh, 1977, p. 81). These measures could be described as "anticipatory protective fortifications."

The tactics of active collusion are aspects of what Freire terms "naive consciousness." Educators assume that the problem resides in students who deviate from the established rules and roles. These students need to be reformed. They need to understand and accept the educators' explanations and do what they are told. If not, they will be justifiably punished: kicked out of class, paddled, converted, detained, suspended, or expelled. As further protection, schools are made into forts. Ultimately, this approach will not work, according to Freire, because it is naive. Reforming individuals, however successful, leaves systemic causes of the conflict untouched: the oppression of students, their variegated forms of rebellion, and educators' active and passive collusion.

This cycle amounts to "educide," similar to the self-destructive act of suicide and the institutionalized destructiveness of genocide. Learning is stunted by oppression. Learning time is halved by sniping in class, and lost through tardiness, truancy, suspensions, and expulsions. Educational funds are redirected into repairs and protection. Everyone exists in a state of mild to intense conflict and stress. Educide, the institutionalized, self-destructive conflicts between educators and students, should stop for everyone's sake.

Winning Peace

With the establishment of a relationship of oppression, violence has already begun. . . . Only by abolishing the situation of oppression is it possible to restore the love which that situation has made impossible (Freire, 1970, pp. 41, 78).

Personally, I do not believe an educational utopia is possible. After all, the word "utopia" is a pun made by Thomas More from two Greek words, *eutopia,* meaning "the good place," and *outopia,* meaning "no place." I do believe that Freire has described a "good place," and that education *can* be made less oppressive, less violent, less rebellious, and more peaceful, cooperative, loving, responsible, and self-affirming.

Our national school rebellion is not a typical rebellion in the sense of an organized political faction vying for control of the country's governance, populace, and resources. There is no national alliance of students for liberation, no national strategy or leadership. Peace cannot be won through a campaign to deny needed resources to the enemy, to defeat armies in major battles, and to conclude the war with a treaty. It is a nationwide grassroots rebellion in response to national grassroots oppression in the schools. The usefulness of viewing the cycles of school violence as a rebellion lies in the clarity such a view provides about basic causes and alternative courses of action.

This is a hopeful perspective. Educators can do something in their classrooms and schools. The first step is to recognize that the war in our nation's schools is not a fact of existence, but a problem to be solved. Then, instead of blaming irresistible external forces or bad students or permissive parents, educators can identify central conflicts in the classroom and school. They can work with students, rather than work on students. Educators can engage in true dialogue, speak true words, raise consciousness, create guides for liberation, facilitate democratic problem solving, reduce stress, and raise minimum competencies, as described in the next section of this book.

Most educators are people of good will, idealistic and committed. Many teachers are aware of the national school rebellion and have become self-appointed members of an educational peace corps that serves their fellow human beings. Like the teachers described in this book, they are demonstrating that the tactics of war can be transformed into democratic education, that schooling can more effectively foster human development and learning, and that schools can become places where it is easier to love.

PART II

SOCIALLY LITERATE METHODS

FOUR

Resolving Discipline Conflicts through Dialogue

Dialogue is more than exchanging information. It is a powerful process for solving problems and embodies a goal of humane, creative living. Dialogue is "the way people achieve significance as human beings." "It is thus an existential necessity." "It is an act of creation." "It is the conquest of the world for the liberation of human beings." "Dialogue is the encounter in which the united reflection and action of the dialoguers are addressed to the world which is to be transformed and humanized" (Freire, 1972, p. 77).

These assertions sound glorious but do not clarify such mundane problems as how dialogue can change a conflictful classroom into an arena of cooperative learning or bring love to an angry confrontation between a teacher and a student. What is true dialogue? How can it help resolve discipline problems?

Antidialogue

At 9:45 A.M. the secretary escorted Lavinia, a Black eighth-grader, into Mr. Belkin's office. As the school disciplinarian, he conducted discussions, made decisions, and took action to ensure safety and order in school. Mr. Belkin motioned Lavinia to sit down. If Lavinia had shown the slightest hesitation, the interview would have stopped until the prerequisite deference had been demonstrated. Mr. Belkin silently read the previous day's referral note.

"So, you wanted to go the bathroom, but the teacher said 'no.' Then you played your radio and talked and danced in your seat and disrupted the class for the whole period. Right?"

"I have a health problem," Lavinia said quietly.

"What's it called?" Mr. Belkin asked sarcastically.

"I don't know. I've got an infection down there," nodding her head downwards slightly.

"Do you have a doctor's note?"

"No."

"What's your doctor's name?"

"I don't know. You can call my mother."

"You should know your doctor's name. Why are you rocking?"

Lavinia stopped rocking momentarily. "I have to go to the bathroom."

"How convenient. Just like yesterday. What hospital did you go to?"

"Ringless Public Clinic."

For the first time Lavinia's health problem seemed plausible to Mr. Belkin.

"We can get confirmation from the nurse," he said dryly.

He wrote Lavinia a pass, sent her to the school nurse, and ordered her to return with a written statement. Whether or not Lavinia had a health problem, the matter of Lavinia's misbehavior remained. After she had left the room, Mr. Belkin walked to his window, looked out at the glazed snow and commented to the visiting educator who was sitting unobtrusively in a corner of the room, "Her brother and sisters were assassins and extortionists." After a brief pause, he continued mockingly. "That rocking was making me seasick. I didn't know the clap did that to you."[1]

In theory, we believe that people should be presumed innocent until proven guilty. As human beings, Lavinia and Mr. Belkin would have liked a relationship of respect, caring, sensitivity, and mutual understanding.

Freire claims that the system of domination prevents this type of loving dialogue.

[Dialogue] cannot exist in a relation of domination . . . . Domination reveals the pathology of love: sadism in the dominator and masochism in the dominated (Freire, 1972, p. 78).

[1]This fictionalized account is based on the observations of Dr. R. Bruce Irons as related to the author.

The sadism of Mr. Belkin and the masochism of Lavinia were not caused by personality quirks, but by the situation. Educators and students merely acquiesce in playing pathological roles in this domination game that begins by giving educators and students unequal power. Mr. Belkin's job demanded that he keep order in school. After years of experience with students who wanted lav passes just to leave class, his disbelief was understandable. After years of following orders in the classroom, Lavinia's rebellion in class was understandable when her legitimate need to use the lav was denied. Her teacher had also assumed it was an escape tactic. Teachers are expected to "control" their classes, which usually means "dominate" them. The objective of daily lesson plans is not "the conquest of the world for the liberation of human beings," but to change the inner subjective reality of students by depositing information in them.

This domination creates antidialogue in classrooms as well as in the disciplinarian's office. R. Bruce Irons describes an illustrative class period in an urban, desegregated, junior high school.[2]

The 7J's start the day in English class. Ms. B., a young, white teacher stands at her desk sorting the students' papers.

8:40–8:45. Students mill around talking and laughing. Two black female students pass out books and paper. The students are mostly in desks, but are up and down.

8:45–8:51. Ms. B. says, "Class!" trying to get their attention. She suggests they will get a "treat" tomorrow if they are good both today and tomorrow. Monica, a black, female student, and her friend make fun of Ms. B.'s suggestions. They mimic her statements and mock her tone of voice. Ms. B. reminds Monica three times, twice asking her to put a book away. Another student asks if Ms. B. and the investigator are married.

8:51–8:54. Ms. B. still is trying to get started with a review. Monica is the center of attention. Students are writing, looking out of the window, and withdrawing. Thirteen of 21 are not paying attention.

8:55. Ms. B. asks for a summary of the story so far. Mark; a black, male student who has been boisterous, volunteers. Monica makes an audible joke. Most of the class laughs.

8:56. Ms. B., "Excuse me, all these little voices, I can't hear."

Vicky, a white student, explains what a "con artist" is.

[2]This description is taken from *Person-Blame versus System-Blame of School Discipline Conflict.* (Irons, 1975, pp. 183–187).

8:58. Ms. B. queries, "Dick (a white student) could you hear Dorie (who had just responded)?"

Dick: "No."

Ms. B.: "Why?"

8:59. Billy, a black, mature-looking young man, comes in. He is returning from "opportunity class." The class studies Ms. B. and Billy. All are silent. Ms. B. says, "Sit here, Billy," indicating a seat in the right front corner. Billy looks at her coolly and walks *very* slowly to the back of the row she indicated. He picks up a chair and brings it back to the front row place Ms. B. indicated. Ms. B. does not respond visibly to his action, although the whole class had become silent, as if expecting a confrontation over Billy's calculated challenge.

8:59–9:07. Discussion of the story continues with wide participation and attention. Donald, a black student who seems to be respected by his fellow students, volunteers and answers. Mark draws a railroad trestle on the board. LaVerne, a black, female student, spells a word. Warren, the oldest, most sophisticated-looking black student, responds when Ms. B. calls on him by saying, "I don't know." Then, he gives the answer quietly. Finally on Ms. B.'s request, he says it more loudly with obvious resentment in his expression and voice tone.

Robert, a black student, and Mark argue about how many ribs a horse has. Darren and Danny, a white student, continue to chat in low voices by the window. Mark is sucking his thumb.

9:10. Monica reads aloud. Fourteen are not attending.

9:12. Ms. B. calls for quiet and again tries to lead discussion about a story. A white female student comes up and stands next to Ms. B. After about three minutes Ms. B. realizes she wants to go to the bathroom and gives her permission.

Ms. B. asks Bonnie, a white student, a question about the story: "Would you please tell us?" Bonnie shakes her head. Ms. B., "Why not?" Bonnie does not respond.

9:14. Ms. B., "Billy, if you don't behave, the class won't get its treat." Donald calls over, "Hey Billy, when you going back to 'Opportunity Class,' next week?"

9:15. Ms. B. calls on Patricia, a black student, who has been reading a fine-print paperback, *Teenage Love Stories,* in her lap. Patricia says, "Huh?" and looks Ms. B. straight in the eye with no pretense of deference.

9:16. Ms. B. tries to catch students' interest with discussion of an unusual barn in the story. At this point there is general talking, joking, tapping, etc. The focus has completely dissipated.

9:17. Billy erases part of a white, male student's drawing. Ms. B. corrects him with, "Be good now, Billy."

9:19. There is no instructional focus at all now. Ms. B. says to Billy, "Write a 200 word composition on the situation." Billy, "Yeah, sure." Ms. B. hands him the paper. Monica yells, "Be quiet!!" to the rest of the class.

9:21. A black, female student moves into the seat next to Monica. Ms. B. sees her and sends her back.

9:23. Ms. B. calls on Patricia again. She is still reading *Teenage Love Stories* inside the class book. Ms. B. talks right on over several conversations, and a purse is being passed up the row after being taken from its owner. Ms. B. pays attention to an *almost* behaving student in the front row.

9:23–9:26. Finally, Ms. B. announces, "Read without talking for the rest of the period." This instruction is ignored at first, but after two minutes *all* the students quiet down. Only one is actually reading the assigned story.

9:26. Ms. B. goes to Warren's desk to encourage him to read. He looks around with an embarrassed expression at his classmates, then pretends to read the book. Class period ends.

Antidialogue is the use of words to dominate people by mocking, mimicking and bribing them, by sarcasm and embarrassment, and by admonishing, ordering, and threatening them. Unfortunately, it is a daily reality for many teachers and students.

Dialogue cannot be reduced to the act of depositing ideas in another, nor can it become a simple exchange of ideas to be consumed by discussants. Nor yet, is it a hostile polemical argument between people who are committed neither to the naming of the world nor to the search for truth, but to the imposition of their own truth. . . . It must not be a situation where some people name on behalf of others. . . . It must not serve as a crafty instrument for the domination of one person by another (Freire, 1972, p. 77).

Dialogue

Just as a situation of domination leads people into antidialogue, a situation of love leads people into dialogue: "Love is at the same time the foundation of dialogue and dialogue itself" (ibid., p. 78). Freire describes six necessary attitudes for dialogue to occur.
1. Love—"Dialogue cannot exist . . . in the absence of a profound love for the world and for human beings" (ibid., p. 78).

2. Humility—"Dialogue cannot exist without humility . . . . Dialogue, as the encounter of human beings addressed to the common task of learning and acting, is broken if the parties (or one of them) lack humility. How can I dialogue if I always project ignorance onto others and never perceive my own? At the point of encounter . . . there are only people who are attempting, together, to learn more than they now know" (ibid., pp. 78–79).

3. Faith—"Dialogue . . . requires an intense faith in people, faith in the power to make and re-make, to create and re-create, faith in their vocation to be more fully human" (ibid., p. 79).

4. Trust—"Founding itself on love, humility and faith, dialogue becomes a horizontal relationship of which mutual trust between the dialoguers is the logical consequence" (ibid., pp. 79–80).

5. Hope—"As the encounter of people seeking to be more fully human, dialogue cannot be carried on in a climate of hopelessness. If the dialoguers expect nothing to come of their effort, their encounter will be empty and sterile, bureaucratic and tedious" (ibid., p. 80).

6. Critical thinking—"Finally, true dialogue cannot exist unless the dialoguers engage in critical thinking. . . . For the naive thinker, the important thing is accommodation to this normalized 'today'. For the critic, the important thing is the continuing transformation of reality on behalf of the continuing humanization of people" (ibid., pp. 80–81).

Several years ago I advocated that our department decrease the number of graduate students admitted to our program. The purpose was to reduce exceptionally heavy loads of advising and committee work so that we could do well what we had chosen to do. In the process of arguing for this policy at every appropriate forum within the department, I found myself consistently in a debate with one of my colleagues whose sensitivity and clinical skills I admired. He argued that the applicants to the program were exceptional. He did not want to deny this learning opportunity to people he derived great satisfaction in teaching. Although this was a policy issue, not a personality clash, it became more and more personalized. In one session I became aware that I could not look him in the eye, nor was he able to look at me. My other colleagues were also aware that a good human relationship was in jeopardy. That night I decided that the rupture of the relationship was not a worthwhile price for a possible policy victory and wrote him a note stating this. He answered my note saying that he had been having nightmares about our increasing inability to talk. My note, he said, allowed us to continue working together.

The exercise of our critical consciousness in dialogue had degenerated into antidialogue, i.e., attempts to dominate each other.

In this instance I resigned from the policy debate. To have done otherwise would have allowed antidialogue to destroy the means and the ends. "Love is at the same time the foundation of dialogue and dialogue itself."

Learning How to Resolve Discipline Conflicts

Educators who attempt to dominate students by imposing rules and punishing infractions perpetuate conflict in the classroom or in the disciplinarian's office. In contrast with the effects of antidialogue, dialogue can resolve discipline conflicts. Put simply, dialogue involves mutual respect in working out the rules that govern relationships.

When Michael discovered his favorite teacher was out for the year and had been replaced by a stranger, he refused to take his seat or take off his hat. In order to establish clear "authority" (a current term for domination), the teacher removed Michael's hat. Angry and embarrassed, Michael stormed out of the room and roamed the halls until he met Carrie Brown. This is her report:

I felt this was a good opportunity for me to use my Social Literacy training. Michael was very upset, almost to the point of tears. He said he felt that the teacher did not have the right to remove his hat and that the way he was spoken to in front of the class was not right.

At this point I told Michael that I would tell the teacher his feelings about the situation. Michael seemed pleased about this. I began to question him as to why he went into the classroom with his hat on, when he doesn't normally do this. Michael hung his head and told me he did this because this was a new teacher and he wanted his former teacher back. I tried to explain to Michael why his regular teacher would not return, and that we had to try to help the new teacher to get used to our situation. I asked the student if he would help me do this. He agreed.

The teacher and student did have a conference the following afternoon to discuss the problem, and they came up with suggestions to help each other.

Teacher

1) Try to be more cooperative with students.
2) Listen to students' view.

3) Avoid verbal confrontations with students as much as possible.

Student

1) Help teacher in the classroom as much as possible.
2) Run errands.
3) Don't come in class with hats on.

The result is that the teacher and students are getting along with each other. Some problems still exist, but they are minimal. The students did overcome the problem of resentment towards the new teacher; and after a lot of discussion, they are accepting the change and cooperating.

Dialogue is hardest when it is needed most: in resolving discipline conflicts. That is when many teachers instinctively engage in antidialogue. Teachers and students need to learn the skills of dialogue so that they know how to work out new rules to govern their relationship in a climate of mutual respect. This is the purpose of "The Discipline Game," a structured set of role plays between a teacher and students involving typical discipline conflicts. (Complete instructions for the game are included in Appendix 2.)

The Discipline Game is an adaption of the Hacienda Game that I had observed in the Ecuadorian mountain village. The process of negotiating resolutions to conflict situations allows teachers and students (who often switch roles in the game) to see problems from new perspectives. The game has been used successfully to prepare preservice teachers for the rigors of democracy in the classroom, to improve the negotiating styles of in-service teachers, to teach students how to negotiate, and to provide a vivid experience for parents who want to know what "the discipline problem" is all about. One's most common realization while playing the game is that the other person has legitimate needs. This tends to soften tones of voice, increases respect, and supports the search for mutually satisfying solutions. In other words, the Discipline Game helps people learn how true dialogue resolves discipline conflicts.

FIVE

Speaking True Words about Central Conflicts

Human existence cannot be silent, nor can it be nourished by false words, but only by true words with which people transform the world. To exist humanly is to name the world, to change it. Human beings are not built in silence, but in word, in work, in action-reflection (Freire, 1972, p. 76).

A cryptic one-liner says it all: "To speak a true word is to transform the world" (ibid., p. 75). Words describing what to do or how to do it are not true words. True words also change "the world." Obviously, Freire is not referring to magician's words like "abracadabra." True words do have power, and speaking them requires power from within us. As teachers, words are our tools. Do we speak powerful, true words? Do our words transform the world?

True Words

For Freire "the world" means far less than the planet Earth. It is external, objective reality in contrast to our inner, subjective reality. "Transforming the world" means changing any part of that external reality—erecting buildings, creating organizations, changing roles, rules, policies—in con-

trast with changing ideas, feelings, attitudes, opinions, beliefs, and preju-
dices.

"To speak a true word" means far more than uttering a factually correct
statement. It is a visible act of creation. Perhaps a more accurate translation
from the Portuguese would have been, "To do a true deed." According to
Freire,

> Unauthentic words [are] unable to transform reality. [This] results when
> dichotomy is imposed on its constitutive elements. When a word is deprived
> of its dimension of action, reflection automatically suffers as well and the
> word is changed into idle chatter, into *verbalism,* into an alientated, alienating
> "blah." On the other hand, if action is emphasized exclusively to the detri-
> ment of reflection, the word is converted into *activism.* . . . Either dichotomy,
> by creating unauthentic forms of existence creates also unauthentic forms of
> thought (ibid., p. 75).

There is a purpose behind Freire's expansion of the meaning of "word." By
contrast he implies that most of the words we exchange in conversation,
that we use to teach, preach, or profess are empty, devoid of transforming
action, mere impotent sound. Empty words let the external world stay the
way it is. A TRUE word involves transforming action. To truly speak a
word is to say it and do it, to mouth it and body it, to make sounds and
to change things. By defining "true words" in this way Freire suggests that
teaching vocabulary should be more than getting students to repeat definitions, that criticizing, bitching, and complaining are like steam escaping
without any transforming power, that to be literate means "knowing how
to" as well as "knowing about," that "the word" is thoughtless if it is only
enacted, that "the word" is passive if it is not enacted.

This definition is challenging but still abstract. It would be helpful to have
criteria for recognizing a "true word," or even a scale for rating the "truth"
value of a spoken word. After further reflection on Freire's statements, it
seems to me that, for Freire, true words have six characteristics.

1. True words are spoken or written

Thoughts, unshared conclusions, silent beliefs, can at best only transform
inner, subjective reality. To have the potential for transforming the world
they must be made public. "Once named, the world in its turn reappears
to the namers as a problem and requires of them a new naming." The
problem in publicizing one's private words is two-fold. First, it takes courage. When children speak in class, they must risk exposing their ignorance.
Similarly, it takes courage for a teacher to criticize a policy in a faculty

meeting and risk the displeasure of administrators who can translate that displeasure into punishment. Second, a safe climate in the classroom or school is needed to facilitate people speaking.

2. True words have existential meaning

The Great Depression" may have existential meaning to a teacher, but not to students. "Drugs" may have existential meaning to students but may not to teachers. When students learn words about events, people, places, or things outside their experience, those words are empty. At best, such words are only factually correct, and at worst implicitly teach students the false notion that learning and experience are unrelated.

3. True words name problems

Empty words state facts of existence. In this sense, a spoken word referring to some oppressive aspect of our experience is not inherently a true word or an empty word. It depends on our attitude toward the statement. Believing that a problem cannot be solved stops action. Belief that it can be solved encourages action. This aspect of true words may vary over time or within a group. It is subtle and alive.

4. True words are heard

More precisely, true words get reactions. In large part this is a political problem. How do we present a real problem so that it is taken seriously? Often, speaking alone guarantees that our words will be ignored. To be a spokesperson for a group often ensures that the words will be heard. Unless words are heard, they are powerless to transform the world, much like silent thoughts.

5. True words are embedded in dialogue

Lecturing is not dialogue. The type of Socratic questioning done in many classrooms, where the teacher knows the correct answer in advance, is not dialogue. Announcements at faculty meetings and over the P.A. requesting sign-ups, may be true information, but they are not true words. Policy statements from the central office may be communiqués, but do not involve communication or dialogue. An order from a supervisor requiring action is a dictum. The person who dictates is, by definition, a dictator. Dialogue involves working with others collaboratively on problems for which the best answers are not yet known. Dialogue occurs among people who respect each other as peers with differing talents, just as different roles are essential for a baseball team. Because of their mutual interest in solving an important problem, team members cooperate. "No one can say a true word alone, nor say it for another, in a prescriptive act which robs others of their words" (ibid., p. 76).

6. True words are a commitment.

True words are a contract or promise in the sense of "giving one's word," "taking your word," "keeping your word" or "breaking your word." Others must be able to count on you to do what you promise. True words involve continued cooperation until the problem is solved.

With these six criteria in mind, I wondered whether I had *ever* spoken a true word. After considerable reflection, I recalled an episode several years ago in which I received a communiqué from an earnest colleague-professor. He had been placed in charge of collecting data on all educational operations of our school of education for a scheduled review by a university-wide committee. It happened every eight years to every school in the university. The communiqué said that, if each of us had kept accurate records of all our students, course numbers, enrollments, publications, service committees, advisees, independent study contracts, projects, grants, for the last eight years, then it would take only eight to ten hours to complete the forms. I respected my colleague's zeal. After all, he had been given the onerous job of collecting and compiling the data and was trying to do his best. I also resented the task passionately.

The previous year a muckraking local newspaper reporter had created the appearance of scandal at the school of education with a series of articles on alleged abuses in expending grant funds and in conducting a humanistic academic program. State and national agencies responded immediately in the then-current Watergate mentality and launched eight separate, simultaneous fiscal and academic audits. As chairperson of one of the school's five departments at that time, I devoted the majority of my year to defending, explaining, documenting, and responding to questions from blue ribbon committees, the FBI, the state attorney general's office, the faculty senate's investigating committee, university and federal auditors. The allegations amounted to an enormous pile of "sum" and almost nothing of substance. For instance, one newspaper article alleged that as much as $15 million in grant funds might have been misspent over the previous seven years. In fact, that was the *total* amount of grants raised by the school during that period. The auditors eventually proved that $29,000 had been embezzled. In perspective, that made our operations purer than Ivory Snow, better than 99.44 percent pure. I suspect the audits cost well over one quarter of a million dollars.

After this most intensive examination of an academic unit in the history of the university, my colleague's request struck me as redundant. Actually, my unspoken thoughts were rather harsher. I wrote him a tart note refusing to comply. I spoke with our new department chairperson and made my case. I also spoke at a meeting and advocated that, as as group, we should persuade the other departments that this was a ridiculous imposition on our time and energy. There was a vigorous discussion, a true dialogue. One professor argued that we should be the first to comply to show the university we had nothing to hide. My passionate, if not loving response: "I see no virtue in our leading a pack of fools."

Most faculty members in other departments were convinced of the necessity of this review and were well along in preparing their dossiers. Our new chairperson, with our support, began the hopeless job of challenging the decision up the university's chain of command. The dean suggested he talk to the provost, who suggested he talk to the vice chancellor, who said, "What academic review? We postponed that because of the extensive reviews last year."

In retracing the chain of command downward we discovered that the dean had initiated the review in response to an ancient policy statement without double-checking it with others. After discovering that the task was not necessary, it was "tabled." I remember thinking how our beliefs can create our own reality. We believed it was necessary (however absurd) and acted. Challenging the "necessity," however hopeless the challenge seemed, was the first step in speaking a true word that transformed the world—a little bit of it.

In this instance I spoke and wrote of an existing problem and was heard by others who joined in the planning and implementation of a solution until the problem vanished. It was like hitting a jackpot in a lottery. I was hooked on protesting absurdities. My colleagues have been tolerant because they are never quite sure whether I am crazy or the situation is. Their patience has also been a good model for me.

Now I have six criteria to use in deciding whether I have spoken a "true word". They can be phrased as questions:

1. Am I willing to speak or write about it publicly?

2. Does the problem have existential meaning for me?

3. Do I believe it is a problem that can be solved or that it is a fact of existence?

4. Am I willing to speak about the problem in a way that ensures it will be heard?

5. Am I willing to talk with others in dialogue and to work cooperatively?

6. Am I willing to make a commitment to keep at the problem until it is solved?

You might find it interesting to talk over this issue with a few colleagues. How often do you speak a true word? Are you willing to speak a true word about one or more of the oppressive rules in your school? Are true words spoken in your classroom, at faculty meetings, by the board of education, by the school disciplinarian in dealing with incidents, in your family and/or other intimate relationships? Can you make any generalizations about where, when, and by whom true words are spoken? Can you think of prototypic examples of true words being spoken? Should public education teach students to speak true words? How important is this as a goal of education? To what degree does public education achieve this goal?

The six characteristics describe an ideal for true words, or synonymously, for being socially literate. Most of us are socially literate sometimes. We have spoken a few true words. That does not make the ideal less desirable. It does mean that a certain humility is appropriate, that we have room for growth, and that we should not use these characteristics to snub others or ourselves (e.g., "You socially *il*literate S.O.B."). The ideal is useful in charting directions, clarifying situations, and as a clearly stated, debatable value position.

Central Conflicts

It is difficult to find an organization's central conflicts. Our team took two years to name and analyze the central conflict in one urban junior high school. Usually, Freire's teams needed several weeks of thorough observation, listening, and discussion to locate the "generative words" that reflected the "generative themes" (central conflicts) in a community. However, with the help of teachers, we have invented a 20-minute method that five or more people can use to identify an organization's central conflicts. It is relatively easy to speak true words about trivial problems. The greater challenge is to speak true words about central conflicts.

This exercise requires that the participants be in the same organization, the same school, club, team, work group, and so on. It is best to have at least three hours for this exercise in one block, or an hour-and-a-half block for steps 1 to 3 and another for steps 4 and 5. The only equipment necessary is newsprint and magic marker or blackboard and chalk, and pencils and paper, plus copies of the essay portion of this exercise. The steps in the exercise are simple and fun. The discussions it generates tend to be lengthy and heated. For this reason, it is particularly helpful to have a designated discussion leader or coordinator for the session.

STEP 1: List the special vocabulary in your organization (5 to 10 minutes)

Every group has its own, unique vocabulary that is often as commonplace to insiders as it is mysterious to outsiders; that is, their shorthand, acronyms, catchwords, and abbreviations. At the University of Massachusetts School of Education, simply to function in conversations and to survive in the graduate program requires that students know the special meanings of mods, LEX's, the 10 forms, comps, division heads, chairpersons, residency, dissertation, Mario. Several words stand out in my memory from organizations in which I have conducted this exercise: "CHCALT" (an acronym for the components of a model for a multicultural education), "hayna" (a derogatory term used by boarding students for those who commuted, equivalent to "hicks"), "Mr. Kelly" (not a man, but a code word in a high school for an imminent crisis signaling all teachers to their battle stations. Over the P.A. it would be announced, "Mr. Kelly is in the building.") In the federal government there are DOD, HEW, DOT, DOA, RFP's, PPBS, and PERT charts, names of places ("the hill"), people (lobbyists), or events (the 18-minute gap) that signify large complexes of issues.

What are the special words in your organization? Make a list of all the words that a newcomer would have to know to understand the daily conversation and to function at a survival level. Brainstorm this list. The more the better. Do not criticize or try to determine whether or not the word really belongs on the list in this step. Take a maximum of 10 minutes.

STEP 2: Prioritize the list (10 minutes)

Usually there are between fifteen and fifty candidate words on the initial list. In step 2 the generative theme is chosen very simply. Each person in the group votes for the two or three words on the list having the highest emotional loading, the strongest affective kick, the highest interest, and controversy value for that person. After the voting, if there is a tie, conduct a run-off election.

In a "sex-role stereotyping" workshop, Dr. Ginger Lapid generated the following list of special words from a group of Santa Barbara, California, high school teachers: girls, you women (said by males), you mother, my old lady, hey man, you guys, that's not ladylike, act like a man, hey boy, chicks, broad, dude, foxy lady, you pussy, boys will be boys, just like a woman, pushy broad, bitch. In a run-off election between "you pussy" and "bitch," "bitch" was selected as the candiate word to describe the central conflict between the sexes in that school.

STEP 3: Is the top word a central conflict?

Freire indicates at least three criteria for deciding whether a word reflects a central conflict. (1) The conflict involves people in different roles of unequal power in the organization. (2) The word signifies a "central" conflict, in the sense that many of the conflicts in the organization are also found in this issue. Or, put differently, if all the conflicts in this one situation were understood fully, most of the important conflicts in the organization would be understood. (3) The conflict is an illustration of "the generative theme of our epoch . . . domination."

To decide whether the top word is a central conflict, (1) list the roles involved in the conflicts; e.g., principal, tenured teachers, untenured teachers, parents group, "Ghetto Brothers," "Savage Nomads," paraprofessionals, etc. Do the roles have unequal power? (2) List the conflicts signified by the word. What does each group want, fear, or have to do? Then decide by a vote whether the whole list constitutes a significant set of conflicts for a newcomer to understand. (3) Can the various conflicts subsumed under this word be seen as illustrations of domination and resistance?

Discussion of these three criteria and questions probably will be heated. Only once have I seen a dull discussion at this point. The word was "humanistic," a designation many claimed described the School of Education where I work. The group was perplexed by what the word actually meant, even though it was used frequently as if everyone knew its meaning precisely. We dropped the discussion, uncertain whether it named a central conflict or not. Yet, over the course of a semester we kept coming back, realizing that the word was used externally for selling the school to others ("This is a truly humanistic place, not a typical, degrading type of graduate education"). Internally it was a convenient, all-purpose club for hitting people when they were not living up to one's own ideal ("You're not being humanistic!"). Most discussions, however, get off to a speedy and vigorous start, though it may take weeks fully to understand the centrality of the conflict. Sometimes it makes sense to end the session at this point and continue with steps 4 and 5 the next session.

STEP 4: Is the conflict a "fact of existence" or a problem?

One group of graduate students with whom I was working decided that the central conflict in their life was designated by the word "dissertation," that schizophrenic event, that watershed in graduate studies, that mental whirlpool, that battlefield between professors demanding high "academic" standards and graduate students eager to do a socially significant piece of work. There was no question that this was a nexus of conflicts, involving two roles of unequal power illustrating the epochal issue of domination. We knew also that this conflict was not healthy. The list of typical graduate student reactions read like a glossary of psychiatric symptoms: loss of sleep, loss of weight, obsessive preoccupation with the task or phobic avoidance of the task, marital problems, nervousness and anxiety, recurrence of bizarre childhood dreams, tics and mannerisms. Clearly, the dissertation was an oppressive situation for graduate students.

Here was a problem worthy of our truest words. Or was it? We decided to rate this central conflict on a 1 to 10 scale. 1 = *Fact of Existence:* No matter how much effort we give to transforming this situation, in all probability we will fail. 10 = *A Problem:* This conflict situation can be solved with the available energies. Our ratings of "the dissertation process" clustered around 3. Basically, we believed that it was a "fact of existence," so intransigent that we should not even bother to try to get it changed.

In step 4, ask each member of the group to assess privately the central conflict on this 1 to 10 scale. Is it an unchangeable fact of existence (1), or a problem that definitely can be solved given the energy to work on it (10)? Then, put the 1 to 10 continuum on a blackboard or newsprint and mark an "X" in the appropriate place for each person's rating. This can be followed productively by a discussion of why people rated it as they did.

STEP 5: Is anyone willing to speak a true word?

Discouraged but not yet defeated, our group decided that we should try to change the dissertation process, even though the odds seemed long. Although we had named a problem, we did not know what was causing it or, therefore, what might cure it. A few students whizzed through without an apparent ruffle. Were they exceptions proving the rule that graduate students are more or less incompetent and unstable? Or were they able to sail through because they did not object to this hazing ritual, this lonely journey through strange territory? Should graduate students be better prepared? Or did the fault lie with faculty members who varied in advising skill as much as students did in their abilities and preparation? Or was this speculation mere person blaming? Was there something about the rules of the dissertation game that caused these pervasive reactions? Should those rules and roles be changed? Although we were not over-confident that our efforts would pay off, the group was willing to continue talking about the problem, to try to speak a few true words about the dissertation process.

After ten weekly, three-hour sessions we had enough clarity to write a short paper with our analysis and proposed solution. Toward the end of the spring semester we presented this paper to a monthly meeting of faculty members and students in our department. Reactions ranged from disinterest by some faculty members, to vituperative anger by several faculty members who "knew" we were launching a vendetta on their personal style of advising. Faculty members took turns asking incisive questions and making erudite "points" as if the discussion was a contest. It was all quite brilliant and an academic exercise in the worst sense. The semester ended. My student colleagues left for summer jobs. The next fall we were all more heavily committed to other projects than to changing the dissertation process. I was left to reflect on what had and had not happened. Obviously, the problem had existential meaning for us, and we spoke about it publicly, in dialogue. But, our final failure was inherent in our initial disbelief that our efforts could succeed. It vitiated our public efforts to persuade others and made it easy to let go of the problem over the summer. Our commitment to transform the dissertation process was puny. In these ways we did not speak true words about a central conflict in our lives.

I have given two examples of attempts to speak true words, a success and a failure. After continued reflection, it seems to me that the "truth" of one's words is mostly a matter of inner determination. One can make words "true" by translating the inner commitments into collaborative action and social change. The results are sometimes surprising, as illustrated by the sudden collapse of the onerous school evaluation. Guesses about the ease or difficulty in achieving a desired change are shaky at best. In other words, more often than we imagine, our pessimism about certain "facts of existence" in our lives may be unwarranted, self-defeating, self-fulfilling prophesies. Inner determination makes the odds against success false through persistent, collaborative, and ultimately successful efforts. This aspect of being socially literate could be called, "the courage of one's convictions." In step 5, it is worthwhile to discuss whether and to what degree individuals in your group are willing to speak true words about the central conflict.

Speaking about Central Conflicts and True Words

When I brought my training as a clinical psychologist into the field of education, I discovered I was a radical, advocating methods for making psychosocial development a true goal of education, not just a "show" goal printed on glossy brochures. When schools came under severe fiscal pressure and violent assault, I became a conservative hoping merely to conserve what was best. Now, I am a "flaming regressive." I would like to go back at least 200 years to the spirit of the Declaration of Independence. The ideals of equality, the right to pursue responsible self-affirmation, and government by the people remain valid even though they have never been translated fully into practice.

The process of declaring independence stands as a model of socially literate, critical-transforming liberation. The systemic problem was named. "Whenever any form of government becomes destructive of these ends, it is the right of the people to alter and abolish it." The causes were listed and summarized: "The history of the present King of Great Britain is a history of repeated injuries and usurpations, all having in direct object the establishment of an absolute tyranny over these states." The initial action was simply to speak a true word: "We, . . . the representatives of the United States of America . . . solemnly publish and declare that these United colonies are, and of right ought to be free and independent states. . . ." At the time, this statement must have sounded theoretically correct but of uncertain "truth," in Freire's sense of the word. Over 35,000 British troops were crossing the Atlantic to crush a Continental Army composed of 7,000 troops, and a majority of colonists continued to play host to British despotism as a fact of existence. The final sentence of this document promised to translate inner commitments into collaborative action and social change: "For the support of this declaration, . . . we mutually pledge to each other our lives, our fortunes and our sacred honor." It took over seven years of war to make these statements into a declaration of true words.

The American Revolution exemplifies a goal of education in a democracy: to help people maintain their inalienable rights by developing their uniquely human capacities to name, analyze, and collaboratively transform oppressive conditions in their lives. This is the meaning of Freire's statement,

For the truly humanist educator and the authentic revolutionary, the object of action is the reality to be transformed by them together with other[s] (Freire, 1972, p. 83).

SIX

Raising Consciousness

One of the greatest obstacles to the achievement of liberation is that oppressive reality absorbs those within it and thereby acts to submerge their consciousness.

(Freire, 1972, p. 36).

All of us are submerged in at least a few oppressive situations. We see few alternatives, feel stifled, unhappy, and victimized. But it is always possible to see the situation differently, to increase our consciousness of causes and new alternatives, and to liberate ourselves.

How can this be done? Freire's answer is brief: "Only as they discover themselves to be hosts of the oppressor can they contribute to the midwifery of their liberating pedagogy" (ibid., p. 33). Freire asserts that we are not powerless victims, no matter how completely convinced we may be of our innocence. Our thoughts, feelings, and actions support oppression just as we are hosts at parties in our homes. We can be the midwife of our liberation by bringing into consciousness the ways we unknowingly are hosts of the oppressive situations that victimize us. Then we can eject these unnecessary, counterproductive thoughts, feelings, and actions from our consciousness. Instead of playing host, we can work collaboratively to transform the oppressive situation.

83

This chapter is designed to help you recognize and understand the subtle and usually self-deceptive tactics of playing host. The first section defines the ways of playing host to oppression. The second section illustrates these states of consciousness in context. Although the focus is on discipline, these illustrations extend beyond school since neither oppression nor playing host is confined to classrooms. The final section consists of several consciousness-raising exercises.

Developing Consciousness of Oppression.[1]

Oppression exists whenever there is economic exploitation or whenever an individual's development is blocked. Many individuals are aware of pain, fear, guilt, anger, frustration, and humiliation but are not conscious of the oppressive situation causing these feelings. They deal with their feelings without changing the situation. They play host to the situation at the same time they suffer from it. Suffering, playing host, and consciousness of oppression develop through stages, as illustrated in the following examples.

Ms. Mack is a paraprofessional. She monitors students during study hall periods. Discouraged but determined, she complained, "They're hell-raisers, talk loudly, don't sit in assigned seats, move chairs. Or they're hall-wanderers, asking for passes to the lav, to their lockers, to the nurse, anywhere to get out of study hall. They call it 'the concentration camp' and 'the prison.' The rule of complete silence really gets them. But what can I do? I'm just a para. The school provides no alternatives." Ms. Mack and her students are absorbed in the oppressive reality of study halls. Their consciousness is submerged in the situation. They do not see that constructive, collaborative alternatives exist to enforcement, compliance, and rebellion.

Ms. Neff has begun to emerge from her submersion in monitoring the prison-halls: "After a month of the typical study-hall problems I couldn't stand it any more. Some of those kids haven't been brought up right. Some are bored because they don't have homework to do, or don't want to do it. I'm a para and was afraid I'd lose my job unless we got some peace in the room, somehow. So I started bringing in the newspaper, magazines, and thermofaxed copies of some word puzzles. I let them work in groups so long as they don't disturb others. They like it better, and so do I, but there are still some problems. I have to carry this huge pile of papers around from

[1]Another description of this development was presented in chapter 1, of this book ("Freire's philosophy of education"). I recommend that it be reread in conjunction with this section.

room to room, and the other day a student sprayed mace in the room just before we got there. But it's better than before."

Ms. Cray another para who monitors study halls, saw the problem differently. She became conscious of an alternative situation, then worked collaboratively to create it. "At a Social Literacy training session I was talking with two human relations club advisers who said that the board of education and the high school had given the O.K. for this club to start. In fact there had been an ad in our school paper for an adviser. I told the principal I'd do it, and he thanked me. The group has been growing each week because we do interesting things, visit other schools, have summer plans, and we'll be the hosts for the city-wide meeting next fall. Some teachers have even commented that the club has had a positive effect on several students' class attendance and attitudes. The club is a lot better than sitting in a study hall for the students and for me."

Each paraprofessional believed that her actions were the natural, logical extensions of what the situation demanded. The external realities of the study halls were the same for all three. What differed was their internal perception, their understanding of the problem; in other words, their consciousness of that oppressive reality. Their actions were the natural, logical extension of what their consciousness demanded. Ms. Mack's response illustrates "magical" maneuvers for playing host by conforming to the dictates of the oppressive situation. (This paraprofessional's name, as well as the other two have been changed. The quotations are genuine.) Ms. Neff illustrates the "naive" style of playing host in which individuals actively reform themselves or others in hopes that the problem will be solved. Ms. Cray exemplifies the "critical" stage in which the person stops playing host and starts to collaborate with others in creating a less conflictful, more loving alternative situation. As people develop through these stages, their problem solving becomes more active, comprehensive, collaborative, and effective. They move from being pessimistic, passive victims in an oppressive situation to creating situations in which it is easier to love and to pursue self-affirmation as responsible persons.

Each stage in this sequence reflects a coherent style of solving problems with a characteristic way of *naming* the problem, *analyzing* the causes, and *resolving* conflicts. In the magical-conforming stage, difficulties are seen as inevitable, unchangeable "facts of existence." The analysis of these "facts" is magical, in the sense that the causes seem to be beyond logical explanation, like a magic trick: historical inevitabilities ("It's the times," "That's the way things have always been") or gross external forces such as fate. Chance, luck or God. The idea of acting to change things causes fears. Instead, people at this stage of problem-solving accommodate. They wait, experience a sense of hopelessness and resignation. This inaction, is a form of passive collusion in maintaining oppressive, conflict-laden situations. Ms. Mack caught the essence of this stage of consciousness when she said: "The school provides no alternatives. I'm just a para. What can I do?"

In the naive-reforming stage, problems are seen to be in individuals who deviate from the systems' idealized rules, roles, standards and expectations. At this stage, individuals either blame themselves for their problems, which causes feelings of inferiority, incompetence, guilt and other types of self-deprecation; or others are blamed, which leads to feelings of resentment, anger and hostility. As a result, individuals try to improve themselves or change others. This is the pervasive mind set of both educators and students toward discipline conflicts. According to Freire, the implicit naive assumption is made that when individuals reform and act properly, then the system will function perfectly and oppressive, conflictful situations will not exist. Because of this belief in the intrinsic soundness of the system, individuals at the naive-reforming stage actively "play host" to the rules, roles, expectations, and standards of the system. As Ms. Neff said, "I'm a para and was afraid I'd lose my job." She changed her behavior, and the situation improved, but oppression continued: "They like it better, and so do I, but there are still some problems." Ms. Neff reversed love and criticism. She criticized the students, their parents for not bringing them up "right," their teachers for not giving them homework, and herself for not being able to run a quiet study hall. Her love for the system was evident in her efforts to make study halls work.

In the third critical-transforming stage, people exercise their critical, intellectual skills in naming the critical (in the sense of "crucial") rules and roles of the system that create unequal power, responsibility and freedom, that place them in conflict and that exploit, oppress or hinder their human development. Groups of individuals analyze the ways they have naively played host to the oppressive aspects of the economic, political, social, school or classroom system. They come to understand how they have victimized themselves and others by their active collusion in supporting the conflict-producing rules and roles. Together, they act to transform those aspects of the system. Ms. Cray made the radical assumption that neither she nor the students were to blame. She loved human beings and criticized oppressive aspects of the system.

In Chart 6:1 these stages are summarized. For a slightly different perspective I suggest you read across the rows comparing the three ways of naming, then the three ways of analyzing, then the three types of action taken. For further insight into the unexpected, sometimes surprising ways to play host, see if you understand how every one of the 16 elements of magical-conforming and naive-reforming consciousness can passively or actively reinforce oppressive rules and roles in a system. For those people who wish to measure or assess the effects of consciousness-raising efforts, a test of critical consciousness is available. (See Smith and Alschuler, 1975).

Consciousness in Context

While the abstract descriptions of stages bring clarity to an analysis of consciousness, they do not convey the passionate commitment that people have to their view of events, nor do they portray the pains of playing host. To understand the dynamics of change requires descriptions of these changes in different contexts. In this section I have attempted to describe some of this richness and complexity as well as to illustrate the categories listed in Chart 6:1.

1. From Feminine to Feminist Consciousness

Magical-conforming consciousness has its advocates. Helen Andelin (1963, p. 6), for example, argues that God's law is the "light to bring [women] out of darkness and guide [them] to this earthly heaven." In her book, *Fascinating Womanood,* Ms. Andelin claims the dominant role of men is sanctified by God's law: "Not only was man assigned the responsibility of leading and providing for his family—but he was given the native ability to fulfill this duty. Woman was created for a different kind of strain and endurance—far different from man's" (ibid., p. 90). A woman's role, according to Ms. Andelin, is to serve her husband, to maintain his authority, and to enjoy her dependence on him. Ms. Andelin claims that women are not thwarted in their human development or exploited. The problem is their failure to accept, endorse, and play their prescribed role. Ms. Andelin thus enthusiastically advocates what Freire would describe as devotedly playing host to oppression.

Being a wife is not necessarily oppressive, nor are all husbands oppressors. However, advocating this single, narrowly defined, subordinate role for all women is oppressive. Both within and outside marriage a broad array of work needs to be done that would be enriched by more female participation and that provides diverse options for the development of women's human potential. From Freire's perspective, Ms. Andelin's specific prescriptions for being a happy wife might be called "fascinating oppression-hood."

A bitter consequence of this way of life is waiting.

CHART 6.1

Developmental Responses to Oppression

	Playing host to the system		Changing the system
	Passively (Magical-conforming)	Actively (Naive-reforming)	Critical-transforming
NAMING THE PROBLEM	NO PROBLEM: 1. Problem denied or avoided 2. Difficulty accepted as a fact of existence	PROBLEMS ARE IN INDIVIDUALS WHO DEVIATE FROM RULES OR ROLES OF THE SYSTEM: 1. Self deviates 2. Peer deviates 3. Oppressor deviates	PROBLEMS ARE IN RULES AND ROLES OF THE SYSTEM: 1. Exploitation, injustice 2. Blocked human development 3. Interpersonal conflict; lack of love
ANALYSIS OF CAUSES	MAGICAL CAUSES BEYOND LOGICAL EXPLANATION: 3. Fatalism, uncontrollable external forces 4. Fears of change	NAIVE BLAMING OF INDIVIDUALS: 4. Accepts oppressor's explanations 5. Blames others: feelings of anger, resentment, hostility 6. Blames self: self-deprecation causes feelings of doubt, inferiority, guilt, pity, worthlessness	CRITICAL ANALYSIS OF SYSTEM CAUSES: 4. Understands how system works 5. Understands all past actions that played host passively and actively
TYPES OF ACTION TAKEN	NO ACTIONS TAKEN; CONFORMING: 5. Pessimism, accommodation to the status, resignation 6. Waiting for change to come from external forces	REFORM INDIVIDUALS TO MAKE SYSTEM WORK: 7. Personal reforms to model oppressor, or live up to standards of system 8. Scapegoating a peer 9. Avoid and/or oppose an individual oppressor 10. Gregariousness with peers; support without action	TRANSFORMATIONS IN SYSTEM OR SELF: 6. Change the rules and roles through dialogue, cooperation, democratic action, scientific approach 7. Self-actualization through personal and ethnic esteem, appropriate role models, faith in peers, boldness, risk taking, reliance on community resources, learning

"Waiting to be a woman. Waiting . . .
Waiting for my great love,
Waiting for the perfect man,
Waiting for Mr. Right. Waiting . . .
Waiting to get married,
Waiting for my wedding day,
Waiting for my wedding night,
Waiting for sex,
Waiting for him to make the first move,
Waiting for him to excite me,
Waiting for him to give me pleasure,
Waiting for him to give me an orgasm, Waiting.
Waiting for him to come home, to fill my
Waiting.
                    (Excerpt from "Waiting," Walding, 1973)

Waiting has its drawbacks, even when women are waiting at work instead of at home. In 1970, 38.7 million of more than 93.6 million workers were women. Traditionally, women have occupied in a few concentrated camps. Almost seven of every ten workers in health, teaching (except college), waitresses and cooks, clinical, and secretarial services are women. The median annual earnings for all fully employed women was 60 percent of the salaries of fully employed men (Ginzberg, 1975, pp. 143–145). Even within the field of education, the development of women's human potential is confined to the poorer-paying, less prestigious, lower levels of leadership. As late as 1970–71, 85 percent of the elementary school teachers were women, but 79 percent of the elementary school principals were men. Almost half of the nation's secondary school teachers were women, but only 3.5 percent were junior high school principals and 3 percent were high school principals. Some 99 percent of superintendents and 97 percent of assistant superintendents are men.

These percentages would be understandable if women did not hold the necessary credentials. However, in 1970–71, women held 46 percent of the master's degrees and 20 percent of the doctorates in education. Nor is it a matter of personality and performance records. Research studies over the last twenty years suggest that women in educational administration are more democratic; rated higher by parents; have higher school morale; act more collaboratively with students, teachers, and outsiders; are more concerned with the objectives of teaching and evaluation; have greater knowledge of teaching methods and techniques; were more confident of their own standards; and produced higher academic achievement than in schools administered by males (Fishel and Potker, 1975; Hemphill, Griffiths and Frederiksen, 1962). It is far more difficult to estimate the extent of women's quiet desperation as they wait.

Dr. Cloteen Brayfield helped a number of female teachers end their waiting periods. She organized a Social Literacy group for women in Connecticut who wanted to become educational administrators. Activities in this ten-session workshop included most of the exercises described in this book. Dr. Brayfield compared the fifteen women in her workshop with another group of fifteen women who were unable to attend the workshops because of scheduling conflicts. Follow-up tests given to both groups showed that Social Literacy training significantly raised consciousness, ego development (the degree to which one's perspective on the world is integrated), and the degree of their professional administrative activity (Brayfield, 1977). One of the participants described to Dr. Brayfield how the workshop inspired her to take action.

As Ellen explained it to me, it was the realization that there were many women in education searching to define what they wanted and *attempting to work through the system* to obtain it, which assisted her to overcome the feelings of personal rejection experienced when she was turned down for the principal job in her own community. Shortly after the workshop ended, Ellen had felt comfortable enough to apply for every principalship she heard about that summer. Three systems ignored her application, one system offered her an interview but not a job, and one system invited her back for three separate interviews before hiring her as an elementary principal in late August (ibid., p. 125).

Even though it is naive-reforming action, there are advantages in *attempting to work through the system* (italics are mine). At least it is action instead of a passive wait for good fortune to strike magically. And it helped a number of women get into the male administrator's club in Connecticut.

2. The Limits of Naiveté

Often a conscious choice is made to work hard at embodying exactly what an oppressive system demands rather than to change those demands. For several years I gritted my teeth as I worked to obtain a tenure at the University of Massachusetts. Problems in my naive-reforming strategy emerged even before the tenure decision was made. The impending and uncertain judgment caused me to doubt my worth because I did not know how others would evaluate it. In my fantasies I heard the personnel committee comparing the candidates with each other and with tenured professors.

Inevitably, the voices concluded I was inferior to someone on every rating scale. I imagined looking for a job in a tight professorial market, having to move my family from a lovely community with good schools. Anxiety and self-pity affected my sleeping and eating and my relationships with my peers who happened to be on the personnel committee. There I was as an adult, having the same feelings I experienced before spelling tests in third grade, before class elections in eighth grade, before final exams and the SAT in high school, before finding out which college, then which graduate school would accept me. In striving to be what others wanted, I was not my own person. I "belonged" to those systems and consistently punished myself in anticipation of their judgments of my worth. The imaginary personnel committee did considerable damage to my self-esteem. Calling this process "self-deprecation" does not do justice to the exquisite variety of mental torture and excess stomach acid produced by actively playing host to the oppressive standards of the system.

The pain of naiveté can stimulate the emergence of critical-transforming consciousness. Whenever you feel inadequate, inferior, undervalued, or guilty for not doing "better," instinctively say to yourself, "Maybe it's not me, but the system." Stop whenever you find yourself angry, resentful, hostile, or judgmental in conflict with a peer. These feelings are clues that some oppressive aspect of the sytem may be victimizing you and your friends in mysterious ways, and that it may be possible to solve the mystery, stop playing host, redirect aggression, and democratically change that aspect of the system.

Malcolm X succeeded within the system, then experienced pain from his naiveté.

In the second semester of the seventh grade I was elected class president. It surprised me even more than other people. But I can see now why the class might have done it. My grades were among the highest in the school. . . . I was proud; I'm not going to say I wasn't. In fact, by then, I didn't really have much feeling about being a Negro, because I was trying so hard, in every way I could, to be white (*Malcolm X,* 1964, p. 31).

That year Malcolm decided he wanted to be a lawyer. Mr. Ostrowski, his teacher, tried to help him understand and live within the system.

Malcolm, one of life's first needs is for us to be realistic. Don't misunderstand me, now. We all here like you, you know that. But you've got to be realistic about being a nigger. A lawyer—that's no realistic goal for a nigger. You need to think about something you *can* be (ibid, p. 36).

Initially, Malcolm's pain was a physical reaction.

It was then that I began to change—inside. I drew away from white people.
I came to class, and I answered when called upon. It became a physical strain
simply to sit in Mr. Ostrowski's class (ibid, p. 37).

Malcolm's emergence from naive thinking was slow. He was a pimp, thief,
convict, and a minister preaching against the devil white man, before he
reached a fully critical-transformist view.

3. Constructive Criticism

For Freire, criticism is constructive when it is aimed at oppressive aspects
of the system, rather than at individuals. This perspective is clear in Malcolm X's later view.

The white man is not inherently evil, but America's racist society influences
him to act evilly. The society has produced and nourishes a psychology which
brings out the lowest, most base part of human beings (ibid, p. 371).

Malcolm X worked on an international scale to raise consciousness, but not
everyone needs work on the international system to make a difference.
Oppressive systems exist at many levels: systems of international relationships, state and national political and economic systems, school systems,
schools, departments, and classrooms. Problems at any level can be seen
from a magical, naive, or critical perspective. The essential task of consciousness raising is to help people stop playing host either passively or
actively and to start collaboratively reconstructing critical aspects of the
oppressive system.

Lee Bell and Rochelle Singletary were coordinators of the Social Literacy
group at Fox Middle School in Hartford, Connecticut. In a written report
and subsequent conversations with the author, they reported: "Lack of
communication among different clusters (small teams of teachers and students) in the school prevented us from sharing our expertise. Some people
came up to us at various points in the Social Literacy sessions and said, 'Oh
yea, I knew that, and I've always done that in my classroom.' The ideas and
successes we heard in this way somehow had never gotten shared with other
teachers who were very frustrated by the same problems and didn't know
that someone else already had designed a very successful solution." Ms. Bell
and Ms. Singletary supported their peers when they criticized the system.
"Scheduling encourages isolation and staying with the same group all day.
As a result, teachers often only talk to those in their immediate cluster or

house. House, staff, and cluster meetings often are superficial and never become real discussions of real problems." To construct a set of conditions that fostered communication, Ms. Bell and Ms. Singletary took several steps: "(1) Identified which clusters have planning meetings at the same time and provided a list so teachers would know this; (2) encouraged them to share that time once in a while by providing materials for discussion; (3) met with team leaders to get successes that were collated and shared with others, and identified experts in the school as resources for others; (4) used part of a faculty meeting to share the results in order to stimulate more verbal sharing."

Ms. Bell and Ms. Singletary encountered the resistance of destructive criticism in several forms. They said, "Many people were pessimistic and felt that discussion would solve nothing since the administration would do what it wanted anyway. Some (teachers) didn't want to be bothered." This magical criticism often seems like an immovable object to those who want to transform some part of the system. Naive criticism seems like an irresistible negative force. Instead of sharing ideas and solutions, peers often criticize each other, paternalistically and maternalistically, behind their backs. "You know, Sam Pilton can't control his classes. I solved that problem long ago. He talks about being nondirective. It's another crock of crap he learned in graduate school." Sometimes this backbiting is slightly better organized and even more naive. Teachers meet informally at a local bar to blow off steam while injecting alcohol. It does ease tensions from day to day and does provide adult companionship after several hundred contacts with kids. But these bull sessions would more accurately be called "steer" sessions since their transforming power has been castrated. Gregarious steer sessions play host actively by helping people tolerate oppressive conditions.

By contrast, Social Literacy groups are an all-purpose tool for raising consciousness. They encourage dialogue with peers and help in speaking true words. They provide support for taking action and tangible support through team work.

For Freire, critical consciousness is a uniquely human activity.

[Human beings] differ from animals which are beings of pure activity. Animals do not consider the world; they are immersed in it. In contrast, [human beings] emerge from the world, objectify it, and in so doing can understand it and transform it with their labor (Freire, 1972, p. 119).

As human beings we can "consider the world," criticize it, and transform it. The more we exercise these uniquely human capacities to emerge from our immersion, the more fully human we become. In Freire's view, raising consciousness and increasing humanness are synonymous.

Consciousness-raising Exercises

The exercises in this section are intellectual rehearsals for full critical consciousness in action. They are designed so that you can work on them alone, but they are most profitably done with a group of peers. In a larger group, individuals can get more practice and time to talk by breaking into subgroups of three to five. As an introduction to these exercises, participants should read the preceding section of this chapter.

Each of the situations described below was reported by a teacher. Interspersed in each narrative are suggested discussion questions to stimulate your understanding of the stages of consciousness. Take 15 to 30 minutes to discuss the most interesting situation. If there are enough groups, try to cover all situations. At the end of the session it is often helpful to reassemble in the large group and "go around." This involves letting every person share with the group their completion of the following sentence stub: "The most interesting (or useful or important) thing I realized during this session was that. . . ."

SITUATION ONE: A counselor was asked to help resolve a conflict between a chronically boisterous girl and her male teacher. After she said to her teacher in class, loudly and with passion, "I love you," he sent her to the front office for unchivalrous disciplining. The class was thoroughly amused by the situation. (WHAT WOULD YOU HAVE DONE IN THIS SITUATION?) The teacher and the counselor generated the following alternatives to solve the chronic problem:

- The teacher and the student should talk it over with the counselor present.
- The social worker should talk with the girl's mother.
- Talk with the girl's other teachers to assess the extent of the pattern and share ideas.
- Have the girl see a psychiatrist.

(FROM A CRITICAL-TRANSFORMING PERSPECTIVE, WHAT IS WRONG WITH THESE SOLUTIONS? WHAT POSSIBLE CLASSROOM AND/OR SCHOOL-WIDE PROBLEMS DOES THIS INCIDENT SUGGEST?)

SITUATION TWO: Total havoc reigned in a low-division seventh grade junior high school science class. No work was done. Students wrestled and talked constantly, and there were interracial conflicts. The teacher stated, "The students know that I want them to behave and learn, but they also know that I will not use either detention or punishment papers to try to coerce them to do the correct thing." (DO YOU AGREE IN PRINCIPLE WITH THIS TEACHER? WHAT WOULD YOU DO IN THIS SITUA-TION?) "The major problem is school-wide. The seventh graders already know that the 'game' at school is to get away with a great deal of havoc without getting too much detention or punishment." (ASSUME THIS TEACHER'S ANALYSIS IS CORRECT. CAN YOU THINK OF FIVE GOOD WAYS TO BEGIN TRANSFORMING THIS SCHOOL GAME CRITICALLY?)

SITUATION THREE: A teacher refused to allow a student to go to the lav because the student had tried to escape from class at every opportunity. The student turned out the lights in retaliation. The class got angry at the student, told her to sit down and "stop bothering the teacher." The student took her seat and did her work. The teacher commented, "The most impor-tant thing for us to do in the classroom is to get the majority of the students on our side and the rest will follow suit." (IS THIS DEMOCRATIC OR OPPRESSIVE? ARE THE STUDENTS PLAYING HOST?)

SITUATION FOUR: "As a teacher in Upward Bound, I helped one of my students get placed in a faster track math class during the regular school year. The administrator in charge of scheduling was very cooperative. However, the guidance counselor in charge of testing called me in, ques-tioned my judgment and did it in a one-sided, directive fashion. I was shocked by the reproach and its lack of validity. I was too angry to respond then, and left the office. I went back the next day, confronted the counselor with my perceptions and feelings about her style. I feel that the best ap-proach to a problem is to confront the individuals directly, honestly, and openly. (IS THIS THE BEST APPROACH? WHAT ARE THE ADVAN-TAGES AND DISADVANTAGES?)

SEVEN

Creating Guides for Survival and Liberation

The choice is always present: to survive by playing host to an oppressive situation, or to liberate oneself with others by transforming it. The activities presented in this chapter make that choice explicit by considering and criticizing oppressive rules in your situation. Before presenting these techniques, however, it may be helpful to illustrate the choice between survival by magical submersion in mysterious rules and liberation through critical transformation of oppressive rules.

Students in Ms. Fallon's class studied less than 15 percent of the time in her class. They met consecutively during two of the three lunch periods. The class was a physically dangerous place, more like a free-fire zone in a combat area, than a combination English and Music class in a junior high school. There was no discernible difference between English in the first period and Music in the next. Anarchy was continuous. Most students wandered around the room talking, braiding hair, joking, playing the dozens, standing on desks, or fighting, while two or three students worked quietly with Ms. Fallon at the front desk. She seemed happily oblivious to the general disorder. When asked, Ms. Fallon said, "No, I don't have a discipline problem." The principal, who had observed her "classes," disagreed. He suggested that she join the Social Literacy group.

The Social Literacy group got to know Ms. Fallon and in the process discovered that (1) she was a long-term sub, (2) she had been trained as a

Music teacher, not as an English teacher and (3) had never taught before. Her sole previous work experience had been supervising a tobacco-picking crew in Massachusetts, where leaves for the outer wrappers of cigars are grown. From this perspective her teaching style was understandable. In the fields each person knows what to do and is expected to work without constant direction by the supervisor, who remains available for individuals who need special help. Ms. Fallon did at her desk what she had done in the fields.

Most important, however, the Social Literacy group realized that Ms. Fallon had been assigned to this class in the middle of the year without any orientation. She did not know the formal rules of the school or the informal rules that mean the difference between being a bumbling outsider and an accepted team player. "Her" problem was not a deficient personality, professional incompetence, or a faulty teacher-preparation program. Ms. Fallon did not even know the rules for survival in the school.

Ms. Fallon was submerged in an oppressive situation. She barely survived. Ms. Lee Bell emerged from it, turned on it, and liberated herself, her students, and substitute teachers. Ms. Bell taught remedial reading in a lab setting using complex equipment. She knew that when she was out, students felt they had a vacation from work. Many subs believed their basic job was to baby-sit. Sometimes students played the game "Drive the sub crazy." Ms. Bell presented this problem to her students, who said they did not like a stranger in the room and felt disoriented. "We brainstormed a list of rules for a sub and posted them on the board. We also listed the things students could do to help each other and the subs to make class run more smoothly. For example, (Sub rule) "Don't yell at us. Ask us if you don't understand something, and we will help you.' (Student rules) 'If a classmate needs help, help her or him.' 'Be patient when subs are in the room. We're the experts and need to be tolerant.' After returning from a two-day workshop, Ms. Bell reported that, "The sub said the classes went smoothly. The students said they felt better knowing they had a plan. I praised the students for the responsibility they showed and for helping each other. Now we use the same rules all the time for sharing responsibility."

Ms. Bell's simple solution to this chronic problem was based on critical, liberating assumptions that the situation could be transformed, that students wanted to learn, that they wanted a plan for learning, and would be more committed to the plan if they were involved in creating it. They invented liberating rules. The objectives of the exercises in this chapter are (1) to specify precisely what is required for mere survival in the situations and (2) to specify precisely what rules in the situations are oppressive. Obviously, the latter provide clear targets for liberating action. Each exercise can be done in 45 minutes to an hour in a group of three to ten people. Larger groups should break down into groups of this size. The exercises can be done with *any* ongoing group: a class, teachers, administrators, a family, a club, a church.

1. Name and analyze the formal rules

Formal rules typically are written down some place (e.g., teachers' contracts, handbooks, and so on) or are public, commonly acknowledged rules. Here are several rules from one school:

Students may not share lockers.

Don't run in the hallways.

Students must have a pass outside of class.

No eating, drinking, or chewing gum in class.

Never give a student a key to a class or leave a class unattended.

Teachers may not leave school during lunch.

No hats on in class.

Assaulting a teacher or student is an automatic suspension.

Take attendance every class.

First, brainstorm a list of the formal rules for about 10 minutes. Remember: the more the better; no criticisms or discussions during the brainstorming session; write them all down. The list does not have to be complete.
Second, discuss this list of rules in terms of the following comments and questions.

· Not all formal rules need to be followed. There is a law in Boston, for example, that you can be arrested for walking your cow on the Boston Common *if* you are not carrying a shot gun. Which of the rules on your list *must* be followed to survive? Which *should* be followed? Which rules are only on the books?

· After examining their school rules, one group concluded that the formal rules oppress students. They were made by adults without significant participation of students. They were made for the benefit of adults to control students and to maintain safety, as interpreted by adults. Are your rules oppressive for students? Are they good for students? for adults? Can rules be both oppressive and good?

2. Name and analyze the informal rules

Typically these rules are *not* written down and are seldom discussed publicly, even by teachers in the safety of their own homes, but they are crucial to survival in the school. These are the rules for avoiding problems, for getting things done and done efficiently. If a new teacher knows these rules, many months of fumbling can be saved. For instance, in one school everyone knew that the first thing to do in the morning was to say hello to Pat. Who's Pat? Yes, the head secretary in the front office. Violating this rule resulted in delays in getting phone messages, erratic delivery of memos, delays in processing requests for materials, etc. Although these rules are informal, they exist and are important. Here are a few informal rules for survival from one school:

Never park in the principal's space.

Get to be friends with the custodian.

It's okay to bitch, gossip, and complain in the teacher's lounge, or lunch room, but never discuss a serious educational issue.

Never make a suggestion in teacher's meetings; you may be put on a committee.

Never give up material you have. You'll never get it back.

A female teacher should not be seen talking to a male teacher more than twice a week. Otherwise gossip will start.

Don't criticize until you have tenure.

Never admit you have problems teaching. Blame it on the students.

Pull all the window shades in the front of the building to the same length.

Never visit another teacher's classroom.

Don't appear to be liberal.

Don't hassle the football players.

Don't appear to be affluent.

Always wear a bra.

Don't let your unshaved legs show.

First, take 15 minutes to brainstorm a list of as many of the informal rules as possible in your school. Remember, *do not discuss, analyze, or criticize this list during the brainstorming portion.* A scribe should write all of these rules in plain view on a blackboard or newsprint and number them. Write down every rule anyone suggests. Get at least fifteen informal rules.

Second, let each person vote for the three most toxic, least liked rules on the list. This can be done in less than 5 minutes by a public count of raised hands.

Third, discuss each of the three worst rules in terms of the following questions:

Does this rule facilitate learning?

Does this rule foster collaboration among teachers, regardless of tenure status, sex, race, or role?

Why do these rules exist? In what ways do you "play host" to these rules?

Fourth, take a vote to see how many people in the group are sufficiently interested to spend time at another session developing a plan to implement the new rule or rules.

3. Name and analyze the rules of the "ethnic relations" game

In one workshop attended by a large, ethnically diverse group of teachers, we developed a variation of the "informal rules" exercise.

First, divide into groups of ethnically similar people, maximum size of six if possible; e.g., Afro Americans, Hispanic Americans, Jewish Americans, Anglo Americans, etc. Each group may define its common ethnicity as it chooses.

Second, brainstorm a list of informal rules you follow to survive in the ethnic relations game in your school (15 minutes).

Third, vote for the most important five rules (5 minutes).

Fourth, discuss these five rules:

Do you like these rules?

What does it help you get? avoid?

If you could change a rule to be ideal, how would you change it? Rewrite it. (10 minutes or more)

Fifth, count off in each group to the number in the group. Form new groups by number (all 1's together; all 2's together; . . .) These will be maximally diverse ethnic groups.

Sixth, each person in the new group should read the rules she/he brings.

There should be no discussion or comments until after all the rules are read. Then an open-ended discussion follows (30 minutes or more).

Seventh (optional), have the original groups re-form to discuss their reactions to the ethnically mixed discussions.

Eighth, close with each person completing the following three sentences in writing:

"What I learned from this exercise was_____."

"I would like to_____."

"The support I need is_____."

All individuals should be given a chance to read their sentences to the large group if they choose (10 minutes or more).

To give you an idea of the types of informal rules mentioned by black and white Americans at this workshop, here is a partial list:

Activate our built-in radar system and tune them out.

Resent the attitude of whites that black parents don't want the same things for their own children.

Be friendly but don't go out of your way.

Resent being used as a token nigger.

Beware of the "con game."

Stay out of "their territory."

Relate on superficial level so as not to be offensive.

Visit minorities on their own ground and make the first step toward physical contact.

Try to listen rather than talk.

Make sure I don't give more privileges to minorities than to others.

Be careful-watchful looking for signs of being offending.

Tend to propagate phony friendships.

Do not touch.

Avoid associating too much because you will be viewed as an artificial liberal.

Avoid conflict at all costs.

All whites are prejudiced to some degree so deal with it accordingly.

Always be more cautious with blacks in what you say and do.

Avoid identifying expressions—"these people"—.

Psyche out how a member of a minority group is relating to me.

Be aware of balancing any group situation ethnically.

Bend over backwards to give minorities a double chance.

Sit on your own feelings and allow racial remarks to go by when you are in the minority.

Don't confront minority people because you will be called a racist.

Some of these rules are clearly identified with specific ethnic groups. Some are not. Many were sincerely offered *and* offensive. Thus it is important to do this exercise in a trusting, supportive climate, if possible, and allow sufficient time to reach closure. That may require up to two hours. If there is sufficient time and interest, a second session can make plans for change in the third and fourth steps of the previous exercise: analysis and planning for change.

4. Name and analyze the rules of the sex role game.

By following the same steps as in the previous exercise, but dividing into groups of men and women, or boys and girls, it is possible to name and analyze the rules of sex roles. The following illustrative rules are divided into the age levels from which they came.[1]

Junior High School

Girls	Boys
Wear the uniform of the group— surfer, sexy, or straight Have long hair Don't touch Make good grades Have a "best" friend	"Hang ten" Tease girls you like Wear jeans Don't sing during music Don't be teacher's pet

[1]These rules were generated in Title IX workshops conducted by Dr. Ginger Lapid in Southern California.

High School

Girls	Boys
Wear suggestive T-shirts	Wear long hair, denims and John Deere hats
Have boyfriends	
Have a good tan	Have lunch money to go off campus
Wear halter tops, beach thongs, and blue jeans	Carry cigarette papers and the "right" kind of condom
Never beat your boyfriend at games	Come to class stoned after lunch

College

Women	Men
Be soft, curvy, and attractive	Don't be a mamma's boy
Catch a husband	Have an interest in sports
Don't sweat or swear in public	Be assertive around women
Don't be a jockette	Be sexually aggressive and/or talk about it
Don't want to support a family	Be independent—love them and leave them
Home and family come first	
Be intuitive and emotional	Be mechanical
	Be buddies with men but don't bare your soul

5. *Analyze your classroom rules*

Dr. Rodney Hammond has suggested six rules for classroom rules:

1. Involve students in making the rules.

2. Keep rules short and to the point: e.g.,
    Keep your hands to yourself.
    Walk in the room.
    Raise your hands to speak.

3. Phrase rules positively. Identify the desired behavior rather than the punishable behavior.

4.   Lable the rules in context: e.g., those rules apply "to independent work" or "to when a substitute teacher is here."

5.   Remind the class of the rules frequently, at least at first, but not when they are breaking the rules.

6.   Post rules in a conspicuous place.

To implement rules, Dr. Hammond suggests a golden rule of teaching: "Catch kids being good." Rather than rewarding bad behavior by attention and punishment, try to ignore it. Instead give lots of reinforcement to those who are following the rules when they are following them. Some effective forms of reinforcement are verbal praise, smiling, a soft touch, nearness, tokens, points, or desired activities (Grandma's method, in other words: "You can go out to play when you have finished the dishes").

Sit down with a colleague and share assessments of your classroom rules. How many of the six "rules for rules" do you follow? In implementing your rules do you reward the positive or punish the negative? To build commitment to classroom rules, the involvement of students in making them is critical. Not to do so is both counterproductive and undemocratic. How do you involve students in making and revising the class rules? You might also want to consider whether the school rules governing your behavior are consistent with Dr. Hammond's rules for classroom rules. Does your principal catch you being good, give you plenty of reinforcement, and ignore your bad behavior?

These five activities do not solve problems. They do help pinpoint what needs to be changed in order to become liberated from oppressive situations. To stop here is to remain an arm chair analyst, a mere spectator and victim. Are you willing to speak a true word about one or more of the oppressive rules in your situation?

LB 3011.04 1972

B Bodl

ocation | Account No. | Copies

945

1

EIGHT

The Nuclear
Problem-Solving Process

Singlehandedly, she was responsible for a major share of the junior high school's disciplinary referrals to the front office—a true educational assassin. But she was nearing retirement, everyone said, and deserved support for her forty years of service. It was too bad that she hadn't kept up with the times, the desegregation of the school, the "new types" of students with so many problems at home. She just didn't understand their dialect, their ways of joking. It was an unfortunate situation, everyone agreed, but what could be done?

The principal ignored this typical explanatory trash and did the obvious. He went on to observe "the assassin" in action. The problematic pattern, its systemic cause, and a possible solution became clear after one period and one conversation. She loved to work individually with students, disliked lecturing and did not do it well. However, the desks were bolted down, making it difficult to do anything but lecture and patrol the aisles monitoring seat work. So she lectured poorly; got a poor response; threatened, which only made matters worse; then kicked students out of class. The principal realized she and her students were being victimized by bolts. After discussing several alternatives, he suggested she join three other teachers the next semester in a "quad." That way the teachers' roles could be differentiated. She could work with individuals while the others, who liked lecturing and did it well, could handle the large groups. After discussion with the other three teachers the quad was established and the assassin's referral rate dropped to zero.

This sequence illustrates the nucleus of socially literate problem solving. Starting from an incident or an individual, you identify a problematic pattern. Alternative solutions are considered that change "the system," i.e., the rules or roles in the situation. These system changes are proposed for discussion with all those involved so that a democratic, mutually satisfying, permanent solution can be adopted. The nuclear problem-solving process is a 20-minute activity that helps people go through this sequence. It is sufficiently short and effective for two teachers to help each other twice in a typical 43-minute free period. There are also interesting variations in the nuclear problem-solving process as a format for individualized counseling, as a problem-solving process with a class of students, or even in democratically resolving recurrent family conflicts. The nuclear problem-solving process is "nuclear" both because it contains the irreducible core of Social Literacy that can be applied in numerous situations, and because it is extremely powerful, like a nuclear reaction, with beneficial effects.

This chapter contains instructions, illustrations of six criteria you may use to evaluate the degree to which the solutions are socially literate, and a simple report form to keep a record of the problem, the alternatives you considered, and the solution that worked.

The Process

Nuclear problem solving can be done alone, but it is more effective and fun to do with at least one other person. In larger groups we recommend that several simultaneous subgroups of two, three, or four, each work on a problem of their choice. That way, more problems can be solved and everyone can participate more actively. Before beginning, each group should choose a "problem poser," someone who is willing to describe a specific problem and who wants to get a socially literate solution. After this person is selected, the group works toward a solution in four 5-minute steps.

STEP 1: Name the problematic incident

In the first 5 minutes the problem poser describes a specific conflict in as much detail as possible. The problem poser is the only one who speaks. The others listen as carefully as possible, trying to understand what happened. One colleague keeps time and signals when the 5-minute period is over. The problem poser must stop immediately. In subsequent steps, the problem will be explored further from other perspectives. Thus the incident need not be described completely in this first step.

The problem incident may be an interpersonal conflict, a classroom problem, or a school-wide difficulty: for example, a tardy student who disrupted class, a student who constantly wants individual attention beyond the teacher's available time, an out-of-control classroom, a troublesome school rule requiring all teachers to be hall monitors during the 5 minutes between classes, a deadly dull faculty meeting.

In describing the incident, the problem poser may wish to respond to the following questions. If the questions are helpful, use them. If not, the problem poser should simply describe the incident as fully as possible.

What was the problematic incident?

> Who was involved? What happened? What did you and the other person say, do, think, and feel?

What led up to this incident?

> What was the prior history? What experience in the problem poser's life preceded the incident and set the stage for this incident? What experiences in the other person's life that day set the stage for this incident?

What were the consequences of the incident?

> What was the sequence of events after the incident? How did you feel afterwards? How do you think the other person felt afterwards? What else do you think will happen if this conflict is not satisfactorily resolved?

STEP 2: Identify patterns of conflict

Dealing with incident after incident is endless and often ineffective. There are thirty to fifty discipline incidents per period. There is no possible way to respond to and resolve them all. Patterns of conflict must be identified and eliminated if the overall level of conflict is to be reduced. Socially literate problem solving focuses on patterns, not on incidents.

The purpose of step 1 was to start with a grounded, real event. In step 2, the objective is to uncover one or more patterns illustrated by that incident. In the simplest terms, *a pattern is any event that occurs more than once.* Obviously, it is advantageous to identify broad, but not cosmic patterns if a significant improvement is to be made. An incident may exemplify several patterns in interpersonal relationships between students, between the teacher and student, in a teacher's behavior, in the organization of classroom activities, or in school rules, policies, and informal norms. Here are a few examples of conflict patterns: the milling game at the start of classes, students forgetting pencils, rough housing and running in the hall-ways, widespread tardiness to school, a long-term repetitive conflict be-tween teachers and the school counselor or administrator, inadequate time to prepare for class.

Mr. Milt Van Vlack moved from a specific incident and vague sense of the problem to specific patterns. For twelve years he had been an A-V specialist. In September he went back to classroom teaching. Just before Thanksgiving he had a particularly bad day, after several trying weeks, and became convinced he had lost his touch. No teaching or learning was occurring because he could not control his classes. To locate the problems more precisely, Mr. Van Vlack placed a TV Portapack in the corner of his room and videotaped three classes. In reviewing the tapes he identified three patterns: (1) There was an average of twenty-one interruptions per period. (2) The longest span of uninterrupted time he had in which to teach was 3 minutes. However, most students were not paying attention because the momentum of disruptions was overpowering. (3) finally, the vast majority of interruptions were not under his control: they included, calls on the phone from the front office, P.A. announcements, students entering class late, hallway commotion. Mr. Van Vlack concluded, to his relief, that his original self-deprecation was misplaced and that his students were being victimized as well. Beyond that, probably other teachers and classes were suffering from the same problematic pattern.

During the second 5-minute period the task is to get off of the incident and on to patterns. Take 5 minutes to list as many possible patterns as you can that are illustrated by the incident. Do *not* try to agree on the most important problematic pattern to resolve. In step 3, you will come back to the patterns from another perspective. Remember, try to get away from the incident and individuals. Focus instead on patterns involving several peo-ple, a whole classroom, or the entire school.

The following questions may be helpful to ask the problem poser:

How does this incident illustrate a pattern?

> Has this incident occurred before? Have you reacted in this way before? Has the other person? Has the type of incident occurred with other people involved? Is this pattern for the class? For other teachers? For the whole school?

> If this pattern were described as a game, what would the title be? How would you "make points?" How would the other person "make points"? If you were to write a rule book so that another teacher could play this game exactly as you did, what would those rules be? What would be the rules for the other person(s)?

Please complete each of the following three sentences as many times as you can.

What I really wanted in this situation was. . . .
What the other person(s) really wanted in this situation was. . . .
The basic conflict was. . . .

STEP 3: *Brainstorm alternative, system-blame solutions*

Socially literate solutions to discipline problems blame the system and change it rather than blaming individuals and attempting to change them. *By a system-blame solution, we mean changing the RULES and ROLES that govern people's behavior.* These may be the implicit rules and roles in classroom games such as "milling," "the pencil sharpener game," etc., or the explicit rules and roles in the classroom or the school. For instance, the Social Literacy group at Fox Middle School in Hartford examined a seemingly endless parade of specific discipline incidents. Students were testing the limits almost everywhere, trying to see what they could "get away with." However, instead of instituting a mass crackdown on individual students, they searched for and found a system-blame explanation: The school lacked a consistent set of rules. This led to extensive person blaming. Teachers accused students of taking advantage of the situation and blamed other teachers for not enforcing the rules. Administrators blamed teachers, who returned their accusations in full measure by claiming that administrators were inconsistent in their enforcement. The Fox Social Literacy group catalyzed the participation of the entire school in generating a list of basic rules to be included in a new student handbook. Each "house student council," "cluster group," "special area group," the secretarial staff, and administrators suggested at least five rules to be included in the handbook. A representative committee pulled these suggestions together for school-wide discussion and approval. This democratic process helped make the new rules workable, consistent, and cooperative.

When the problematic pattern exists in the classroom, the rules and roles there need to be changed. For instance, Wynn Young, a teacher at Duggan Junior High School in Springfield, Massachusetts, was on the verge of quitting. As a retired naval officer who had been teaching for fifteen years, he *knew* the meaning of discipline and had a reputation for being a tough disciplinarian and a budding Mr. Chips. One year, however, one of his classes was chronically out of control. Students were throwing everything: chairs and books on the floor, paper airplanes, nails, punches, and insults. After meeting with his Social Literacy group, Mr. Young, in desperation, decided to try a collaborative problem-solving process with his class.

"I hate coming to this class. And I think you hate coming to this class, too." Mr. Young's honest opening statement stunned the class into silence. "I don't expect you to be angels or to learn everything, but I would like the atmosphere to be such that you and I enjoy coming to class. Maybe it's my fault for setting up too rigid rules. I'm going to try something. For the next two days we're going to forget about the subject matter. We're going to discuss how we can improve the situation. I want you to suggest the rules for the class. As long as it's within what the school board says is OK, we can try it."

The class brainstormed thirty rules, some of them "crazy," e.g., no work. However, after further discussion the list was pared down to fifteen, mutually agreed-upon rules, such as,

Homework only three nights a week.

Fewer referrals to the front office.

More movies.

Instead of yelling, Mr. Young should just look at us.

Work in teams of two or four.

Do research reports.

Use more educational games.

The rules went into effect the remainder of the week. Teachers walking by the classroom noticed the drop in noise level and asked what happened. "It's not perfect," commented Mr. Young, "but compared to what it was before, it's like night and day." The next week Mr. Young was ill and out of school for several days. One of the students told him later that, during the weekly prayer meeting at his home, they had prayed for his recovery. On returning to the class he was greeted by applause and a large sign on the blackboard, "Welcome back, Mr. Young."

"I almost keeled over. There's more to teaching than disseminating information. This is what makes teaching worthwhile."

Even when the problem is in a systematic interpersonal conflict, identifying alternative rules and roles for the relationship is useful. Joe DiChiara, a physical education teacher at Bulkeley High School in Hartford, Connecticut, was having a recurrent problem with his star basketball player. So were other teachers. The young man refused to follow the rule of "no hats on in school." At one point a conflict with a teacher developed, a threat was made, and the young man was suspended. Mr. DiChiara was asked to intercede. Rather than force compliance with threats or entice compliance by appealing to the needs of the basketball team, Mr. DiChiara decided to see if this was a conflict between the school rules and some "implicit" rules governing the student's behavior. In discussions with the student both sets of rules were clarified. The rule helps the school identify outsiders and monitor students' moves in and out of school. The student countered with the fact that he had joined a Jamaican group over the summer. "Wearing the hat," he said, "is part of my religious belief and practice." Mr. DiChiara continued a collaborative problem-solving approach with the student by considering the available alternative solutions:

1. Continue wearing the hat in school and take the consequences.

2. Get out of the group and follow the school rule.

3. While in school, follow the school rule. When outside of school, follow his religious practice by wearing his hat.

4. Attempt to change the school rule for everyone.

The student picked the third alternative.

"I felt that after my conference with the student, he really understood all implications and was happy to pick #3. Since then his attitude is great, his attendance and academic work are better, and he seems to have matured a great deal in the past month."

Changing rules and roles rather than individuals tends to be more efficient and just. Instead of blaming persons and being in an adversary relationship, system blaming encourages cooperation between people in conflict as they try to change some aspect of the system that bothers both of them. It is helpful to generate a large number of alternative rules and roles for consideration. In step 3, participants conduct a 5-minute brainstorming session to *identify as many rules or roles as possible in relationships, classrooms, the school, or school system that could be changed to solve the problem.* Keep four rules in mind as you brainstorm.

1. Generate as many alternatives as possible, but at least ten. Don't worry about quality. The best ideas can be selected later. The ideas should be stated briefly.

2. There should be absolutely NO evaluation of alternatives during this phase, e.g. "Yes, but I tried that and. . . ." "That wouldn't work because. . . ." The problem poser should record all suggestions, however silly or implausible. The best alternative will be refined in the next step.

3. Let your imagination soar. Wild ideas often contain a crucial element of a creative solution.

4. Let yourself build on other people's ideas by suggesting a variation or modification. The problem poser also may suggest alternatives.

STEP 4: Develop democratic plans for the first step in implementing one solution

The objective of this last 5-minute period is to help the problem poser develop the enthusiastic feeling that, "Yes, that's something I'm going to try tomorrow. It looks like it could work." To move toward that existential state the problem poser selects one of the brainstormed, system-blame alternatives that appears to have the greatest potential for resolving the conflict pattern. Then the colleagues help develop that alternative into a plan of democratic action. What obstacles may arise? How can they be overcome? What support does the problem poser need to carry out the plan?

It is possible for adults to select a solution and impose it on students without their participation. However, this undemocratic process tends to be counterproductive. The planning should include activities desiged to involve all those people who occupy the roles or play by the rules to be changed. Fox Middle School had a miniconstitutional convention. Wynn Young took two days with his class. Joe DiChiara sat down with his star basketball player. This type of democratic collaboration helps make the eventual solution mutually satisfying and more permanent.

Remember,

1. The problem poser chooses the alternative to be proposed.

2. Plans should involve democratic collaboration.

3. At the end of the 5-minute period, exchange phone numbers and a time to find out what happened. This acts as an incentive for the problem poser to take action, and as a source of additional help if the original plan runs into unexpected difficulties.

The examples of problem solving all focus on collaborative efforts to change rules and roles that define patterns of conflict. The examples also illustrate useful variations in the nuclear problem-solving process. It can address conflicts between two individuals, in a whole class, a school, or even at a district-wide level. It can be done by a group of teachers, with students, or even include parents. It can be accomplished in 20 minutes, or the steps may be extended over a longer time period. No matter what variation is tried, however, the steps and intent of the Social Literacy process remain the same: begin with a specific conflict, identify the pattern it illustrates, collaboratively search for changes in the conflict-producing rules and roles, and develop a mutually agreed-upon solution.

Evaluating Socially Literate Problem Solving

The nuclear problem-solving process is a tool and only a tool. It can be misused. The best guides are a steadfast commitment to dialogue, mutual respect, and a desire to actualize the socially literate ideal of democratic action. Then the nuclear problem-solving process may help reduce the number of victims in school and increase the number of loving relationships.

It may be useful to have a simple scoring system to help evaluate the degree to which problem solving is socially literate, not for the purpose of setting olympic Social Literacy records, or for the purpose of one person's judging another. The "scoring system" is meant as a tool to check over work and to identify what is essential. The questions below can be used as guidelines after a nuclear problem-solving process, after using any of the other Social Literacy problem-solving techniques, after developing a plan of action, or after the implementation of any solution.

1. What is the problem?

Treating each conflict or problem as if it were a unique event is a typical response but is inefficient. A pattern is any problem that has occurred more than once. The more frequently it occurs, the more important it is to resolve the pattern. Or put differently, it is most efficient to focus our energies on significant patterns. Patterns may involve a student or a teacher, a "typical" conflict in a classroom that involves a number of different students over time, or it may be a school-wide pattern. *Score +1 if the problem is a pattern.*

2. Where is the problem?

Whenever we want individuals to change so that they act properly or play by the rules, we are assuming that the problem is in individuals. Whatever the justification, whenever we name the problem as *in an individual,* we implicitly or explicitly blame them. Any problem can also be seen as being *in the system.* A system consists of the rules that govern the roles in any situation. The rules and roles can be explicit, public, and stated, or implicit and nonverbalized. Did you identify the problem as being in conflict-producing rules and/or roles, or in a misbehaving person? *Score +1 if the problem is in the rules or roles of a situation.*

3. How many system-change solutions did you consider?

Did you consider the problem as an interpersonal conflict pattern, and as an illustration of a more general classroom conflict pattern, and also as an example of some troublesome aspect of regular school functioning? What are the implicit and explicit rules and roles at each level of the pattern? At any level there are several alternative rules and roles that might resolve the problem. *Score +1 if you considered several alternative changes in rules and roles.*

4. Is the problem-solving process democratic?

It may be effective, but it is not democratic for one or more individuals to impose rules and roles on others without those others having a chance to participate in determining the rules and roles. Changes in the rules and roles should be negotiated with those involved. Dialogue, rather than prescription, should be the ideal. *Score +1 if those people affected by the rule or role change were involved in determining the change.*

5. Is the solution mutually agreeable and satisfying?

This question simply asks whether the people involved like the solution. Does it meet some need they have in a way that does not violate someone else's needs? Often we ask students to change their behavior to satisfy adults' needs or for the common good. While this is important, it is not enough. Can a solution be found that is satisfying to all the individuals involved? At a minimum this requires knowing what the various needs are and checking to find out if they are met. *Score +1 if the solution is mutually satisfaying.*

6. Is the solution sustained?

Obviously a problem is not solved if a solution is attempted but does not work, or if a workable solution is implemented, but the problem comes back. Keeping at the problem is the key here. *Score +1 if the problem seems to be permanently solved.*

Summary of the guidelines for socially
literate problem solutions

		SCORE	
		0	+1
1.	What is the problem?	An incident	A pattern
2.	Where is the problem?	In individuals	In rules and/or roles
3.	How many system-change solutions were considered?	One	Several changes in rules and roles
4.	Is the problem-solving process democratic?	Not everyone affected was involved in solving the problem	People affected were involved in solving the problem
5.	Is the solution mutually agreeable and satisfying?	Not everyone's needs are met	The solution is satisfying to everyone
6.	Is the solution sustained?	The problem has returned	The problem has remained solved

Obviously, this is a crude six-point scale: Each guideline really refers
to a dimension, not an either/or criterion. Any incident can illustrate
patterns at one, two, or more levels; rules and roles exist at all those
levels; there is a difference between considering one, two, ten, or twenty
alternative solutions; sometimes not everyone can or wants to participate in the problem-solving process, nor is it often that solutions are
completely satisfying or permanently solved. Therefore, use these guidelines to the degree they are helpful in orienting you or providing perspective on your work. The scoring system moves in the direction of
being more objective about what constitutes a "good" socially literate
solution.

We assume that each Social Literacy group will want to keep these
six criteria in mind. While it is true that the immediate concern of the
Social Literacy group is to solve specific, troublesome, common prob-

lems, the simultaneous larger purpose is to actualize certain values: to reduce the pain and victimization people experience, permanently to increase the amount of mutually satisfying social interaction, to increase people's humanness by engaging them in the uniquely human processes of collaboratively naming, analyzing, and changing the systems that govern their lives. The six guidelines are reminders of these underlying values.

Reporting Socially Literate Solutions

We also assume that each Social Literacy group would like to help other teachers and students benefit from their successes, learn about a problematic pattern similar to ones they face, understand your thoughtful analysis of systemic causes, the array of alternative solutions you considered, and what you did to solve the problem democratically, in a way that was satisfying to everyone involved. This can be done simply and quickly by describing the problem and solution in a brief report. There are many uses for this report: as a permanent record of the groups' work; as a resource bank of solutions for educators or students with a problem, as the "final report" to complete a preservice or in-service Social Literacy course.

As you describe your success story, the key question in mind is this: "What should I write that will help another teacher like myself?" To facilitate this process we have suggested six specific questions to which you may wish to respond. These questions are amplified and explained in the previous section. However, there is nothing sacred about the six questions or their sequence. If they are helpful in describing your experience fully, use them. If not, don't. Some teachers have found that working with another teacher is particularly helpful in getting a complete story. One teacher asks the question and records the answers while the other teacher is freed to concentrate on what happened. Then the teachers switch roles. You should do what works best for you in creating a full and useful report.

1. What is the problematic pattern? Can you also describe a recent incident that illustrates the pattern?

2. What are the systemic causes of the problematic pattern?

3. What alternative system-change solutions were considered?

4. How did you democratically seek and implement a solution? What obstacles were encountered?

5. Was the solution agreeable to all or most of the people involved? What were other results?

6. Has the solution been sustained? That is, is the solution applied consistently and continually? Is the improvement stable?

NINE

Mainstreaming and Raising Minimum Competencies

To illustrate variations in the nuclear problem-solving process I am pleased to share two applications with you. In the first, Tara Sartorius and a group of intern art teachers[1] focused on problems in classrooms in which students with special needs are placed. Ms. Sartorius described the group's efforts by responding to the six questions in the Social Literacy report form.

1. What is the problematic pattern? Can you also describe recent incidents that illustrate the pattern?
    The problem is the inability of certain students to function in a classroom situation and the intern teacher's inability to meet all students' needs. For example,

· I was helping some students with their work when I looked up to see Bill push Richard. Richard fell backward between two tables, hitting his head on one. I rushed over to the crying boy to make sure he was all right —then I sent Bill to the office and Richard to the nurse.

· Before class, Dick and David were having a pencil fight. I warned them that I'd take their pencils if they continued. They didn't stop, so I took their

---

[1] The other members of the group were Alison M. Alcorn, Shawn Allen, Charles Erb, Stephen E. Gustuson, Laurie Rose Neurzer, Suzanne Schmohl, Elizabeth Sponagle, and Lea Zarate.

121

pencils. They proceeded to steal pencils from other students' shelves in order to continue with the pencil fighting.

· I asked Susan to sponge off her desk. She went to the sink and got a sponge. When she was walking back to her desk, someone nearby stood up to sharpen his pencil, and Susan pushed the sponge in her neighbor's face.

Ms. Sartorius started student-teaching in a class where she was *not* informed of the six "special education" students assigned to her. The master teacher was absent for the first two weeks of the semester, which left Ms. Sartorius alone with the situation. As an intern teacher she was inexperienced with classroom management and untrained in dealing with the needs of "special education" students. These students demand a large amount of class time since they increase class disturbances and require more help with their art projects.

2.   What are the systemic causes of the problematic patterns?

Art classes are used as a dumping ground or as filler classes by school counselors and special education teachers. The placement of special education students, in general, has a far-reaching effect—more than is believed by the public or admitted by many school systems. These students, historically, have been placed in art education classes because they can reach a higher satisfaction and achievement level than in most required academic classes. With this knowledge and the desire to see special-education students succeed, the administration overloads the art classes. In other words, the class size is standard, based on a head count, but not in terms of student behavior or time required by the teacher. This problem has plagued art teachers for the last twenty years.

3.   What alternative system-blame solutions were considered?

· Pair up special education students with high-ability students.

· Group together the special education students and provide a separate learning situation.

· Provide written assignments to alleviate extra questions.

· Place one special education student with a group of regular students.

· Counsel special education students after school, at lunch, etc.

· Never allow free time in class or give students time to fool around.

· Restructure lessons to attract problem students instead of boring or losing them.

· Convince the master teacher to get involved and help.

· Temporarily change seating arrangements.

- Hold class meetings to solve problems.
- Require more student responsibility.
- Offer other rewards besides grades or points.
- Reward good citizenship.
- Get Social Literacy group to come in and help.
- Hold critiques or art shows.
- Have group meetings on students' attitudes and behavior.
- No more than two special education students per class.
- Special education students have their own art classes.
- Art-therapy training for art teachers.
- There should be art appreciation classes which students would have to take before they could get into a studio art class.
- The classroom environment should be more conducive to artistic efforts.
- Disband the grading system in art (reward the students—give the grade to the parents).
- All special education students should be identified to the teacher before the beginning of any class.
- Establish a Weighted Student Unit for determining class size.
- More counselor aides and resource teacher involvement.
- Special education students admitted on a provisional, trial basis.
- Have administration remove problem: the "special education students."

4. How did you democratically seek and implement a solution? What obstacles were encountered?
   We have proceeded on two fronts: Tara's class and a more general solution.

Social Literacy group participated as aides in the following ways:

1. Group meetings on nonbehavioral problems in the art classroom (e.g., citizenship evaluation, clean-up procedures, etc.).

2. Group meetings on attitude and behavioral problems in the art classroom.

3. One group member brought a motorcycle in for students to draw, several times. Motorcycle used for motivational purposes.

4. Help with outdoor sketching field trips.

· In addition to Social Literacy group aid, a regular teacher's aide was supplied by the administration whenever possible. Basically, the teacher's aide was assigned to the handicapped students.

· Written instructions were developed to aid the students with assignments. Care was taken to make sure instructions were done with the low readability student in mind.

· Increased collaboration between resource personnel, special education instructors, and Tara was established.

· Collaboration between the administration and Tara was strengthened for placing special education students on a provisional or trial basis.

· Alternative approaches to any given assignment were offered to special education students—especially those who had poor motor skills.

As the specific situation became resolved, the Social Literacy group turned its time and energy toward a solution of the general problem. At present, the student-teachers in the education program are collaborating with their master teachers to have the superintendent of the Santa Barbara School District implement the Weighted Student Unit (WSU) program. Basically, the WSU would balance the placement of special education students in any class. For example, if a special education student requires three times as much attention as the regular student, the special education student should fill the space of three regular students. This would allow every student, in any given class, an equal opportunity for learning.

Given—each special education student's WSU is equal to three (3) students

Given—legal size of class should not exceed twenty-eight (28) students

Present Class Situation	*WSU Class*
6 - spec. ed. = 18 students	6 - spec. ed. = 18 students
22 - regular = 22 students	10 regular = 10 students
28 Total = 40 students	16 Total = 28 students

To date we have taken the following steps:

· Library research on the definition, placement, facilities, needs, and reaching of special education students.

· Created a specific proposal in the form of a petition which has been signed by the Santa Barbara art teachers, interns, special education teachers, other resource personnel, and a number of other teachers.

· Contacted State Senator Rains and Assemblyman Gary Hart for possible implementation on a statewide level.

· Contacted the California Federation of Teachers and other organizations currently interested in the implementation of WSU.

· Obtained information from Idaho, Utah, and Washington, where the WSU is in operation.

· Wrote and distributed a proposal and explanation to teachers, administrators, school board members, and university faculty to lobby for support.

· Wrote a short statement of support that can be used for letter and telegram support of any legislation that may be presented to the public.

5. Was the solution agreeable to all or most of the people involved? What were the other results?

6. Has the solution been sustained, i.e., is the solution applied consistently and continually? Is the improvement stable?

As this book is being written, there are almost daily developments in the campaign for a WSU in Santa Barbara and California. The final questions, therefore, cannot be completed now. Several facts are clear, however. Even inexperienced, "powerless" interns faced with an out-of-control class and a system stacked against them CAN make a difference by working together. Second, numerous alternative solutions are usually possible at a classroom level and there are several levels at which the problem can be addressed: individual, classroom, school, school district, state. Third, less obvious is the effect of collaboration on the morale of the intern art teachers. They have been transformed from a collection of separate, slightly depressed individuals completing a heavy load of required courses into a coherent group of enthusiastic educators. Finally, it should be obvious that not every nuclear problem-solving process leads to or demands a change in a state law. But, the nuclear problem-solving process is powerful through the collaboration it facilitates, through the problematic patterns it addresses at several levels, and through the systemic changes it promotes in a broad array of educational situations.

The second example illustrates a year-long variation of the nuclear problem-solving process designed to increase basic literacy.[2] The Jacksonville, Florida, schools had been getting warnings for months. In April and May,

[2]This description was published in substantially the same form in (Alschuler and Flinchum, 1979).

1977, the *Jacksonville Journal* and *Florida Times-Union* carried stories about Jacksonville's own test of basic skills that preceded Florida's literacy test by several years: "High school Seniors try test one more time," "227 Seniors told they'll flunk because of two tests," "Graduation Validity Questioned." By the next October, statewide data showed that Jacksonville's failure rates of 45 percent in mathematics and 14 percent in communication ranked 57th and 64th among Florida's 68 counties. Again, newspapers caught the tenor of public reaction: "Dismal school test scores," "Concerned parents flock to Ribault (High School)," "Scores do not fairly portray Stanton High School role." Stanton and Ribault had the highest mathematics failure rates in the city (94 percent and 80 percent, respectively) as well as the highest communications failure rates (52 percent and 44 percent). A shocking number of these eleventh graders were unable to demonstrate minimum competency in such basic skills as using a city map, completing a check and its stubs, determining the time between two events, or solving problems involving weight and measurements. While educators debated the degree of validity and bias in these tests, the public demanded remediation and the rest of the country watched Florida as a test case of the effects of statewide literacy testing.

Superintendent Herbert Sang argued that eleventh grade was too late. During the three years under his conservative, no-nonsense leadership, Jacksonville schools adopted a uniform discipline code, created a uniform curriculum across all schools, set up a massive testing program second in size only to that of New York City and established minimum competencies to be attained at every grade level. According to Sang, "In Jacksonville, we have truly done away with social promotion. The key word is expectancy. Children have a way of rising to the level of expectancy." His policies seem to be working. Over the last three years an increasing number of schools have been accredited, based in part on improved test scores. Having anticipated the "dismal" scores at Stanton and Ribault High Schools, Sang focused attention on one of the major feeder schools, Northwestern Junior High School. He wanted to know why Northwestern students were not achieving, and what could be done about it.

Northwestern could have been a leading candidate for the worst junior high school in the country. Battle fatigue took its toll. The yearly teacher turnover rates hovered around 30 percent. Conflict between the 1,300 students and 79 teachers was so intense that each year there were nearly 7000 referrals to the front office for disciplinary purposes. Interracial misunderstanding may have been a factor. Jacksonville's court-approved desegregation plan allowed Northwestern's student population to remain 100 percent black, while a subsequent ruling required all schools in the county, including Northwestern, to achieve a 70 percent white, 30 percent black teacher population. The new principal at Northwestern, Milton Threadcraft, a young, dynamic black administrator, was determined to improve the physical facility, unite the faculty, develop pride in the student body, raise student achievement levels, and reduce discipline problems.

To study and to help improve education at Northwestern, Superintendent Sang hired Andrew Robinson, dean of the School of Education at the University of North Florida, and himself a graduate of the Jacksonville schools. With $44,000 from the school system and a university grant of approximately $36,000, Dean Robinson brought together a diverse group of faculty members[3], consultants, intern teachers, and graduate students under the direction of Professor Betty Flinchum. They carried out a socially literate plan to improve education at Northwestern.

It would have been possible to analyze performance data to identify the individuals most in need of help. For instance, 9 of the 79 teachers were responsible for over 60 percent of the discipline referrals. They might have been singled out for training or termination. Similarly, those students most frequently in trouble or with the lowest achievement test scores might have been put into special classes. However, instead of using the data to name and blame individuals, the Stanford achievement test scores, obtained yearly, were examined for problematic patterns plausibly related to systemic causes. The seventh grade test scores were typical of all three grade levels. At the end of seventh grade, the mean score in reading at Northwestern was at the 18th percentile against national norms, and at the 21st percentile in mathematics. Forty percent of the seventh graders read below the third grade level, and 96 percent scored below grade level in mathematics. The Stanford achievement test is a "power test" not dependent on the speed of student's work. Nevertheless, a majority of the seventh graders did not finish the last third of the test in the time provided because many were nearly illiterate and most were poor readers. The most obvious proximate causes were inappropriate curriculum objectives geared too high for students, thus guaranteeing failure, frustration, and discipline problems.

During the summer of 1977, faculty members from the University of North Florida worked with department heads at Northwestern Junior High School in revising educational objectives in reading, science, social studies, and mathematics to make them realistic, obtainable in one year, and educa-

---

[3]Including Alfred Alschuler, Bernadine Bolden, Marianne Betkouski, Thomas Clawson, Lorraine Daniels, Jimmy Greek, Donna Keenan, William Merwin, Bette Soldwedel, Ann Stoddard, and Ann Tillman.

tionally significant. For example, item analysis of misspelled words on the Stanford achievement test led to the creation of spelling objectives related to those patterns of error. The entire faculty was oriented to the revised objectives during the summer of 1977. During the school year, teachers were supported in implementing curricular changes through additional teacher-interns in many classes, through regular consultation by university faculty members, and through a weekly, three-hour in-service course taught by the UNF professors. Topics in this course were designed to help make the new curricula work: how to structure instructional time, how to construct tests and evaluation procedures, how to manage the classroom, how to improve techniques for questioning, how to make better use of alternative instructional media.

The results of this collaborative effort were detectable in several areas. Teacher absenteeism went down from an average of 8.9 days in the 1976–77 school year to 7.2 days in the 1977–78 school year. At the end of the school year, the teacher turnover rate was half that of the previous year, reflecting higher staff morale and providing a more seasoned, stable group of teachers for the next year. Student attendance went up slightly from an already high average daily attendance of 92.7 percent in 1976–77 to 93.1 percent in 1977–78. The most important data, however, are portrayed in the following graphs:

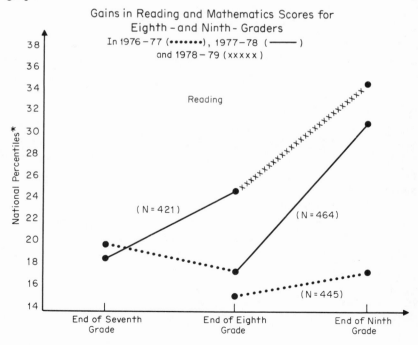

Gains in Reading and Mathematics Scores for
Eighth - and Ninth- Graders
In 1976 − 77 (••••••), 1977−78 (———)
and 1978 − 79 (x x x x x)

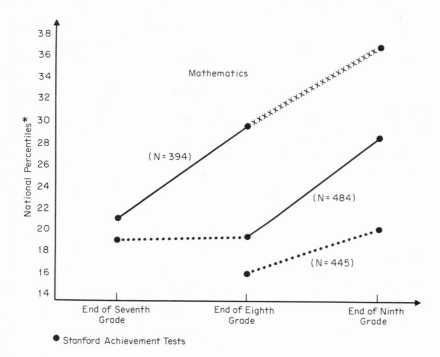

● Stanford Achievement Tests

In both graphs, the slope of the solid lines represents the gains of the eighth and ninth graders during the project year. They contrast with the gains of the eighth and ninth graders the previous year, represented by the slope of the broken lines. The gains are related to the curricular changes and project activity, not to differences in the students from one year to the next. This can be seen by comparing the performance of the eighth graders prior to the project (the broken lines on the left-hand side of each graph) with their performance as ninth graders during the project (the solid lines on the right-hand side of the graphs). Gains in both reading and mathematics for both eighth and ninth graders went up sharply during the project year. The curricular improvements continued to help students, as can be seen by the slope of the upper right hand lines (XXX) the year after the project changes were made.

Northwestern Junior High School is not yet a paragon of educational virtues. The discipline referral rate remains unacceptably high and the test scores, although up, are still well below the national average. This year socially literate solutions are being devised for these problems.

The effort to raise minimum competencies was not particularly fancy, complex, innovative, or hugely expensive by today's standards. In retrospect, several well-known ingredients of successful programs appear to have made contributions: A prior history of efforts at change in the school system, educational leadership committed to make improvements as shown by their behavior as well as their words. Perhaps most important, a precise problematic pattern was named, the curriculum was changed rather than individuals, an eclectic array of methods were used, there was multi-level collaboration, and the solutions were mutually agreeable and sustained over a two-year period. It was a socially literate strategy designed to solve a crucial educational problem—helping students attain a minimal level of literacy and numeracy.

TEN

Conquering Burn Out, Battle Fatigue, and Frenzy

Mr. Nicholson ran to his car in the heavy rain and headed for school with only 25 minutes to make the half-hour trip. He knew the principal watched for latecomers from his office window and made a note in the offending teacher's file. Such incidents came up at discussions about merit pay increases. Extra hundreds of good deeds were expected in return for one's minimal salary and went unreported. The risk of an accident almost seemed equal to the risk of a bad mark to Mr. Nicholson as he sped along the slick highway in the morning rush hour traffic. When he was in the school parking lot, only one minute late, he ran for the building, hoping that the principal either wasn't there, or understood that sometimes teachers are late for forgiveable reasons. As soon as he passed through the large metal fire doors, Mr. Nicholson realized he had left his bag lunch in the car. He cursed silently, turned around, and raced back in the pouring rain to unlock his car, retrieve his lunch and get to class a little later and a lot wetter. He was all the way to his room, looking for his keys when he realized that in his rush he had left them hanging from the lock in his car door, swinging in the rain. Students were milling at the home room door. They did not care if they ever went in, but Mr. Nicholson knew that the principal did care: "Congested halls are a hazard." So once again, he made the trip to his car, not even running. He could not get wetter, be much later, or grow more frustrated. These events set the tone for the day. He was short with students and teachers alike. His caged frustration barked and growled for no apparent reason. He sent two students to the front office for minor offenses he normally tolerated and cracked down on everybody else.

The same day, the daughter of one of Mr. Nicholson's colleagues, Mrs. Harold, had not been sufficiently considerate to get sick before 6:30 A.M. The district policy gave teachers until that time to request a substitute for the day. After 6:30 A.M. it was better to report to work in an acute stage of the bubonic plague than try to get an exception to the policy. At the last minute Mrs. Harold arranged for her neighbor to care for her daughter, but Mrs. Harold kept wondering whether the 101° temperature was going up or down. She kept making simple calculating errors on the board in her math class that were corrected gleefully by her students. It was embarrassing. When Mrs. Harold passed her friend, Mr. Nicholson, and didn't "see" him, he "knew" it was a deliberate insult. He wondered what the hell he had done to her.

Tension, stress, anxiety, and depression are not unique to teachers. But the conditions in public schools intensify these problems. Everyday there are several hundred students to greet by name, encourage by a smile, and teach individually. Paperwork, lesson plans, and red tape take twice the time provided by the one free period. Extracurricular activities, committees, and moonlight jobs push teachers to the limits of their physical endurance. Frenzy becomes a life style, until battle fatigue and burn-out finally consume teachers. According to a Teacher Health Survey conducted by *Instructor* magazine in 1976, stress is the worst health problem teachers have. Stress takes several forms: frenzy, battle fatigue, and burn-out. These are not just labels, but clinical syndromes of specific symptoms. What are the problematic patterns of stress? How do you recognize the signs of stress? What are the systemic causes? And what can be done to alleviate stress in the lives of educators and students?

Naming the problematic patterns of stress

Frenzy occurs when educators try to get too much done in an impossibly short time. They act as if *dead*lines meant death for those who do not finish on schedule. They push themselves, their colleagues, and their students to a frantic pace. Here are eight signs of frenzy:[1]

[1]From *Type A behavior and your heart* (Friedman and Rosenman, 1974).

· chronic sense of urgency (impatience with how others operate and their rate of work)

· thinking about and doing several things at once

· active attempts to complete discussions quicker by dominating conversations, determining topics, and by being preoccupied with one's own thoughts about what comes next instead of listening to others

· hurried speech

· constant rapid movements (pacing, eating, drumming fingers, tapping feet)

· characteristic nervous gestures (tics, clenched fists and jaw, pounding on table, grinding teeth)

· vague guilty feelings during periods of relaxation because one is "doing nothing"

· overconcern with getting good things in contrast with being a good person

It is the "Chicken Little" complex. Belief that disaster is imminent causes frenzied rushing about and mobilizing others. Frenzy can be contagious. Unfortunately, as in the story, others often pay the price. If frenzy is constant and long term, it (rather than the feared disasters) can be disastrous. People who experience chronic frenzy are three times more likely to have a coronary heart disease.

"Battle fatigue," another response to stress, is described by Alfred Block (n.d.), a psychiatrist who studied 253 "battered teachers," educators who suffered from physical or sustained psychological assault. According to Block, this assault on normal human sensibilities consisted of the constant threat of murder and rape. Physical assault and injury occurred to a majority of these teachers, as did theft. Their school climate included bombings of buildings, vandalism, destruction of equipment, fights between students and gangs, locker searches that revealed drugs, dynamite, knives, guns, and ammunition. Overcrowded classes in desegregated schools on hot fall and spring days are tinderboxes for explosions of violence. When disruptive students are sent to the front office, it is often the teacher who is blamed for an inability to control the class or to get along with an ethnically diverse group of students. Prolonged work in schools' frontline trenches, Block argues, causes the classic syndrome called "battle fatigue": (1) impaired morale, (2) sense of futility, (3) malaise and depression, and (4) hypochondriacal symptoms, such as complaints of fatigue, weakness, dizziness, blurred vision, irritability, sensitivity to the weather, and gastrointestinal problems. Whether one calls this "combat neurosis" or a normal response to an acute psychotic situation does not change the suffering of "battered teachers." Everyone agrees that the victims need help and that the "war" in schools should stop.

A more frequent response to long-term stress is burn-out, "a common frailty of many people whose jobs require them to give too much, too often, to other people in need" (Maslach and Johnson, 1979). This syndrome "frequently occurs among individuals who do 'people work'—who spend considerable time in close encounters with other people under conditions of chronic tension and stress."

Here are a baker's dozen signs indicative of burn-out. None of these red flags in itself proves that a person is burned out. But the more signs there are, and the more intense they are, the more serious the case of "burn-out" is likely to be. (Incidentally, marriages can be "burned-out" too. You may wish to think about an intimate relationship in these terms.)[2]

1. EMOTIONAL EXHAUSTION Burned-out teachers have as much energy and utility as a dead light bulb. According to C. Maslach (1976), they feel drained of energy, and "lose all concern, all emotional feeling for the persons they work with." They lose interest in helping and in being successful.

2. DETACHMENT Because so many students have so many problems, burned-out teachers protect themselves by detachment. They distance themselves from students' problems in many ways: e.g., using derogatory labels for large undifferentiated groups ("The seventh period class are my dummies"), or by describing complex, multifaceted human beings who have unique personal histories in terms of a single symptom ("They are slow readers"). Sometimes detachment is reflected in becoming less available to help.

3. CYNICISM AND NEGATIVITY Teachers may begin to distrust and dislike students or begin to believe they deserve the problems they have. Burned-out teachers also express cynical, negative opinions about their own work: "I'm not helping anybody." "I've gotten very callous."

4. SEPTIC TANK Teachers feel like a septic tank filled to the brim with other people's problems.

5. VULNERABILITY TO DISEASE This includes psychosomatic problems like ulcers, back tensions, and headaches in addition to colds and sicknesses. Absenteeism is higher among burned-out teachers.

6. CLUTTER This may be physical clutter, such as a messy style of piling

---

[2]Several of these signs were suggested by Bert Bertram and John Curtis at the Florida Personnel and Guidance Association Convention, November 17, 1978 in a workshop on "Burn out".

files on one's desk, or it may be a mental sense of an overwhelming number of little tasks that need to be done.

7. BOREDOM At one time the job may have been new, challenging, and joyful. Burned-out teachers are bored. They find the job filled with dull routines that demand little creative energy.

8. FEELING PUSHED AROUND Burned-out teachers often feel resentful that they have so little control over their work life. Memos, phone calls, bells, paperwork, deadlines, contractual obligations seem to own all of their thoughts, feelings, and actions. Early in a teacher's career these same conditions were merely irritating aspects of daily life in school beyond which there remained considerable freedom.

9. FEELING IMPRISONED There is a special form of claustrophobia in which a person believes that particular job cannot be done by anyone else, even though the person does not like or want the job. It is a feeling of being locked in a work situation.

10. WANTING TO QUIT In the words of a recent popular song, this is wanting to "take this job and shove it." But for a variety of reasons the burn-out does not quit and does not stop wanting to quit.

11. TROUBLE IN INTIMATE RELATIONSHIPS Often burn-out spreads into one's home life and intimate relationships. There is greater irritability and less "quality" time with loved ones.

12. RIGID BOUNDARIES In order to keep job burn-out from contaminating personal life, rigid boundaries are often established. Personal life is not discussed at school and vice versa.

13. SUBSTANCE ABUSE A frequent symptom of burn-out is increasing dependence on coffee, cigarettes, drugs, and alcohol to chemically alter feelings of boredom, the symptoms of stress, or to numb one's sensitivity to the pressing demands of needy students.

Regardless of the type of stress (frenzy, battle fatigue, or burn-out), the severity, or who experiences it (teachers, administrators, or students), it is helpful to identify the causes and to reduce them.

Finding the Systemic Causes

Broadly analyzed, there are two areas of stress, one's personal life and one's professional life. Since the sources of stress in these two areas are different, it is appropriate to look in both places for causes, and if appropriate, develop two separate plans for reducing the major causes. Stress in either area affects one's effectiveness and enjoyment of life twenty-four hours a day.

1. Finding personal causes of stress

T. H. Holmes and R. H. Rahe (1967, p. 216) have developed a list of forty-three common causes of stress that effect our social adjustment. Their research has shown that the more stress one experiences, the greater the chance of having an illness or an accident. Before adding up your stress score, please keep several points in mind. (1) A high stress score does not automatically mean you will be ill or have an accident. Statistically, however, the chances are increased. (2) Check those life events you have experienced within the last twelve months. Because the definitions of each life event are so brief, please be conservative in checking events. If you're in doubt, don't check it. (3) Remember, there are numerous ways to reduce stress. The first step in stress reduction is locating the causes.

Scientists have concluded that you are definitely alive if your total score is between 0 and 149. A certain amount of stress is normal and healthy in creative, developing human beings. Scores between 150 and 199 indicate a "mild life crisis." Scores between 200 and 299 reflect "moderate life crises" and over 300 "major life crises."

It helps to talk about your personal stress score with others. Whether you are alone or in a group, take some time to consider any of the following questions that seem productive for you.

Do you see any patterns in the causes of stress?
Did some event trigger several stresses?
Do the stresses form a linked chain of events?
Are the stresses totally separate or are a number of them related in some way?

Which of these events did you have any control over the causes (e.g., change of living conditions)? Which events occurred independent of your actions (e.g., death of a close friend)?

Which of the events you checked are temporary and will resolve themselves in time? Which events may continue until you resolve them?

How have you been handling stress? Can you make a list of what happens when you experience the stress and what you do about it? Share your list with a friend.

On the basis of your reactions to these questions can you identify a life event or pattern of events or a set of reactions that you would like to change?

Rank	Life Event	Value
1.	Death of Spouse	100
2.	Divorce	73
3.	Marital separation	65
4.	Jail term	63
5.	Death of close family member	63
6.	Personal injury or illness	53
7.	Marriage	50
8.	Fired at work	47
9.	Marital reconciliation	45
10.	Retirement	45
11.	Change in health of family member	44
12.	Pregnancy (self or spouse)	40
13.	Sex difficulties	39
14.	Gain of new family member	39
15.	Business readjustment	39
16.	Change in financial state	38
17.	Death of a close friend	37
18.	Change to a different line of work	36
19.	Change in number of arguments with spouse	35
20.	Mortgage over $10,000	31
21.	Foreclosure of mortgage or loan	30
22.	Change in responsibilities at work	29
23.	Son or daughter leaving home	29
24.	Trouble with in-laws	29
25.	Outstanding personal achievement	28
26.	Spouse begins or stops work	26
27.	Begin or end school	26
28.	Change in living conditions	25
29.	Revision of personal habits	24
30.	Trouble with boss	23
31.	Change in work hours or conditions	20
32.	Change in residence	20
33.	Change in schools	20
34.	Change in recreation	19
35.	Change in church activities	19
36.	Change in social activities	18
37.	Mortgage or loan less than $10,000	17
38.	Change in sleeping habits	16
39.	Change in number of family get-togethers	15
40.	Change in eating habits	15
41.	Vacation	15
42.	Christmas	12
43.	Minor violations of the law	11

2. Finding causes of stress at work

Conduct a stress hunt.[3] The stress hunt is a four-step process that involves

a. Generating a long list of the most stressful experiences in the daily lives of a group of teachers (or students or administrators) by means of a brief questionnaire;

b. Summarizing these diverse stresses into about ten categories;

c. Asking teachers (or students or administrators) to rate the intensity of each category every day for one to two weeks;

d. Rank ordering the stresses in terms of what individuals find most-to-least stressful.

The stress hunt has the advantage of finding the shared stressful aspects of your work situation.

Generating the list of stressful experiences

It is common to hear administrators speaking for teachers and, similarly, teachers for students. One purpose of asking people directly is to break this oppressive norm. We need to know what administrators, teachers, and students think in their own words. This procedure can be done with a group as small as four or as large as sixty or more.

The key question is, "What are the three most stressful experiences in your daily life in school?" You may wish to distribute this question with an explanation to all teachers in school, or all the students in your classes. In our own work, however, we have often found that a key stress is the amount of clerical and paper work. If the stress hunt is perceived as another piece of "paper work," many will refuse to respond, or do so without a serious thought passing through their cortex. Be sure to keep responses from teachers, students, and administrators separate since the commonalities and differences need to be noted. While it is helpful to get this information from all three groups, focusing solely on teachers and only those teachers in the Social Literacy group can be an adequate source of data. If people want their responses to remain anonymous, that request should be respected.

[3] This technique was suggested by the work of Fred Stopsky and developed in collaboration with Nellie Santiago-Wolpow and teachers in the Van Sickle Junior High School Social Literacy group.

If you have four or more people in a new Social Literacy group, you may want to extend the key question into a more extensive set of interviews. Here are some possible questions:

When you finish the school day, how do you feel?

At what points during the day do you feel most tired? Most energetic?

What were three rewarding, joyful experiences today?

How do you deal with your fatigue during the day?

Do you have another job after school?

What happens when you reach home after school?

Have you had other jobs besides teaching? What rewards did you obtain from those jobs that you don't receive from teaching and vice versa?

How could the work environment be redesigned to help teachers be more effective and happier?

Have each person in the group interview one other person, writing down a two- to five-sentence description of each stressful and each rewarding experience on separate pieces of paper. After everyone has been interviewed, have each interviewer introduce one person to the entire group emphasizing "little known facts about. . . ." and what common stresses and satisfactions were shared by this person. It is quite remarkable and too frequent that teachers need to be introduced in meaningful personal ways to those people they work with everyday. This is a good priming activity for an early Social Literacy group meeting.

Categorize the stresses

As you read through the list of stresses, some will be unique, but most will seem clearly interrelated, common stresses associated with schools almost anywhere. Choose two people from the group to formulate ten to fifteen (maximum) relatively independent, nonoverlapping categories into which you can place most (i.e., 90 percent or more) of the stresses elicited from the interviews or questionnaires. In giving names to these categories, try to stick with the words most frequently used by the individuals. For efficiency have two group members take the set of stressful situations and categorize them while the rest of the group continues an informal discussion of stress in school. Here are fifteen categories that have emerged from numerous groups of teachers. Not all of these categories may be relevant to your group, and you may have several unique categories.

1. Clerical work

2. Interruptions that disrupt the class

3. Discipline problems with students

4. Lack of equipment and materials

5. Lack of teacher input into decisions

6. Rigid curriculum

7. Destruction of school property

8. Conflicts with school administration and poor working conditions

9. Problems with parents

10. Class size

11. Lack of planning time

12. Problems with other teachers

13. Lack of problem-solving mechanisms

14. Feeling of impotency

15. Problems with sexist and racist attitudes and actions

This categorization process is not rigorous, elegant, or highly precise. Nor, correspondingly, is it meant to be difficult. This list is a first rough set of categories of stresses identified in terms meaningful to your group. This same process can be followed in generating a list of stresses from administrators or students.

Here is a typical list of common stresses in the lives of students in a Santa Barbara, California, junior high school:[4]

1. Getting up in the morning

2. Going to classes

3. Being bored

4. Hassles with teachers

5. Homework

6. Getting bad grades

[4]My thanks to Gary Mason and his students for sharing this list.

7. Taking the bus

8. Having to respond in class

9. Food in the cafeteria

10. Not being prepared

11. Hassles with classmates

12. Being tardy

In a recent survey of 1,200 Oregon school administrators, Boyd Swent and Walter Smelch (1978) found that the following ten stressful situations were most frequently cited among the thirty-five situations listed on their questionnaire:

1. Complying with state, federal, and organizational rules and policies

2. Participating in meetings that "take up too much time"

3. Trying to complete reports and other paper work on time

4. Trying to gain public approval and/or financial support for school programs

5. Trying to resolve parent/school conflicts

6. Evaluating staff members performance

7. Having to make decisions that affect the lives of individuals whom I know (colleagues, staff members, students, etc.)

8. Feeling that I have too heavy a work load, one that I cannot possibly finish during the normal work day

9. Imposing excessively high expectations on myself

10. Being interrupted frequently by telephone calls

Collect base-rate data on levels of stress

In order to identify which stresses are most intense for the most number of individuals, ask each person in the Social Literacy group to fill out the stress form (sample below), every day *the minute school ends,* for five to ten consecutive days. If students are filling out the stress form, they will need a few minutes at the end of class. The sample form below is completely filled out for illustrative and explanatory purposes.

SCHOOL STRESS FORM

Ratings: 2 = very stressful
1 = stressful
0 = not stressful

Name _____   Date Started _____

Stress	1	2	3	4	5	6	7	8	9	10	TOTAL	RANK
1. Clerical and paper work	2	2	1	1	1	1	2	1	1	1	13	3
2. Interruptions that disrupt class	2	2	2	1	2	2	2	1	2	2	18	10.5
3. Discipline problems	2	2	1	2	1	2	2	2	2	2	18	10.5
4. Lack of equipment and materials	1	0	0	1	0	0	1	1	0	0	4	3.5
5. Lack of teacher input into decisions	1	2	0	1	2	0	1	2	0	1	10	6
6. Rigid curriculum	0	0	1	0	0	1	0	0	1	0	3	2
7. Destruction of school property	0	1	0	0	1	0	1	0	1	0	4	3.5
8. Conflict with school administrators	1	2	0	2	1	2	0	0	1	2	1.1	7
9. Problems with parents	0	0	0	1	0	0	0	1	0	0	2	1
10. Class size	2	1	0	0	0	1	2	0	0	0	6	5
11. Lack of planning time	2	1	2	1	2	1	2	1	2	1	15	9
TOTAL	13	13	7	10	10	10	13	9	10	9	104	

OTHER TYPES OF STRESS:

Rank order the stresses

Every day each person can calculate a column total to indicate the individual level of stress that day. At the end of a two-week period a "Total" row can be obtained on the stress form for each type of stress. This indicates the relative importance of each type of stress for each person. To summarize this numerically, use the RANK column (at the far right of the school stress form). Rank order the stresses from 1 (lowest total) to 11 (the highest total). (If two or more totals are tied, give those stresses the *same* rank calculated as the average of the ranks of those stresses, if they had been different and consecutive.)

To obtain the rank order of stresses for the group as a whole, add the ranks for each person for each stress using a group stress priorities form. This total is in the next to last column at the right. At the far right, we have rank ordered the eleven totals from lowest (e.g., stress #11) to highest (stress #3). In this example "discipline problems" (#3), "interruptions that disrupt class" (#2), and "lack of equipment and materials" (#4) are the three most important stresses affecting teachers.

Some groups have found this two-week rating process too time-consuming and unnecessary. One alternative method is to rate the stresses for only one week. Another alternative obtains a rank order in less than 5 minutes. Once the list of stressful situations is named, have members of the group

Stresses	GROUP STRESS PRIORITIES FORM										Total	Rank
	Individual's ranking for each stress											
	1	2	3	4	5	6	7	8	9	10		
1	8.5	11	8	6	7	2	6	8	11		67.5	8
2	10.5	10	10	8	10	4	8	10	9		79.5	10
3	10.5	9	11	10	10	8	10	11	10		89.5	11
4	3.5	6	9	10	10	10	11	9	7		75.5	9
5	6	4.5	7	10	8	11	9	1	8		64.5	7
6	2	4.5	3.5	7	1	9	7	3	5.5		45.5	6
7	3.5	8	5.5	5	4	7	1	5	5.5		44.5	5
8	7	1	3	3	4	5.5	3	7	3		36.5	3
9	1	7	4	3	4	5.5	5	6	4		39.5	4
10	5	2	1	1	6	3	4	4	1		27	2
11	8.5	3	2	3	2	1	2	2	2		25.5	1

either vote for the three they consider most stressful, or have them rank order the stresses. In all variations the objective is to find the most stressful situations so that collaborative action to reduce stress can be focused and maximally useful.

Another variation is to conduct this same procedure, but to identify satisfactions. This can be done simultaneously with the stress hunt with the dual goal of reducing stress and increasing daily satisfactions. The stress hunt is not limited to school. One group's interest in this process was multiplied when they developed a group stress form in relation to their marital, family, and/or love life. In these variations the objective is for each group to discover what its prime stresses and satisfactions are, named in their own words. This forms the basis for action plans that will reduce stress and increase enjoyment of life.

Planning the Battle against Stress

As in war, individuals are victims; their pain needs to be reduced. But if the war is to be won, a battle plan must be developed and implemented that coordinates the energies of many victims. In her article on burn-out Ms./Dr. Maslach comes to a common conclusion: "Many of our subjects did not know that other people were experiencing the same feelings they were: each of them thought their personal reaction was unique" (Maslach, 1976, p. 22). Most often, each teacher's reactions are not unique, yet most teachers secretly fear that they are incompetent or crazy or both. These hidden fears compound the problem. Conversely, talking with one or more colleagues is reassuring, and the act of collaboration overcomes one of the primary causes of stress—teachers' isolation. Ms./Dr. Maslach comments on her findings that show "burn-out rates are lower for those professionals who actively express, analyze and share their personal feelings with colleagues" (Maslach, 1976, p. 22). Sharing concerns in response to the stress hunt or in one's personal life tends to change the locus of the problem. "I'm not alone or unique. It is a common problem. It is not primarily my personal inadequacy. Maybe there is a systemic cause and systemic solution."

Once you have identified the pattern of stresses in your personal and/or professional life, do steps 3 and 4 of the nuclear problem-solving process —brainstorming changes in rules or roles of the system and making a democratic plan. Or, as an alternative, turn complaints into objectives. Do this with a trusted friend. For 5 minutes generate the largest possible list of honestly felt complaints illustrating the stress. These may be complaints about oneself, others, or the system; they may be silly, or as ridiculous as you want. The objective is to create a long, complete list about a common stress. The other person in the pair writes down all the complaints. In a second 5-minute period switch roles of complainer and scribe. Next, select one to three complaints from the list which, if resolved, would noticeably reduce stress. This should not be a huge problem, but one about which something can be done. Take about 5 minutes. Then, translate the complaint into a desirable objective (e.g., from "I'm harassed by my supervisor" to "improve the relationship with my supervisor"). Decide what steps to take, the obstacles to expect, and the help you will need.

Often it does not take much work to reduce stress once the common stresses are located. In one school both teachers *and* students rated interruptions as the most stressful daily event. In that school, P.A. announcements and students coming late to class were two frequent types of interruptions. Both were reduced by changing some rules; e.g., students agreed to start class more quickly and with less hassling in return for 5 minutes free time at the end of class. Other successful efforts to reduce patterns of stresses have included

Creating a crisis intervention team that could mobilize quickly to deal with major disruptions in school.

Making a "first aid" pact with three to five other teachers who agreed to be available for any kind of help, from sick children to car keys dangling in the rain.

Rotating teachers more quickly into and out of the most stressful situations: lunch hall monitoring, study halls.

One family decided the TV was a major source of stress, sold it, and spent more time relaxing together and talking quietly.

Whatever pattern of stresses you plan to attack, remember the criteria for socially literate problem solving. Consider rules and roles to change, not people. Proceed democratically. Then, the overall level of stress is likely to be reduced in a lasting, mutually satisfying way.

Socially literate solutions differ markedly from the lonely efforts and temporary relief advocated in popular magazines:

Meditate daily to achieve a calm, detached perspective on events. ("If I had time to meditate, I wouldn't have the frenzies!").

Develop your physical fitness. When you are in shape, the daily drain is less draining and, when needed, you are better able to sprint. ("Terrific. If I had the time, the first thing I'd do would be to catch up on my sleep.")

Pamper yourself. Buy some clothing. Eat a banana split. Go to a movie. Treat yourself nicely. You'll appreciate it. ("And I'd be a poor, fat, well-dressed movie addict.")

Take a sick day. After all, according to *Instructor* magazine, stress is the number one health problem of teachers. ("I don't know about your school, but in mine it takes triple the effort to catch classes up and calm them down if I miss a day.")

Some individual efforts may be helpful. Here are several more to consider:

Set more realistic expectations for yourself. Don't put on Superman's cape or Wonder Woman's cape. You can't help, cure, or teach everyone. There are limits; accept them.

Get additional training in a needed competency area.

Holler for help from a friend, colleague, or therapist.

Learn to manage your time even more efficiently. Helpful books on the subject are readily available.

Beautify your environment. Make it a place that is pleasant to see, touch, and smell.

Divert your attention: Chop wood, work in your garden, stroll in the woods, see a movie, paint, pay attention to your children.

Try a little cosmic humor. After you have cried, shaken in frustration, and had your anxiety attacks, laugh.

Give strokes. You will be surprised how good you feel when you compliment people, praise their work, or give them a pat on the back or a hug.

Do your own thing: scream, cry, beat pillows with tennis racquets, jog to exhaustion.

Quit. If all else fails, consider getting into a radically different line of work.

While each of these "cures" may alleviate a symptom for an individual, they allow the major stresses to remain, causing more stress the next day for others as well. Socially literate solutions reduce the causes of stress in basic ways that satisfy many people.

ELEVEN

Problem Solving in the Classroom

Achieving socially literate solutions to classroom problems involves the same steps we followed in our six-year effort to unveil and recreate positive discipline, as well as in the twenty-minute nuclear problem-solving process: (1) collaboratively name the central patterns of conflict, (2) analyze the rules and roles of the system that cause these conflicts, (3) democratically transform these oppressive aspects of the classroom. Socially literate problem solving in the classroom integrates all of the techniques, skills, and concepts presented in this book. As in the previous chapters, I will present examples of the steps, then comment on the significance of the whole process.

The steps and the results

Lou Loomis's students thought she was a good teacher, not the greatest and not the worst. As a committed and experienced science teacher, Ms. Loomis always wanted to improve. After several months' involvement with a Social Literacy support group, she decided to try collaborative problem solving in one of her classrooms because she wanted "to do more learning and get more structure in observing what I was doing, plus plain old curiosity." She began with the stress hunt. The following excerpts are from her daily log and from a transcribed interview about her "experiment."

As soon as we started, I changed my status. "Who wants to hand out papers?" When the hands went up, I responded, "Now you decide who'll do it." I sat down with the group to do the game. For reading the stresses, they'd all caught on and picked a reader with my participating in the selection as a peer. You could have heard a pin drop during the reading of the stresses. Then one of the students, who'd already played the game in another class, said, "Now we put them into categories!" Just as that task was completed, the bell rang.

First of all, I found out I was back in the same old bag, being judged. I tended to view it the same way I would have reviewed an administrator's evaluation of me. But by the time I got home with the data and had dinner and sat down and looked it over in the evening, I was able to deal with it simply as information. I could get some goals from this information. In preparation for the next day I counted the number of items in each category and put the tally on the blackboard at the beginning of class:

Course content	20
Student behavior	14
Coldness of the room	11
Teacher behavior	7
Miscellaneous	4
Chairs	2

At the beginning of the second day I said we needed a chairperson and a recorder. Since three people wanted to be chairperson, one was chosen for that day, and it was suggested that the other two be used on subsequent days. This was unanimously and immediately accepted. After about five minutes, the chairperson said she'd rather be recorder, and the recorder volunteered to chair.

It was decided to work on "chairs" first since it looked like the smallest problem. The outcome of the chair problem was a committee to see if modern chairs could be obtained for the room. Then a student said that the two comfortable chairs in the room should be used and that she should have one every day since she thought up the idea. After discussion, there was a vote, and she won. Then it was agreed that the other chair should rotate in alphabetical order. The suggester was immediately given her chair. The one with the circulating chair wanted to start the next day since the class was more than half over.

Under miscellaneous, "noise next door" was mentioned. After some talk, it was suggested that we keep track (no, I did not mention looking for a pattern), and one student had the bright idea of marking the calendar daily.

Also under miscellaneous were "length of class" and "freedom." Suggestions were: five minutes rest at end of period; lesson plan on blackboard; write up experiment one day, do it the next. These were accepted.

"Coldness of room" the students decided was a school problem which we couldn't deal with at the moment; so we moved to "teacher behavior," and I was saved by the bell.

By the end of the second day I was enjoying the process thoroughly— particularly being part of the group. I could raise my hand, participate, make motions, etc. I was listened to along with everyone else.

The next three days were taken up with review for exams, but I adhered to all the new rules that had so far been agreed upon.

The day after exams, one student asked: "Are we going to finish what we were doing before exams—teacher behavior stresses?"

The first comment was that I talked about blacks too much. I said, "Have you learned anything from what I said?" All said "yes." Then a deluge of conversation followed. The final outcome was that there should be lots more talk on the subject, not less.

The next problem was that the teacher explains things too fast. We decided that students would take turns starting class and getting people settled down to listen. Students would say right away when they didn't understand something. I hadn't been getting any feedback from them and was working on the assumption that when I didn't hear anything, it meant that people understood. That gave me a whole new insight. The information doesn't belong to the teacher. It doesn't belong to the student. It just indicates an area where you can get together.

The last day of negotiations we started on three student behaviors. If students don't have materials or need to go to the bathroom, they take a pass and just say where they are going. During questions, Ms. Loomis will ask specific people. Otherwise, all can answer general questions. I expressed my feeling that it was degrading for people to raise their hands to do what they had a right to do. The problem of people standing in the doorway was solved by an agreement not to do so.

It was decided that the problem of students not doing homework couldn't be solved by any class rules because this was up to each person as an individual.

The final category, "course content," which had the greatest number of "stresses," was solved the quickest. Many items were rejected as not real problems, e.g., "If this is a science room, why aren't there any animals?" "That's silly, this course is about physics."

Then, not in the stress hunt at all, came comments asked about the room: 1. The fish tanks weren't taken care of well enough. I agreed and admitted I wasn't a fish person. Were there people who could help me? Yes, there were, and we got a tank committee. 2. The room decor needed more changing. This subject produced considerable discussion. (Mind you, my room is over, rather than underdecorated). One group said everything in the room was useful, and they were content; another group wanted a continuously changing decor in addition to the materials on display that are used for daily work. From the second group came an 'interior decorating committee.'

The next day I showed the new rules on a transparency for review and approval. One student volunteered to make a ditto for everyone. The rules have been duplicated, and each student has a copy.

Next Monday, we will have a discussion to go over things and explore items that have developed as we work with our rules, e.g.: Is any change needed? Any problems? How come none of the committees have done anything?

I have now completed two weeks of classes. Our new setup allows everyone to function. I love it and so do the students. So far it has been more fun than a picnic.

One of the most significant experiences for me personally occurred when I joined the group. I realized that in giving up my role of leader I was not losing everything. I still had a voice. I could still be recognized. The other exciting thing was that in the new setup, frivolousness had a much shorter life-span. One can be constantly frivolous with a dictator, but not so when the group is working together. IT WAS FASCINATING TO SEE THE PRINCIPLES OF SOCIAL LITERACY EMERGE AS THE GROUP DEVELOPED AND FUNCTIONED. THE PRINCIPLES DID NOT NEED TO BE TAUGHT AT ALL. IT WAS AS IF THEY WERE ALREADY THERE IN THE MARBLE, AS A SCULPTOR SEES THE STATUE EXISTING IN THE PIECE OF ROCK.

A major block to the creation of democratic classrooms is teachers' fear of losing their authority, and that with democracy will come a loss of control, less learning, and unreasonable demands endorsed by a majority. Typically, these fears are unwarranted. Authority is the power to authorize. Teachers do have the legal authority to order students to work and to evaluate that work. In practice, however, students often resist, evade, or ignore this autocratic authority, reducing learning time in classes by over 50 percent. Students must give their consent, by cooperation, for learning to occur. In this sense, students always authorize or do not authorize in the classroom the legal authority given to teachers. Ultimately, learning is a result of shared authorization. Ms. Loomis, for instance, did not lose her legal authority when she gave up her autocratic leadership style; she gained the public authorization of the students for cooperation in the classroom, and there was evidence of significant improvement. The group settled down faster with a student starting class. Ms. Loomis had more time to work with individual students. The free lav and locker passes were used less often. On her final exam, this "experimental" class performed significantly better (according to our statistical analysis) than another class taught by Ms. Loomis in the same grade of comparable ability.

Author-ity also is a characteristic of authors, experts who speak true words. As Ms. Loomis discovered, she did not have to teach her students this capacity. "It's in the marble, as a sculptor sees the statue existing in a piece of rock." Under her democratic leadership, the class spoke true words: they spoke publicly about their shared situation in a way that was heard. They focused on rules and roles, not on changing people, and committed themselves to keeping their word. They engaged in true dialogue: loving, trusting, with humility, in good faith, hopeful, and critical. This liberated them all, including Ms. Loomis, from conflict and oppressive aspects of her previous domination. As she said, "Our new setup allows everyone to function. I love it and so do the students." Her classroom became a place where it was easier to love.

This type of democratic problem solving is the essence of Social Literacy. It is not a monumental achievement available only to true master teachers. The "system" to be transformed need not be the macro-socio-politico-economic arrangement of the world. The concepts of Social Literacy do not even need to be taught directly. The methods need not be complicated or rigid. The process is simple, despite my encasing it in polysyllabic, philosophic language. It can be quick, easy, and enjoyable. Start with one of the techniques presented in this book. Try the nuclear problem-solving process one day after you or students have encountered a problem. If the four steps become too complex, just do the last two, brainstorming alternative rules and planning. Or, start with the stress hunt to name the problems. Drop the daily tabulations, if that becomes a burden, and move directly into solutions for the stresses, as Ms. Loomis' class did. Create a survival guide with the class, then vote on the worst informal rule, one that most needs changing. Try a discussion of why that rule exists, and how every person in class maintains it actively or passively. Or, locate and analyze a central conflict designated by the special vocabulary of students. Then try to overcome it collaboratively. Play the Discipline Game to teach people how to negotiate and to get new ideas for solving common problems. Participate in a Social Literacy support group of teachers, even if that group is only one other person you meet occasionally. This peer cooperation is helpful in generating other methods for engaging in democratic problem solving in the classroom when you run into inevitable or unexpected problems. Social Literacy is not a set of techniques, however. Modify or drop a technique if it is not facilitating the process of collaborative problem solving aimed at making situations more loving and conducive to development. The following two examples illustrate this flexibility.

Raymond Cerins, a Hartford High School sociology teacher, decided to use an inquiry approach in one of his classes.

It seemed to me that it would be a refreshing break, but didn't turn out that way. There was once a great deal of participation in this class, but it seemed to be breaking down. The same problems that were bothering me, also bothered the students. I decided to try the nuclear problem-solving technique with the class. We went through each step and came up with many solutions which were narrowed down to one which has worked very well. We mutually decided to revert back to the traditional text which was successful at the beginning of the semester. The interest and participation quickly returned. The main point here is that the students had some input in deciding what direction the class was going to take.

This same "main point" is central when techniques like the nuclear problem-solving process don't work. A reading teacher in a Springfield Junior High School, who wished to remain anonymous, reported that

Students in the advanced level course find reading boring. They have come from the number one group of readers in the elementary grades and don't know why they must take reading in junior high. One class grumbled so badly that I told them if they could think of something better, I would listen. To aid them in doing this, I tried to teach them the nuclear problem-solving technique. This proved disastrous. When they were in groups, the talking got unbearable. No one heard the instructions. Time limits could not be adhered to. Some students caught on, but the majority used the time to clown.

Next, they reviewed the (Glasser) film, "Classroom meetings." They were bored, but when it was over, we discussed how a class meeting could be used. That class ended with my saying that when they were ready and had an agenda prepared, they could submit it to me, and I would arrange a place for a meeting.

A couple of classes came and went. One day, some members of the class began to grumble, "You said we could have a say about what we would do in reading class. We want a classroom meeting like you said." They said they had an agenda and now was the time and the classroom was good enough for a place.

Because the period was lunch time, this class met one half hour, then went to lunch and returned for another half hour. To quiet them, I said if they worked quietly on the assignment before lunch, the meeting could take the second half.

While they worked, I quickly listed what I needed from the students. After lunch I gave each student paper to take down a few facts: What time period we were talking about, the number of class periods left, and the number of hours the class was planning for, the course requirements that were necessary, such as "assignments must be related to reading." and "some time must be spent working on reading skills."

Students took over from there. Most wanted free reading, books *they* chose to read. They settled who would be responsible for supplying reading materials, what materials would be satisfactory, etc. Keeping order in class was discussed. Record keeping and reporting of reading work was settled, how much and when skills would be worked on was settled.

What I agreed to and what they agreed to do were spelled out and signed by those willing to participate. Those who wished could continue with the way things were.

It was decided that 30 of the 90 minutes of reading a week would be spent on learning and refining reading skills. The students have worked harder and more conscientiously on the work and have accomplished more in way of mastery than when almost 100 percent of the time was supposedly alloted to learning skills, almost none to free reading. What was a noisy, inattentive class with seemingly endless discipline problems is now great to have. On reading day they come into the room like gangbusters, throwing gym clothes, chasing, ranking, etc. When the bell rings, most find their seats, open their books and in less than five minutes the room is silent. Doors can be opened, the teacher can take care of other matters, counting papers, planning. Grades are up and so are attitudes and relationships.

This teacher, like Ms. Loomis and Mr. Cerins, renegotiated several items after the new system had been in operation for a while. This does not indicate failure. On the contrary, it shows a continued commitment to the process of democratic problem solving in the classroom. This process, rather than any specific technique or solution, is a viable, valued way to reduce conflict and increase learning.

Problem-posing Education

Learning how to overcome oppression in interpersonal relationships, classroom organization, and the school is one ultimate goal of education as well as a means for improving education. This goal cannot be reached by teaching students *about* critical problem solving. The teaching-learning enterprise should *be* critical problem solving. More specifically, Freire indicates three characteristcs of problem-posing education that differentiate it from banking education:

1. Teachers and students engage in dialogue.

In most schools, the teacher, convinced of his wisdom, which he considers absolute, gives classes to pupils, passive and docile, whose ignorance he also considers absolute. [Problem-posing education] is a live and creative dialogue in which everyone knows some things and does not know others, in which all seek, together, to know more. (Freire, from an undated circular sent to the coordinators of culture circles in Chile).

2. Teachers and students attempt to speak true words about central conflicts.

The starting point for organizing the program content of education or political action must be the present, existential, concrete situation, reflecting the aspirations of the people. . . . We must pose this . . . situation to people as a problem which challenges them and requires a response, not just at the intellectual level, but at the level of action (Freire, 1972, p. 85).

By contrast, banking education presents content unrelated to students' needs and situation. Education

becomes an act of depositing in which the students are the depository, and the teacher is the depositor. Instead of communicating, the teacher issues communiqués and makes deposits which the students patiently receive, memorize and repeat. This is the banking concept of education (ibid., p. 58).

3. The meta-goal of specific problem solving is to develop critical consciousness, not magical or naive consciousness.

The more students work at storing the deposits entrusted to them, the less they develop the critical consciousness which would result from their intervention in the world as transformers of that world (ibid., p. 60).

The difference between problem-posing education and banking education is like the difference between participating on a research team and reading a research report, or working on a committee in contrast with listening to a policy statement, or collaboratively resolving a live classroom conflict instead of studying the dead battles of the Revolutionary War. It is the difference between a teacher who is a team captain and one who is the team owner. It is the difference between making the rules and abiding by them.

Problem-posing education is known, in part, under other names: the inquiry method, the discovery method, the inductive, experienced-based methods that characterize the "new" curricula. But in problem-posing education, students do not solve a prescribed sequence of substantive problems in order to "discover" preexisting knowledge in preestablished disciplines. Problem-posing education addresses problems-in-living, "political" problems, rather than problems in mathematics, physics, or biology. Answers have to be invented; they cannot be discovered like a buried treasure. It is closest in theory and practice to Dewey's democratic education.

Freire advocates problem-posing education as a liberating alternative to a banking education that domesticates people. Personally, I see problem-posing education as *one* alternative in our schools. In addition to liberation, love, and critical consciousness, there is value in learning about people, about things, and about events remote in time and place that are not immediately oppressive. These subjects matter, too. Learning about them only by inquiry and invention can be cumbersome, unnecessarily time-consuming, and restrictive, i.e., oppressive. It seems indisputable that problem-posing education is not appropriate all the time for all disciplines at all age levels. It is also indisputable that the existing wall-to-wall banking education, from kindergarten through graduate school, from the alphabet to zoology, is equally inappropriate and oppressive. Balance and diversity are needed. Loving, critical problem solving deserves a larger role as a method of education in schools and as a legitimate goal of education in our democracy.

TWELVE

Problem Solving in a Street Gang

Several hundred students were passing between classes near the gym area. A fight broke out and turned into a small riot. A teacher, in her sixth month of pregnancy, stepped in and managed to stop the fighting. Several male teachers watched this episode. They said they admired her but that getting involved in that way could be a hassle. They remembered what happened to their vice principal. He was assaulted by a student in the hallway. Two teachers had witnessed his nonviolent restraint of the kicking, pushing student. Lawyers represented both sides at the hearings. Nasty questions were raised about his character. In the end, the student didn't even get a reprimand. Within a week of the small riot near the gym, one student stabbed another student. It happened so fast that the teacher in the class did not have time to decide whether or not to intervene. The following Monday another teacher stayed late to work with three female students. They tried to take her purse. When she resisted, one student took a knife, and slashed her forehead, eyebrow, and cheek. This sequence of violence caused teachers, teachers' unions, parents, and the board of education in Hartford to demand a crackdown on violent or disruptive students.

Calixto Torres, a teacher at Quirk Middle School in Hartford, did not passively observe from the sidelines nor did he step up the punishment of deviating students. He "joined" the Ghetto Brothers, a youth gang. I found out about his efforts to do problem-posing education in this street gang at the monthly meetings of the Social Literacy Institute, a year-long project funded by the U.S. Office of Education. After three interviews (from which the following edited dialogue was taken), I realized that Calixto Torres was Enrique Tasiguano's North American counterpart. After six years I had found another superstar "teacher." This time, however, Mr. Torres helped me see that superstardom was available to any teacher. The power is in the process of problem-posing education, not in the personality of the teacher.

Joining Up

We sat in an isolated corner of a large meeting room, facing each other, almost head to head in order to hear above the noise of sixty other teachers talking in their school's Social Literacy group meeting. Mr. Torres was in his late twenties, of medium height and slender build. As I listened, asking him occasional questions, what I noticed most were his intense black eyes and debonair, trim mustache, which contrasted with his gentle, matter-of-fact tone of voice. Sometimes I had trouble hearing him.

The Ghetto Brothers had been around the school. The year before, they were the cause of many discipline problems in the area, especially after school. They would come from the high school into the junior high school area. When our kids were coming out, they would loiter, harass, and threaten our kids and would not get off the premises.

An article about them, written by a colleague of mine, said the Ghetto Brothers were responsible for a particular discipline problem at another high school. I was not aware of that particular article, even though I am the director of this Spanish community newspaper. When it was laid out, I didn't have enough time to review it. I'd been out sick. When I came back, I was told by the vice principal that on three consecutive days a group of youths had wanted to talk to me. The kids know who I am. I'm around the neighborhood all the time.

Calixto, how did you feel when you found out they wanted to see you?

To tell the truth, I was a little bit scared. I know they mean business when they set out to do something. By then, I had some idea of Social Literacy, so I said to myself, "If I can deal with the situation in a nonthreatening way, then maybe we can get somewhere. But if I assume a defensive position, I think they'll see through that." And I knew I hadn't done anything to them.

When they came over, I said, "Let's sit together and see what the problem is. Let's solve this collaboratively."

And what did they say?

They said they were willing to do that. They came after school, two of them, the president and vice president of the gang. They said, "You guys can't do that. Who gave you permission to do that? Who gave you permission to print that? You can't print that unless we give you permission to print it!" They were going to kick my ass if I didn't do something about it.

Did you think that was a serious threat?

Oh, yeah. They could have smashed my car. Somebody could have pulled a gun. They could have done anything they wanted to. But then, I said, "What is the problem?" They said, "These things are not true. Another gang caused this." I said, "What do you want to do?" "We want to communicate in a more positive way. What can we do to create a positive image?" At this point it was very ambiguous; I didn't know where they were coming from. I said, "Look, this is your community paper, too. If you want, why don't we sit together and write your opinion in a letter to the editor explaining your point of view. I'd be willing to do that."

They said they were satisfied with that and wanted to know if they could come back the next day, bring some other people and talk about this. I said, "Fine." We met again the next day, and they asked me to be their counselor. I was asked to meet with them on Saturday.

I had a rendezvous at a particular meeting place. There was a young club member (they don't think of themselves as a "gang" but as a family, or organization, or club) who blindfolded me and took me to a basement, a stereotypical gang meeting place with a bulb hanging over the desk where the president sat. Everything was dark. There were about forty kids. I started looking around and saw familar faces—faces of suspended kids, kids who had been sent to the alternate learning center, kids who had dropped out of school, a lot of kids I knew were considered disruptive and dangerous. I don't think there is a teacher alive who could have kept those forty kids there for two hours and maintained the order and organization they had. There was absolutely no fooling around, no smoking, nothing. To my understanding, most of the self-contained cl.ssrooms that have this type of "disturbed" kid don't have more than five or six of them at a time.

Calixto, that seems incredible to me. It sounds as if they only were disturbed in school. Maybe they were disturbed *by* school. Apparently, the club got them to cooperate. How did they do it?

The club has established rules—not written down or anything. They have a system by which rules are made, dues are collected; members who get out of line get a "zipper." A "zipper" is a demerit. So many zippers and you get a "bounce." A "bounce" is corporal punishment. A discipline committee, composed of seven to nine bigger kids, has a minute clock. The person to be bounced is in the middle of the group and for one minute this person is punished, kicked, punched, anything. I saw it happen.

I believe one student member had broken the rule by fighting with another member of the group. If they have a grievance, they are supposed to talk about it. The time for a grievance is at a meeting. If you have a confrontation with another member, you have a chance to explain yourself. This explanation was not acceptable and justified, so he was bounced. I felt very uneasy. It is very difficult to sit by and watch. It was not my intention to tell them what to do. I had to keep my mind on what my purpose was in being there. It was a terrible experience. You can feel the pounding, like the rain, for 60 seconds. The kid came out bloody and crying. He tried to hold back his tears. When he finished, he just flopped all over the place. One of the other fellows tried to hold the boy up, to comfort him, but was told to stop. The boy knew he was responsible for his actions, and he had to take the consequences. I knew that at any time, if they really wanted to get back at me, they could, and there were some kids who had something against me. It was a dangerous situation.

Solving problems

After my first interview with Calixto Torres I realized the extent of my ignorance about gangs. Gangs existed in the fifties while I was in high school but had disappeared, at least from public view, during the civil rights and antiwar movements of the 1960s, or so I thought. Were the Ghetto Brothers an anachronism in Hartford, or simply Hartford's version of a new gang movement in the 1970s? This question was answered almost immediately by Senator Birch Bayh's report of the Senate subcommittee to investigate juvenile delinquency. Titled, "Challenge for the Third Century: Education in a Safe Environment—Final Report on the Nature and Prevention of School Violence and Vandalism," this document was published in February 1977, within a few weeks of my first talk with Calixto Torres.

Although gangs are not a pervasive phenomenon, schools in those cities experiencing a resurgence of violent gang activities "are also feeling the effects of the return of the armies of the street." Apparently, the modern, criminally oriented gangs not only protect their turf but also have protection rackets, conduct planned robberies of businesses and homes, and are even involved in drug traffic. These gangs seem to have modeled themselves after the rich and powerful syndicates of organized crime. They are dangerous. In contrast with gangs of the 1950s, modern gang members have access to increased fire power—rifles, sawed-off shot guns, hand guns, semi-automatic and fully automatic rifles, pipe bombs, and occasionally even a home-made bazooka. Instead of the "rumble," today's gangs have "hit squads" that make lightning-fast raids on rival territory to attack individual enemies from speeding cars. In a ten-month period during 1974 the approximately 140 gangs operating in Los Angeles "were involved in over 1,600 violent crimes including 51 deaths, 885 assaults with a deadly weapon, 294 assaults with intent to commit murder, 279 kidnappings, 19 rapes, 8 fire bombings, and 99 cases of shooting at an inhabited building" (Bayh, 1977, p. 41). Not all illegal gang activity is violent or confined to the streets. Junior and senior high schools are major arenas for recruitment, protection rackets, and narcotic rings. Fortunately, "not every gang of youngsters is engaged in violations of the law; many groups are perfectly law abiding and even helpful in the school and community" (ibid., p. 43).

I wondered what kind of "club" the Ghetto Brothers were, and just how dangerous the situation was in which Mr. Torres had placed himself. These questions were answered in my second interview, again in a corner of a large room during the noisy planning of eight schools' Social Literacy groups. I asked him, "What were the Ghetto Brothers doing when you became involved?"

They were planning a theft. They needed money to buy jackets. Nobody would give them jobs, but somebody from the suburbs, an Anglo, offered them money for this theft. That upset me very much. I said, "Look, if this is your decision, after explaining what the consequences are, then I will step outside, because I might be liable." They said, "No." I should stay because I was part of the family. They trusted me and they had no reason to doubt me. I said, "Well, O.K., but I'll have to tell what I know if I'm questioned." They understood this.

We talked about the fact that they were victimizing their own community. They were victimizing themselves. The ideal thing was to set up a system to get funds for the club without victimizing themselves. There had to be some other ways, some things available in the community. I said to them, "Let's set up a committee. I'll find a meeting place and time where a committee can meet." They themselves set up a committee of their leaders to plan legal ways of getting money for their group. They came up with different ideas like a car wash, setting up a corporation, washing windows, getting a bank account, and selling Puerto Rican flags. They went out and generated some advance money from the Red Cross. We also got somebody to donate aluminum cans.

We wrote an article about these legitimate money-making efforts. After the article was published, some agencies came to them asking for help. Around Christmas time the Red Cross asked if they would distribute clothing and gifts to children in the neighborhood. We also have a group that has just finished taking a first aid course. Those who are 17 will be getting instructor courses so that they can go on and teach the others.

The Fire Department also expressed their interest. So, we set up a meeting to see what could be done, what they could offer the kids and what the kids could offer them. The basis for collaboration was the very critical problem of fires in Hartford. It affected the Spanish-speaking community to a great degree. Arson and false alarms were hurting kids' own parents, their own sisters and brothers, aunts and uncles, the place where they live. The Ghetto

Brothers wanted to get the community on their side. They wanted to do something. They wanted to show some new patterns of behavior that were positive and constructive. We have initiated seminars. In fact, today they are having their second seminar with Chief Thomas and Captain Stewart. There will be some films. There was a preliminary meeting for a few of the kids, and it went off very well. They motivated the other kids to go. In fact, they made it mandatory for a whole club to go over today.

The firemen are afraid of having the kids being involved directly in the fires but feel that there can be a lot of service in public relations work, in teaching the community the things they need to know about fires and how to prevent them. During emergencies they would be identified with cards and helmets and things. They would help the Red Cross treat people in the immediate area and help firemen relocate people or get emergency service to people, like food.

The fire department had a list of fire boxes to watch. The month the Ghetto Brothers began keeping their eyes open for small kids who pull the alarms as a game, the number of false alarms was reduced incredibly. The firefighters had been contemplating removing the fire boxes prior to that, but decided to leave the boxes in.

The problem is much greater than false alarms. The fire department was saying that every time they go to a fire, they were getting hit with bricks and bottles. They don't have any Spanish-speaking firemen in the department. There is a lack of communication between the department and the community, and there are negative attitudes on both sides. We are trying to change these patterns and behavior by bringing together the Fire Department and the community. The Fire Department system can be transformed by these youngsters who, at one time, were on the other side of the fence. Now, Chief Thomas has opened up the Fire Department headquarters to the Ghetto Brothers for meetings. This is a whole turnaround now.

That's impressive, Calixto, I said (imagining a youth brigade at the periphery of all fire department activity). Has your work with the Ghetto Brothers also influenced what's happening in school?

Yes. There was an appendix to the gang, a junior gang, that came to me and asked me to be their treasurer. They went to the vice principal of the school and got a system where anytime there was trouble brewing involving their members, the vice principal should contact me so that we might set up a collaborative process. This was their idea. We averted many fights and confrontations. We had one situation where a student had dropped out of the gang some weeks before. Some of the members were looking for him to bounce him. You can't just drop out. The rules don't allow it. This particular student was afraid to go home. He had gone to Mr. Chicarillo, the vice principal, and Mr. Chicarillo came to me and explained what had happened. So that day, I walked out with him, and sure enough, there were the fellows. We got together, and I asked them what the problem was. I got their point of view. We were able to come to an understanding that this fellow had not been advised previously of the consequences of dropping out and that it was unfair because he did not know the rules.

There was another case where a kid had a girl friend. She said that the gang was going to get on this kid and beat him up. Again, we were able to solve this. The problem was not this particular student and the gang. The problem was the girl friend who was creating these rumors. So, the pattern was established that if they heard rumors at any time, they would ask individually whether he had said it. Then they would meet on it, find out the facts, and work out some kind of solution.

We are trying to move towards collaboration, to discussion, to finding out what are the basic problems. The principals are more involved now with the club. There is a working relationship. Because they have worked out cooperation between the school and the club, the principal has let them use the facilities of the school. The club has established new rules and patterns they want to follow to avoid creating any bad situations in school. In fact, they even offered their services to help protect both the students and the teachers from other students.

A month went by before my next interview with Calixto Torres. During this time the Ghetto Brothers were getting increased favorable coverage in the press and on television. I was eager to find out whether the Ghetto Brothers were going to carry out an earlier plan to incorporate.

"What's new with the Ghetto Brothers?" I asked as soon as our third talk began.

They are going through a transformation, a search for new goals. They are thinking about disbanding and reorienting their efforts. Originally, they wanted to develop a positive role in the community. In our dialogues, different ideas came out and were put into practice: working with community groups, dialogue with community people, working with the Fire Department, getting first aid instruction, this type of thing. Because of their collective efforts I was able to help them get part-time jobs. At the same time, a lot of the violence began to diminish—violence against other community people, violence against their own peers who were not in the gang, even bouncing their members.

As confrontations arose among members, there was more dialogue, and more philosophical argumentation pro and con. They began to discuss what was just. For example, one fellow had an argument with another fellow who wanted to leave the gang. The vice president asked one member to beat up this fellow. This was against the rules. There were rules that governed leaving, either a fine of $25.00 or a bounce. Some of the kids I least expected were posing these questions: Was it just to punish the fellow who wanted to leave and at the same time let the vice president, who incited this thing, get away with what he was doing—not following the rules and making decisions without consultation with the group. They felt that both the vice president and this individual were guilty. The vice president was reprimanded. The fellow was let go, and there wasn't any violence.

I think that they have seen positive results in the recent things they have done. People are willing to listen to them and work with them. They are joining other organizations. Some of them are working part-time at jobs and are doing very well. Some of them are participating in a fraternity run by one of the local churches, and some of them are working with a group of civil rights lawyers in the community. They want to do the legwork for this group. But they may go back in a couple of months depending on how much collaboration they get from these agencies. If they feel they are being left out and are not participating, they will form their union again.

The Facilitator Role

When these interviews took place, I was impressed by the events and Calixto Torres' courage. Now, over a year later, as I near the completion of this book, the implications are becoming clear. For instance, the development of these youths is cause for deep optimism. In school, they raised hell and made it so difficult for classes to function that they were labeled "disturbed," "disruptive," "delinquent," and were exiled from school. The Ghetto Brothers exercised powerful leadership and effective control of their members. (Apparently they had learned something from their exposure to schooling!) But they were organized to achieve their goals through illegal, violent, oppressive, and dehumanizing methods. Over time, they were able to substitute legal methods that were self-enhancing and contributed to community welfare. These transformations within school would have been considered a miracle. It was inconceivable to me that forty "disturbed" students in a self-contained classroom without a teacher would organize anything besides holy havoc. It was just as inconceivable to many teachers that within months these hellions could become candidates for Hartford's "young men of the year" award. In retrospect, these events demonstrate again that dramatic human development can take place when the situation is transformed, the rules are changed, and the "teacher's" role is collaborative. At most, Calixto Torres was an adviser or a counselor. He preferred to see himself as a facilitator. In editing the three interviews I was particularly interested in discovering how he accomplished so much. What was his magic formula?

They originated the role. That is, they decided how much they wanted me to be involved. This is very informal, yet formal. They have their own rules. They make their own rules.

My role is to facilitate the meetings and be a resource when they need information. I sit in the background, and I listen and then give them feedback. I don't interfere with all the things being said. I try to see that they are all on the same wave length. "Is this what you are saying?" "How are you going to solve these problems?" "Are you blaming yourselves or is this some kind of pattern that can be changed?" I ask questions and let them think about what to do. Sometimes I have alternatives in mind, but I don't give any answers. The answers come from the kids. I made it clear that I was not there to tell them what to do, but to help them do what they wanted to do. They feel I am not pushing them around, or putting anything over them.

We Puerto Ricans suffer from paternalism. How can I help liberate them if I am only going to perpetuate this attitude? It became clear to me, so painfully clear, that some of the counselors and agencies who have been working with these kids have been paternalistic. They are reformers. They want to change the kids and talk down to them. I think their condescension might do harm to the kids. They turn the kids off. These kids have been in school for many years and people have told them what to do. That didn't seem to make any difference. They still didn't do what was right. My telling them what to do was not going to change anyone or anything.

In collecting these statements from my interviews with Calixto Torres I realized he shared an attitude with others whose stories have filled this book: Enrique Tasiguano's work in Ecuador, Milt Van Vlack's videotaping of his classes, Wynn Young working his way out of chaotic classroom conflict, Joe DiChiara talking man-to-man with his star basketball player who wore the "religious" beret, Tara Sartorius and her art intern colleagues, Clotean Brayfield working with aspiring female administrators, Lee Bell and Rochelle Singletary coordinating communication among faculty members at Fox Middle School, Lou Loomis, Raymond Cerins and the anonymous Springfield teacher who successfully posed problems in the classroom, and many more. Calixto Torres spoke for them all when he said, "There is a hell of a lot of potential in the kids. If we are to be socially literate, we must believe in the potential of the kids and the people we are dealing with. They can be masters of their own lives. This has a liberating effect."

Freire agrees.

In order to be a good [facilitator] you must be convinced that the fundamental effort of education is the liberation of human beings and never their "domestication. You need, above all, to have faith in human beings, to believe in their possibility to create, to change things. You need to love. (Freire, undated circular sent to coordinators of culture circles in Chile).

APPENDIX 1

How to Start, Lead, and Participate in a Social Literacy Group

Social Literacy groups may involve three or four teachers in a school who meet regularly, or the entire faculty of a school system during a one-day, in-service workshop. Social Literacy concepts and techniques may be one segment of a preservice teacher-training program or an entire university course. The setting, purpose, membership, and frequency of Social Literacy group meetings vary widely. Regardless of the particular situation, there are three basic roles: the initiator (a teacher, principal, assistant superintendent in charge of in-service education, professor of education, etc.), the workshop session leader, and participants. The recommendations for each role in the following sections may be excessive. To err on the side of too much advice seemed better than to hinder people with too little advice. If you think a recommendation is inappropriate or unnecessary for your situation, modify or ignore it.

How to Begin: Notes to the Initiator

Several people may be enticed by the idea of a Social Literacy group, or perhaps you are a sole, curious reader toying with the notion of organizing

NOTE: This appendix is adapted from *Teaching Achievement Motivation* (Alschuler, Tabor, and McIntyre 1970).

a group. No matter how the group begins, one person generally takes responsibility for getting it started.

As the initiator, your first task is to learn enough about the material to recruit other course members by convincing them that these experiences may meet their needs. To acquire background information on Social Literacy and what its possibilities are, we suggest that you reread the Preface and Chapters 1, 2, and 3. Then prepare for an introductory meeting.

When you begin recruiting within a school system, start with members of the administration. They can often supply incentives such as in-service credit, tangible help like money for books and resources, and the essential, intangible help of their own enthusiasm. Encourage members of the administration to participate. If they work alongside teachers, you will have a doubly effective Social Literacy group. Moreover, the exercises and discussions that occur in the group about discipline, teaching styles, and classroom and school situations are valuable, shared experiences. Later, when you conduct democratic problem solving with students, administrators will be more willing to support the effort fully. They will understand what you are trying to do, what it requires in terms of time, space, and facilities. They will be able to remain unruffled through the logistics of transforming your classroom.

The total Social Literacy group, ideally, can include three to thirty or more persons who have volunteered because of special interest and favorable impressions from your advance information. The group should be small enough to work in a close, straightforward way over a period of time. Thus, groups of more than fifteen should split into subgroups to facilitate interaction. In these working groups there should be a mix of men and women, a variety of subject matter specializations, talents, ethnic backgrounds, personality types, and ages. This makes for a richer exchange of ideas. An already formed group, however, such as members of the guidance or physical education or social studies departments, may decide also to form a group. In this case the group has the advantage of a common focus on content, problems, and teaching styles and a greater chance for effectively implementing new ideas.

Group meetings can vary in length, just as the number of meetings can multiply, depending on the direction the group takes and the involvement members feel. Various schedules are possible, from long weekend retreats (Thursday evening through Sunday evening), to a series of weekly meetings, or some combination of the two. It might be useful to present these alternative schedules to people when you describe the course initially, so that they know the group will not take more time than they are willing to give. A definite schedule can wait until the first meeting, when the group can make a joint decision about the time and the location of future meetings.

Let us assume that you have progressed through the sequence just described: you have read appropriate chapters in the book, and you are comfortably familiar with Social Literacy. Perhaps the administration is receptive to the idea of allowing teachers some released time and in-service credit for tackling this independent project. Several teachers are interested in the course and are willing to devote time. You have scouted out room possibilities and invited all those interested to an hour-long introductory meeting. The purposes of the meeting are to help interested teachers decide whether they will participate in the group and to make plans for getting underway.

A list of goals and guidelines we have kept in mind when starting groups is presented below. The list is our contribution to a pool of topics and issues —yours and ours—from which you can draw to create a first meeting that will accomplish your own goals.

1. Set a tone and atmosphere that is comfortable and evocative. The group has natural selling points. People have found it fun, interesting, and worthwhile. Avoid creating pressure. Create conditions that make people want to accept an invitation (e.g., describe a sample exercise, or have the principal express enthusiasm).

2. Give a brief sketch of the background, rationale, and potential benefits of a Social Literacy group.

3. Discuss what the group can accomplish: resolving troublesome classroom conflicts, reducing stress in the classroom and school, increasing learning time, increasing student achievement, creating more democratic orderly classrooms, teaching collaborative problem solving to students, improving the rules and roles in the school, providing interpersonal and emotional support, raising consciousness of how to reduce conflict and making schools an easier place in which to love.

4. Indicate what the group is like. Try to convey the experiential, relaxed, participatory climate. Give examples of the course contents: role plays, games, exercises, discussions. Within the course there will be opportunities for people to pursue their own special directions. Explain how the course will be run. If this is a group of teachers, there will not be an instructor; instead everyone will share the leadership role by taking turns for each session.

5. Be prepared to consider questions about housekeeping details such as the following: Is anyone taking overall responsibility? Who will lead each session? Where will it be? What is the schedule for the course? Will there be any credit given, or compensation? If it is a university course, students may want to know what is required to pass (e.g., two written reports of socially literate solutions to discipline problems—see Chapter 3 for details). These housekeeping details can be handled in a short follow-up meeting by those people who decide to join the group. It is important to assign a leader for the first two sessions so that everyone has ample time to prepare.

6. Decide on the focus of the first session or two. We suggest that you take the chapters of the book as the session topics, but there is nothing rigid about this sequence. In your first session, Chapters 1, 2, and 3 provide substance for a discussion of Social Literacy and a good background for all other chapters/sessions. Your group may wish to explore a few of the subsequent chapters or only a few of the topics within each chapter, or to develop these skills in a different sequence.

An alternative to designing your own course exists in the set of audio tape cassettes, "Resolving classroom conflicts", distributed by the Publishing Division of the National Education Association (Room 509, 1201 16th Street N.W., Washington, D.C. 20036.) This eight-session set is based on chapters of this book. They provide useful directions for sessions, or examples to use in designing your own sessions.

How to Lead a Session: Notes to the Facilitator

When you are leading a session, your assignments will range from mundane assembling of materials to the subtle creation of a tone and atmosphere that helps the session click. You must perform some duties yourself, while the group shares other duties with you. To be more specific, let's consider your role as a three-stage process: planning the session, guiding the session, and leading the evaluation at the end of the session.

Planning for the session

Before the session, you are like a production manager responsible for staging. The following types of preparation will help the production come off successfully:

1. Read about your session far enough in advance to tell the group about the reading they should do before the session.

2. Understand the game or experiment directions so that you can clarify the objectives and sequence of activities for the group and keep the session from bogging down in details.

3. Make some arrangements for refreshments, if that is in order. Provide for the comfort of the group. At minimum have a break halfway through the session.

4. See that any necessary materials are available and set up properly before the session begins.

An important ingredient for the success of any session is an enthusiastic, open-minded attitude. When you are the leader, accept the fact that you can prepare only up to a point. You are not going to be the teacher leading the class in lockstep through an outlined plan of the day. You will be more like a director who has set the stage for the activity about to begin. After careful preparation, relax and breathe deeply. (Physiologically, taking enormous breaths is one of the best ways to relieve tension.)

Guiding the Session

Begin the session by briefly explaining the purpose, writing the two or three objectives on the board, and describing the sequence and approximate time periods for the activities. You should run the exercise or activity efficiently so that there is ample time for discussion, but you should not be so glued to the schedule that you are seen as a drill sergeant. Rather, try to be attentive to people's involvement and enjoyment. Careful advance preparation and a certain amount of agility will carry you gracefully through the mechanics of the activity. Try to move to each next step shortly after energy has peaked, not when the group is exhausted.

As discussion leader, you will be working with everyone else to gain insights. Consequently, you will be called upon to "play it by ear" a good deal of the time. From prior reading you should be ready with questions to stimulate the group's thinking. But be prepared to modify, or even discard parts of your plan. There is an important distinction between preparation and planning. Adequate preparation will help you use your knowledge to facilitate the group's functioning. It will help you improvise on where the group has decided to take the discussion. Planning that is too specific is likely to cause resistance. The real skill of the discussion leader is to make what happens in the situation relevant.

Besides helping the group accomplish its goals, you must also accept responsibility for "group maintenance" and be watchful of the *group process:* How is the task being carried out? What are the interactions in the group? Is everyone contributing? If they are not, why? Are people apathetic, angry, distracted? For example, if someone constantly digresses or dominates the group, that affects everyone else and is a matter of group concern. To tolerate it under the pretext of "getting on with the job" will let the group decay. Usually the best time to take up and resolve these interpersonal issues is during the evaluation period of each session.

In any group, personal energy can manifest itself in defensive, destructive behavior or in a supportive, productive manner. Progress on a group task is contingent on good working relationships within the group, and ideally on openness, trust, and support among members. Everyone should feel responsible for creating this working atmosphere, but you in particular can contribute most to the creation of this climate by practicing the specific leadership behaviors listed below:

· Listen superbly, and encourage the rest of the group to do the same. A good way to check how well you are listening is to see if you can paraphrase to yourself what the speaker said.

· Never compete with members of the group or struggle to have your own ideas heard. As leader, you are present for *their* benefit. Later, as a follower, you can attend to your concerns. The best rule of thumb you as leader should remember is to hold off your comments until everyone else has finished. Often, others will make your point and feel good about contributing.

· Use every member of the group. This means inviting participation of the shy or reluctant (with eye contact or perhaps a nod of the head) and tactfully suggesting some boundaries for those who tend to dominate the group ("Thank you, I've got the idea.").

· Intervene in ways that clarify what has happened. When the time feels right, paraphrase what has been going on and what has been said. Identify points of confusion and questions that seem to be left hanging. You do not need to resolve the confusion yourself. For example, you might say, "Could someone summarize the alternatives that have been mentioned so far?" or, "I'm not sure I understood your last point—could you say a little more?" or "Could someone else give me their understanding of what was said?"

· Help members develop that habit of personalizing comments, especially those that affect other group members. Help people to take responsibility rather than blaming others. For example, another way for a participant to say "You monopolize the group," is to say "I would like to talk more, but I find it very uncomfortable trying to stop you." The second remark is fairer, because the person addressed can stop talking graciously without losing face and feeling attacked. Further, help people avoid making comments to no one in particular. Often it is helpful to say something like, "Can you address that comment to someone in particular in the group?"

· Prevent anyone from being "put down." The leader should help the group be positive by stressing the value of ideas and comments, not the potential pitfall. First say what it is you like about a person's idea, no matter how bad it is, then say what concerns you. This procedure recognizes that people will disagree, but also that good ideas often are lost because people are not willing to look at them carefully.

· Try to be a "barometer" for the group. If you feel tension vibrating around people, express that feeling. Depending on your own sense of the situation, your own style and inclination, that expression might be humorous or perfectly straight, but it should open the possibility of talking about what is wrong and relieving people's feelings. Conversely, if people are really tuned in and enjoying themselves, join in. Help sustain it.

· Keep the pace energetic and lively. You are accustomed to working with groups of students and know that the energy level and involvement of a group often mirrors your own energy for the day. If you are alert and involved, the group is more likely to be enthusiastic and interested. Start on time and aim to finish at a given time. Avoid the kind of laissez-faire leadership that lets a group languish and then forces everyone to catch up madly by being stingy with time later. You can decide when to push and move people on, when to let the group settle down to relax or hassle over a point. People may well look to you to indicate when to break a silence or when to allow for time to think and feel. Or they may need the relief of hearing someone say, "We've been working pretty hard; let's stop for coffee." This kind of pacing depends particularly on the leader of the session.

Evaluating the session

During the evaluation phase of the session members of the group as a whole consider how they are doing in terms of:

· Learning about socially literate solutions to common problems

- The effectiveness of the session just concluded, and

- Working relationships and cooperation within the group

The evaluation is not simply an evaluation of the leader as such, nor is it a final comment on a finished product. Instead, it is more like the process a person goes through in steering a boat. The end point is known, but the winds, tide, and current all necessitate constant adjustments and attention to steering. Allow enough time for people to fill out the evaluation form. Five minutes usually is enough. Then a series of simple hand counts can summarize the numerical aspects of the evaluation. Another 5 to 10 minutes to discuss the evaluation results will be helpful to the group and the leader of the next session. When the agreed-upon stopping time has been reached, a useful way to obtain closure and a summary is to "go-around." Have each person in the group complete one of the following sentence stems: "What I found most interesting today was . . . ," or, "What I learned today was . . . ," or, "The most useful thing I learned today was. . . ." Then, present your own 2- to 4-minute summary of the session, reviewing the objectives of the session, what actions were taken to reach those objectives, what were the key concepts and general conclusions. It may be useful to prepare some of this summary during your planning before the session.

Any group engaged in a long-term project experiences a range of success. There will be periods when people are less involved than at other times, and sessions where conflict is unavoidable. On some days the feeling will be one of enjoyment and accomplishment. Accept the highs and the lows in a way that allows you to learn from both of them. Careful attention to the evaluation process will help you do that. As leader, you will be responsible for engaging the group in the evaluation activity and organizing the comments into a useful form that can be passed on to the next leader.

Your final task as facilitator is to ensure the continuity of the group. Is there agreement on the purpose and activity for the next session? Has the next facilitator been chosen? Make sure the next facilitator has all the evaluation forms to study. Does everyone know the time, place, and preparation, (if any)?

How to Participate in Social Literacy Group: Notes to Members

Your group will be unique. No one of you can be sure what is going to happen. The combination of personalities, the decisions made along the

SOCIAL LITERACY GROUP EVALUATION

The purposes of this questionnaire are to help the group improve its functioning and to provide the leader of the next session with specific questions

	Poor		Fair		Good		Very Good			Excellent
1. Overall, how would you rate today's session? (circle one)	1	2	3	4	5	6	7	8	9	10
2. How valuable was today's session?	1	2	3	4	5	6	7	8	9	10
3. How interested are you in the techniques and concepts you learned today?	1	2	3	4	5	6	7	8	9	10
4. How well were the stated objectives met?	1	2	3	4	5	6	7	8	9	10

5. Please indicate your degree of satisfaction with each of the following aspects of the session.

	Unsatisfied	*O.K.*	*Very satisfied*
Clarity of the objectives			
Clarity of directions and examples			
Relevance of daily problems			
Work done in small groups			
Pace: neither too fast nor too slow			
Validation of individuals			
Warm, conducive learning climate			
Clarity of the summary			

6. In order to improve the group's functioning in the next session,
    (a) what good aspects of this session should be continued?
    (b) what aspects should be changed? how?

way, the special goals, the room you work in, a dozen quirks and circumstances will make your group unlike any other group.

The directions for the group do not constitute a syllabus. They are more like the outline of a play or the road map of a country open for exploration. This description may appeal to your sense of adventure and at the same time make you a bit nervous. "How," you may ask, "will I know when I've reached the objectives?" Since there is no "expert" you will have to help each other in at least three ways. First, prepare exquisitely well for the session you lead because during that session you are the "expert" for the other workshop members. Second, during the session keep the critical problem-solving sequence in mind. It will allow you to anticipate what will happen and help you coordinate your contributions more effectively. Third, at the end of every session, during the scheduled evaluation period, give frank, specific feedback about how the session went and what can be improved the next session. This advice is as important for others before they lead as it will be for you in preparing to lead your session.

APPENDIX 2

The Discipline
Game Manual

Purpose of the Game

The purpose of the Discipline Game is to introduce players to the process of negotiating mutually enhancing solutions to classroom discipline problems as an alternative to unilateral punishment of students. The process of negotiating solutions also helps identify the needs and desires that motivate both students' and teachers' actions in typical discipline conflicts. This process enables players in the game to see these troublesome situations from different perspectives and usually leads to the realization that the best solutions satisfy legitimate teacher *AND* student needs in mutually constructive ways.

Discussions after the Discipline Game can accomplish several other important objectives of Social Literacy training: development of a vocabulary to name the typical repertoire of student and teacher actions (moves) and the typical discipline cycles in the classroom, initial diagnosis of existing student and teacher needs that are expressed in these games, clarification of the nature of good and bad negotiations, preliminary list of possible solutions to these problems, and consciousness raising about the causes and appropriate responses to classroom discipline problems.

NOTE: Solomon Atkins, James Dacus, and Nellie Santiago-Wolpow helped in developing this game.

Overview of the Game

The game board identifies various places in school where discipline conflicts occur. Players progress around the board by rolling two dice to determine how many spaces they should move. For each type of place on the board the leader will describe a specific situation or conflict that has occurred. After hearing the specific conflict situation, the player may decide (1) to negotiate a solution or (2) to accept a written solution that is then read from the situation manual. If the player decides to negotiate, other players may participate by investing some of their discipline credits, distributed at the beginning of the game. Additional discipline credits are either awarded to them or taken away depending on the success or failure of the negotiations as rated by the principal on a -1 to $+2$ scale. If the player decides to accept the written solution, specific numbers of discipline credits are designated by the situation manual. One major difference between negotiating and accepting written solutions is that players either all win or all lose discipline credits in negotiations. In the written solutions some players always win and some players always lose in that situation. When a player completes one cycle around the board, s/he receives twenty-five discipline credits. The object of the game is to earn as many discipline credits as possible.

The Discipline Game Board, "Pieces," and Places

We decided not to publish this game separately because it would be expensive. We suggest that you purchase some brightly colored oil cloth, or similar material, and create your own game board using felt pens, polaroid pictures or other decorated symbols appropriate to your school.

Each player in the game will need a distinctive "piece" to move around the board. Anything will do: chess pieces, medallions, rings, colored stones, an eraser, eye patch, band aid, hall pass, book marker, belt buckle, etc. A set of poker chips may be used for discipline credits.

There are seven different places represented on the board, each having conflict situations appropriate to it. The specific conflict is determined by finding the type of place in the situation manual and reading the situations in sequence. Read one situation when a player lands on that type of place. Read the next situation the next time a player lands on that type of space.[1]

[1]Note to the principal: As an aid in finding the appropriate type of situation to read, put tabs at the side of the manual on the first page of each type of situation in the situation manual.

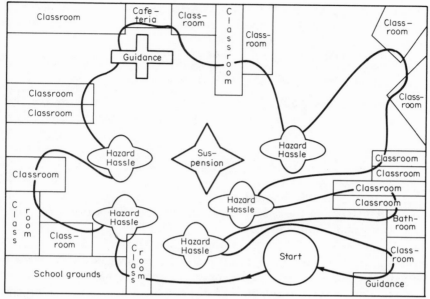

(The size of the board is about 3' X 3')

Classroom. The situation manual contains examples of the types of discipline conflicts that occur in classrooms. There are three sections in each situation: The "situation," the "outcome," and the "basis for negotiation." After hearing the situation, the player must decide whether to negotiate a solution or to accept the written outcome. The written outcome is read *only if, and after* the player chooses to accept it rather than to negotiate. If the player decides to negotiate, read only the "basis for negotiation." Three minutes are allowed for the process of negotiation.

Hazards and hassles denote activities taking place in hallways, stairways, locker rooms. Points are not won and lost in these situations. Rather, they are contributing forces which propel players into other situations on the board.

School grounds contain examples of discipline problems that occur nearby, outside of school. There is no chance to negotiate solutions to problems found here. The outcomes are read from the manual.

Guidance symbolizes the relationships between students and teachers that end up in the counselor's office. These situations are specifically concerned with the student and counselor-teacher relationship.

The cafeteria symbolizes the types of discipline problems which occur in this area of school. The outcomes are random, and no opportunity for negotiated solutions is provided here.

The bathroom illustrates discipline cycles occurring in the bathroom. This place includes no win, win-lose, and win-win outcomes.

Suspensions. Occasionally a student is suspended from the classroom and moves his/her piece to that place for the designated number of rounds.

Roles in the Discipline Game

Up to approximately ten people may play the discipline game at one time and still maintain fast-paced high involvement. If you have twelve or more, play two games simultaneously.

The principal runs the game, has the situation manual, reads the conflict situations (and, when appropriate, reads the outcomes) keeps time on the 3-minute negotiating period and, finally, dispenses or collects the proper number of discipline credits.

Students and teacher. Up to five players are students who take turns in sequence with a "teacher" (a sixth player) rolling the two dice and moving around the board. Whenever a student chooses to negotiate a conflict the teacher *must* negotiate. However, neither teacher nor students are required to reach agreement on the issues.

The jury provides advice to the principal when s/he asks for it. To facilitate discussion after the game, each jury member should (1) keep a record of good and bad negotiating in the game, and/ or (2) make a list of the needs expressed by students and teachers in the negotiations, and/or (3) keep a list of negotiated solutions to the discipline conflicts. The size of the jury should be about three. At some point during the game it may be interesting for the jury members to exchange roles with the students and teacher.

Rules for the Discipline Game

1. Each player receives fifteen discipline credits at the beginning of the game, e.g., one blue chip (10), and one red chip (5) or five white chips (1).

2. The number of spaces each player moves is determined by rolling two dice.

3. In classroom situations after the situation is read, the player has a choice of negotiating or the player may accept the written outcome. If the player chooses the written outcome, it then is read, and that move is over. If the player chooses to negotiate, the "basis for negotiations" is read and there is a 3-minute time period beginning after other players have had a chance to invest in the negotiations. The teacher must negotiate when a student calls for negotiations. When a teacher chooses to negotiate a conflict, s/he may choose any one or more of the students with whom to negotiate. Those students must negotiate.

4. All players may invest in the negotiations, before the discussion begins, by placing one to five discipline credits (chips) on the board in front of them. Any player who invests in negotiations may also take an active vocal role in those negotiations. Those who do not invest may not speak. The principal judges the success or failure of the negotiations on a -1 to $+2$ scale. If a player has invested five discipline credits and the negotiations were highly successful (judged a $+2$) that player gets ten additional discipline credits (10) from the principal. If negotiations fail badly and are judged -1, the player must give the principal five discipline credits s/he has invested. There is one rating for each negotiation. Thus all players (students and teachers) get the same rating.

5. The ratings of negotiations are based on the following criteria as judged by the principal:

   -1 Any negotiations that result in increased misunderstanding, anger, hostility, or conflict.

   0 Any negotiations which end in a stalemate, without apparent willingness to bargain in good faith, seek compromise, or allow the other party in the negotiations any way to meet their needs. Either party in the negotiations may produce a 0 rating for the total negotiations by the unwillingness to enter open, serious negotiations.

   $+1$ At minimum, *both* parties in the negotiations must demonstrate serious intentions to find a mutually agreeable solution by their willingness to listen, to consider seriously the other's point of view, needs and proposed solutions. The negotiating parties do not need to decide on a mutually agreeable solution to earn a $+1$ rating. *However, if players abdicate their self-interests as defined in the situation and basis for negotiation, the negotiations can only be rated 0.*

$+2$ In addition to the characteristics of a $+1$ negotiation, the parties must reach a clear, mutually agreed-upon solution to earn a $+2$. Solutions must reflect a way to satisfy clearly stated different needs of both teacher and students to earn a $+2$ rating.

6. The principal's decisions are final. Obviously there is some room for differences in opinion about the proper rating of a 3-minute negotiation. The principal may request advice from the jury or if either party is dissatisfied with the rating, the principal may ask the jury to arbitrate. In this case the jury's decision is final. It is the principal's option about whether or not to call for arbitration and this choice may not be appealed. In any event, it is pedagogically helpful for the principal to explain the rationale for the rating.

7. If a "situation" suspends a student, the student must move to the "suspension room" on the board for the designated number of turns. During this time the player may not speak to any other player. When the suspension is over the player returns to "start" and moves around the board.

8. When a student or teacher completes a round of the board, s/he receives twenty-five (25) discipline credits. The winners are the players with the most discipline credits.

9. The game may continue as long as players feel it is a useful learning experience. Approximately twice around the board is a reasonable period for the purposes of the course.

General Instructions

Introducing the discipline game

Although the game was designed to be used as part of an ongoing Social Literacy training program, it can be used by itself in a wide variety of other contexts, e.g. PTA meetings, board of education meetings, school committees studying the discipline problem, junior high school classrooms. Obviously the purposes will be slightly different in each situation, and will require appropriate introductions. For example, many PTA groups are concerned about discipline problems in schools. The Discipline Game could be used to help parents reacquaint themselves with the array of specific problems at an experiential level and appreciate the difficulties experienced by teachers and students in solving them. Based on this experience, parents should be better informed in discussing useful parent, teacher, student, and administration roles. If the game is used as part of a Social Literacy training for teachers, the first two paragraphs of the introduction, and all of sections entitled "The Discipline Game Board" and "General Instructions" should be read to orient players to the game.

Styles of playing the game.

The principal may wish to try out different roles—authoritarian, democratic, laissez-faire, supportive, etc. If this is done during a single session, it is helpful for the principal to say publicly that s/he is experimenting with a different role to be discussed at the end of the game. An appropriate time to announce a change of style is after players have gone around the board once.

You may also wish to give the jury specific instructions. For instance, you may want to announce that they have a board of highly paid consultants who are available to players for advice on how and when to negotiate and for suggested alternative solutions. Or you may want to use the jury as a mediating group to suggest ways that teacher-student negotiations can be more productive. Or, you might ask each member of the jury to be an analyst-recorder having a particular task: record the full list of expressed student and teacher needs; record the list of proposed and/or accepted solutions, describe the most and least effective negotiating strategies.

If the jury attempts to define effective negotiating strategies, they might keep in mind the following questions: Did the negotiating parties thoroughly discuss the problem or situation? During the discussion did the negotiating parties each make suggestions as to possible solutions? Did the negotiating parties show willingness to move toward a third point of view as a compromise? If the negotiation process proved to be unsuccessful, what factors contributed to the failure of the process? It may be useful to stop the game briefly after the players have gone around the board once to discuss what constitutes effective negotiations.

To add spice to the game you may wish to write out brief role descriptions for the teacher and students that represent some of the student character-types encountered in your school. Or, players can replay situations trying out different attitudes and assumptions to see what effects they have on negotiations. To make the game more relevant to your particular school, create alternative "situations," "outcomes," and "basis for negotiations," to substitute for those in the manual.

If you want to concentrate solely on practicing negotiations, you can dispense with the game board and simply take each "situation" and "basis for negotiations" and role play them. Divide the entire group into triads in which one person plays a student, another the teacher, and the third the jury. Let the group pick the situations they want to role play, time themselves, and discuss their effectiveness. *This format allows for maximum involvement* and can be done with large groups. It is helpful to start this variation of the Discipline Game by asking for two volunteers to demonstrate a 3-minute negotiation in front of the whole group. Read the "situation," the "basis for negotiations," and time the 3-minute negotiation. Then give it a rating from -1 to $+2$ with an explanation. Sometimes it is useful to ask others what was done well and poorly. With this feedback the two volunteers can replay the situation to see if they can improve their rating. Inform the others that that is the sequence and purpose of the role plays, then ask if there are questions. Give the triads about 20 to 30 minutes to role play situations, discuss ratings, rotate roles, role play the situation again, etc. At the end of this period call the group together to pool their conclusions in two columns: What facilitates good negotiations, and what hinders good negotiations. Usually a characteristic in one column has an obvious converse, e.g., "reflect people's feelings" versus "ignore people's feelings." After a list of ten to fifteen characteristics has been obtained, give the triads another half hour to practice using the positive characteristics.

Follow-up

Don't talk the game to death. As a general rule, try to stop the postgame analysis shortly after the energy of the discussion peaks. The experience during the game will be recalled and discussed spontaneously at several other points in the Social Literacy training course. It does not need to be analyzed completely immediately after playing the game.

Your choice of which questions to address after the game will depend on the timing, the context, and the type of people playing the game. Here are some possible questions to initiate the discussion or to keep the discussion lively:

How did you feel in your role?
Did you like it? Dislike it?
How typical was your experience compared to the classroom situation?

What were the needs, desires, goals expressed during the negotiations?
Are these needs good or bad?
In what situations are they good?
In what situations are they bad?

What constitutes good negotiations?

Is it possible to actually negotiate with students in and outside the classroom?

To what degree are teachers afraid of giving up their traditional forms of power?

Is negotiating with students really giving up power?

What are the proposed solutions that come out of negotiations?

Are these feasible alternatives for the classroom?

What effect did the different styles of principal-ship have on students in the game?

What style is more conducive to productive negotiations?

In what ways does the teacher both win and lose in discipline conflicts?

In what ways do students both win and lose in these conflicts?

To what degree are the causes of discipline problems (a) in the students' or teachers' background, home life, or economic situation; (b) in the personality of the student or teacher; (c) in the formal and informal rules in the specific classroom? Depending on your answers, what needs to be changed to resolve these conflicts?

Brainstorm a list of: other types of discipline conflicts in the classroom; the other needs of teachers and students in these conflicts; and other ways to solve these conflicts in the classroom without sending students to the front office.

If these alternative styles of play and follow-up questions seem a bit overwhelming, just remember that the essential purpose of the game is to practice moving toward dialogue. Modify the game in whatever way will be helpful to your group in learning how to include more love, humility, trust, hope, and critical thinking into their communications.

The Situation Manual

The Classroom

SITUATION 1

The student makes the following request to the teacher: "The class is tired after lunch and wants to talk instead of work."

The outcome

The teacher is irritated and refuses the request after a lengthy explanation about the importance of learning the names of the seven continents today. The teacher pays the student two discipline credits because the student succeeded in delaying the lesson by 5 minutes.

Basis for negotiations

Negotiate a way to deal constructively with both the lesson plan and the students' fatigue.

SITUATION 2

The student returns from the bathroom after 8 minutes, having promised to take no more than 3 minutes.

The outcome

The teacher requires the student to come in after school to make up the 5 minutes and also brings down the student's daily grade. The teacher gets five discipline credits from the student.

Basis for negotiations

Returning late from the bathroom is a long-standing pattern. The teacher is always irritated. Students are bored with class. Negotiate a solution that meets the students' and teacher's needs.

CHOOSE THE APPROPRIATE SITUATION (3)

Student: You are sent to the front office for being in a fight in class. The assistant principal says it doesn't matter who started it, and suspends you for one day. (You miss one turn in the discipline game.)

Teacher: The front office has information that your certification is not in order. Pay the principal ten discipline credits and fret profusely.

SITUATION 4

The student calls the teacher a "feckless zebu" in class loud enough to be heard by others.

The outcome

The teacher lectures the student about proper language and behavior, but takes no punitive action. The teacher pays the student one discipline credit for helping the class avoid the lesson on animal anatomy without being punished.

Basis for negotiations

After class the student tells the teacher that s/he puts them down with her lectures about "proper behavior." The students feel that they can't let their true feelings be known so they mutter under their breath. Negotiate a mutually satisfying solution.

SITUATION 5

The English teacher before your class has lectured on the profound significance of silence in communications. The class arrives, sits down, folds their hands in unison, and are completely silent despite your efforts to communicate.

The outcome

The teacher is totally frustrated and punishes the students with a pop quiz. The student pays the teacher four discipline credits.

Basis for negotiations

Establish communications without embarrassment to the teacher or student, and find a mutually agreeable solution to oppressive teacher-power and oppressive student-power.

SITUATION 6

A geography lesson is important for a state exam but is boring to both the teacher and students.

The outcome

About half the class talks and passes notes. The student gets two discipline credits for controlling his/her attention.

Basis for negotiations

Negotiate a way to teach/learn the material in a way that is interesting to both the teacher and the student.

SITUATION 7

The following dialogue occurs between two students:
Student: "Hey Stanley, I hear your brother got suspended."
Stanley: "Ya, man."

Student: "That must make you feel good, cause now you got clothes to wear." The teacher dislikes putting each other down in class.

Outcome

The teacher breaks up the laughing and pays the student two discipline credits for catching the teacher's attention and delaying the class.

Basis for negotiations

Negotiate at least one way to have more fun in class that is satisfying to both the teacher and the student.

Read the appropriate response (8)

Student: Mr. Foureyes sends you to the front office for grabbing a girl-/boy. Pay the principal ten discipline credits.
Teacher: You have sent more students to the front office than anyone else. The principal wants to know why. Pay the principal ten discipline credits.

SITUATION 9

It is late Friday afternoon in an English class. A student gets up and begins to mock-wrestle with another student.

The outcome

The teacher immediately threatens to cancel a showing of the "Last Tango in Paris" scheduled for the sex education class the following Monday. The class suddenly is passive and attentive. The student pays the teacher two discipline credits.

Basis for negotiations

The teacher stops the mock-fight. Negotiate a way to meet student needs for contact, movement, and attention in a constructive process of learning the subject matter.

SITUATION 10

The teacher threatens an inattentive student with having to do an extra worksheet on ancient Egyptian hieroglyphics.

The outcome

The student promises to pay attention and then daydreams the rest of the class. The teacher pays the student two discipline credits for maintaining control of his/her own attention.

Basis for negotiations

Negotiate with the students a way to make ancient Egyptian culture more interesting.

READ THE APPROPRIATE RESPONSE (11)

Student: You are caught cutting science class and sent to the front office. Pay the principal ten discipline credits.

Teacher: You are called into the front office and informed by the principal that you are not allowed to wear denim pants to school. Pay the principal fourteen discipline points.

SITUATION 12

A street-wise student returns to class after a long-term suspension and wants a seat near his/her best friend. The two students have been difficult to deal with in the past.

The outcome

The teacher agrees to the request in order to avoid an immediate confrontation only to be disrupted 2 minutes later by the pair who begin to sing the latest hit song. The teacher pays the student three discipline credits because the teacher failed to establish a constructive collaborative relationship.

Basis for negotiation

Negotiate an agreement that allows the pair to sit next to each other and leads to cooperation with the teacher.

SITUATION 13

During a discussion in the classroom the teacher touches a student as s/he is emphasizing an important area. The student yells immediately, "Don't touch me."

The outcome

The lesson stops. The teacher is surprised, embarrassed, and apologizes. The teacher pays the student five discipline credits for losing face in front of the class.

Basis for negotiations

The teacher and student have different conceptions of what touching means. Negotiate an understanding about when, where and under what conditions touching in class is permissible.

READ THE APPROPRIATE RESPONSE (14)

Student: The teacher and student have had a loud argument in front of the class. You are now in the assistant principal's office. Pay him/her fifteen discipline credits.

Teacher: The principal calls you on the carpet because you are always late for school. Pay him/her fifteen discipline credits.

SITUATION 15

The teacher is called from the classroom for a parent conference. A substitute teacher is sent to cover the class. The students destroy the classroom and reduce the substitute teacher to a warm puddle of tears.

The outcome

The teacher is angry and punishes several students with detention. Even though you are the ringleader, you are not punished. Collect six discipline credits from the teacher.

Basis for negotiations

The regular teacher wants the class to exercise some minimal self-control when s/he is out of the room. The class doesn't want the teacher to be called to parent conferences on their time. Negotiate a mutually agreeable solution to the conflict.

SITUATION 16

The teacher screams at a student to turn around and pay attention. The student says something about the teacher's mother loud enough for some other students to hear.

The outcome

The teacher sends the student to the front office. The principal says that comments about mothers are out of place in school and suspends you one day. Miss one turn in the game and pay the teacher and principal seven discipline credits each.

Basis for negotiations

The students want some time to talk and interact with their friends. They say that the teacher never lets them have any free time. The teacher wants full attention to the subject matter. Negotiate a resolution to this conflict.

SITUATION 17

The P.A. repeatedly comes on and distracts everyone. Students are unable to solve half of the math problems assigned to them.

The outcome

The distraction is a factor in causing the whole class problems on a test. All of the students and the teacher pay the principal three discipline credits each.

Basis for negotiations

Students want the teacher to speak to the principal about the distractions, but the teacher believes nothing can be done about this.

READ THE APPROPRIATE RESPONSE (18)

Student: You spill paint on the floor in art class. Because of your past record you are accused of doing it on purpose and are sent to the front office. You are suspended one day. Miss one round of the game and pay the art teacher and the principal three discipline credits each.

Teacher: Your reading class disrupted the classes on either side of you. The front office wants to know why. Pay the principal ten discipline credits.

SITUATION 19

Students attempt to delay the start of class by participating in a milling game around the teacher.

The outcome

The student is singled out by the teacher who asks if the student is "lost." Everyone in class laughs. The student pays each of the other student players and the teacher one discipline credit each.

Basis for negotiations

Students don't like the work in the class. They attempt to delay it by milling. Negotiate a way in which both teacher and student can win.

SITUATION 20

A student jumps up when the student behind him/her sticks him/her with a pin.

The outcome

The teacher gives the student detention. The student pays the teacher ten discipline credits.

Basis for negotiations

Students seem to get in trouble because they want attention. Negotiate a way in which the teacher still covers the material *and* gives individual attention to students.

SITUATION 21

A student tells the teacher that s/he has a sore throat and is unable to recite in class.

The outcome

The teacher believes the story. Collect one discipline credit from each of the other players and from the teacher.

Basis for negotiations

Try and find some ways in which the student can participate without oral work.

SITUATION 22

The teacher lectures to the class for 5 minutes about bringing pencils and other necessary materials.

The outcome

The students prolong the discussion with many "yes, but" arguments and delay the learning time by 15 minutes. The student collects three discipline credits from the teacher.

Basis for negotiations

The teacher wants students always to bring materials to class. Students believe that the teacher should have such materials as pencils for students who occasionally forget. Negotiate a solution that is mutually agreeable.

READ THE APPROPRIATE RESPONSE (23)

Student: The teacher, principal, and guidance counselor say your records indicate you are a troublemaker. You are assigned to the remedial classroom. Pay the teacher and principal three discipline credits each.

Teacher: You have been assigned by the principal to teach this remedial classroom for one day. Miss one turn.

READ THE APPROPRIATE RESPONSE (24)

Student: You loudly emitted noxious vapors from both ends simultaneously. The teacher sends you to the front office where you get a 10-minute lecture on chewing your food. Pay the principal eight discipline credits and collect five discipline credits from the teacher for successfully getting out of a dull class.

Teacher: The principal finds that you are having a smoke in the teachers' room while your class does "busy" work. Pay five discipline credits to the principal.

SITUATION 25

A student is thirsty and wants to go to the water fountain in the hall. The teacher refuses permission.

The outcome

The teacher refuses permission. The student gets mad and refuses to work. The teacher keeps the student after school. Pay the teacher five discipline credits.

Basis for negotiations

The students want to be able to get a drink of water or go to their lockers when they need to. Negotiate a solution to this chronic problem.

SITUATION 26

A student places a comic book behind a textbook and reads it during class.

The outcome

The student is able to read the comic and put one over on the teacher. Collect two discipline credits from the teacher.

Basis for negotiations

Students would like for the teacher to talk about things that interest them. Negotiate some ways that the teacher can still cover the subject *and* let the students learn about some things that are important to them.

SITUATION 27

The entire class coughs at the same time, to get the teacher.

The outcome

The teacher heard you talking about coughing at the same time. The teacher assumes you are the leader and gives you detention. Pay the principal seven discipline credits.

Basis for negotiations

Students feel that the teacher is too tough and that s/he doesn't let them participate in any decisions about how the class is to be run. The teacher believes s/he is doing what s/he is paid to do. Negotiate a mutually agreeable solution.

READ THE APPROPRIATE RESPONSE (28)

Student: You refuse to stop dancing in class. The teacher sends you to the front office. The principal dismisses you for one day, which is what you wanted from the start. Collect four discipline credits from the teacher, four from the principal, and miss one turn in the game.

Teacher: You are called to the front office. The principal orders you to stop playing hooky from teachers' meetings. Pay the principal eight discipline credits.

SITUATION 29

The student spends the entire class period combing hair, cleaning nails and teeth.

The outcome

The teacher notices this grooming but says and does nothing. Collect one discipline credit from the teacher for being allowed to do your thing.

Basis for negotiations   .

The teacher says that even though this is a personal hygiene class, theory must precede practice and asks the student to read about the causes of tooth decay. The student says s/he already knows about "that stuff." Negotiate a mutually agreeable resolution to the conflict.

SITUATION 30

The teacher catches the student passing a note to a friend. The note says, "Look, the teacher's underpants are showing."

The outcome

The teacher reads the note substituting "your" for "the teacher." Collect three discipline credits from the teacher for successfully interrupting a deadly lesson, but pay each of the other players one discipline credit for being embarrassed.

Basis for negotiations

The student wants to be able to talk with other students occasionally during class. The teacher wants to maintain control and attention to the lesson. Negotiate an agreeable compromise.

SITUATION 31

A student does a Lenny Bruce routine and calls the teacher's attempts to stop the act "police oppression."

The outcome

The teacher sends "Lenny" to the front office "jail." The incident, how-ever leaves the teacher drained of energy and angry. No discipline credits change hands.

Basis for negotiations

The student believes that the teacher's standards of obscenity are Victo-rian and that the true "obscenity" is the absence of sex in any of the text-books. The teacher feels that this topic should be dealt with elsewhere, not in mathematics class. Try to resolve the issues in a mutually acceptable way.

SITUATION 32

A student falls asleep during class.

The outcome

The teacher makes the student stay after school for 40 minutes despite the student's protest that a family crisis kept him/her awake all night. The student pays the teacher four discipline credits.

Basis for negotiations

The student's family problems interfere with learning in the classroom. The teacher believes s/he can or should do nothing about the student's home life as this is not the teacher's responsibility. Negotiate a mutually acceptable course of action.

SITUATION 33

The teacher catches a student passing a reefer to a friend in class.

The outcome

The student is sent to the front office and suspended for the duration of the year. However, the student makes $300 selling dope to classmates after school. The principal pays the student twenty-five discipline credits for effectively controlling his/her own attention and for the school's failure to provide sufficiently relevant, attractive subject matter.

Basis for negotiations

The student says that if the teacher sends him/her to the front office a long-term suspension will result and the student will deal in drugs on the street. If the subject matter were relevant and attractive the student wouldn't be risking a suspension by passing pot in class. The teacher considers this an irrelevant argument and an attempt to avoid taking personal responsibility. Attempt to resolve this conflict of viewpoints.

SITUATION 34

Students keep getting up out of their seats. When the teacher finally threatens to send several students to the front office, one student quotes the following passage from the Declaration of Independence: "Governments are instituted among men, deriving their just powers from the consent of the governed." Further, the student says that the teacher is King George and the class is tyranized.

The outcome

The teacher asserts that students are minors without these rights and until the teachers are overthrown, the current rules will remain. The student pays the teacher four discipline credits for allowing their attendance to be controlled unilaterally.

Basis for negotiations

The teacher and student get into an argument about constitutional law and classroom control. Try to resolve this debate.

SITUATION 35

A student refuses to work in class.

The outcome

The teacher manages to make the student look silly in front of the class. The student must pay each of the other student players one discipline credit each.

Basis for negotiations

The student won't work because the teacher treats students like babies. Can you work out the problem?

READ THE APPROPRIATE RESPONSE (36)

Student: You are suspended for one day for throwing a rancid piece of meat back over the cafeteria counter. Miss one turn.

Teacher: You call in sick, but really need the day to do Christmas shopping. The principal finds out and docks you one day's pay. Pay the principal twenty discipline credits.

SITUATION 37

A student sitting near the teacher's desk as punishment for a recent classroom crime asks the teacher to let him/her sit in the back where there is more room to spread out the work.

The outcome

The teacher agrees and the student works hard. The principal pays three discipline credits to the teacher and to the student.

Basis for negotiations

The teacher is afraid that the student will be disruptive again. The student is quite sincerely trying to work. Establish trust.

SITUATION 38

The class arrives angry because the previous period math teacher gave them a snap quiz. They complain angrily to the teacher and won't get down to work.

The outcome

The teacher tries to be sympathetic and listens for 5 minutes. Because of lost learning time, the teacher pays the student five discipline credits for effectively shifting the content of the class's discussion.

Basis for negotiations

The students do not want any snap quizzes in the teacher's class. The teacher believes this is the best way to ensure that students will keep up on their homework. Negotiate a mutually acceptable solution.

SITUATION 39

Fire drill! The principal pays all students and the teacher ten discipline credits for allowing them time to manage their own attention. (No negotiations)

SITUATION 40

The student pulls out a knife.

The outcome

The teacher sends the student to the front office, where the principal discovers that the student has been intimidated by a gang of students. The principal takes decisive action to control the explosive situation and pays the student five discipline credits for helping to defuse the problem.

Basis for negotiations

The student claims the knife is for self-defense against the gang that is out to get the student. The teacher half believes the story but knows the school's policy that anyone caught with a weapon is automatically suspended. Negotiate a solution to the teacher's ambivalence.

Hazards and Hassles

1. STUDENT: Before school you find out that your worst teacher is absent. Move ahead two spaces.

TEACHER: Before school you find out that the kid who gives you the most trouble is out for the day. Move ahead two spaces.

2.   STUDENT: You run to the cafeteria, don't get caught, and get in front of the line. Move ahead two spaces.

TEACHER: You go to the teacher's room and find that the principal has bought donuts for the faculty. Move ahead one space.

3.   STUDENT: You forget your book and are able to sleaze the teacher into letting you into class. Move ahead two spaces.

TEACHER: You drop some papers in the hall and some students help you gather them up. Move ahead two spaces.

4.   STUDENT: There is name calling on the bus and you don't get involved. Move ahead one space.

TEACHER: You hear about a fight on one of the buses but you are not on bus duty. Move ahead one space.

5.   STUDENT: You forgot to lock your locker but find that you haven't been ripped off. Move ahead one space.

TEACHER: Your union representative tells you that the pay increase for next year is a good possibility. Move ahead one space.

6.   STUDENT: AND TEACHER: You slip on the stairs and sprain your ankle. You are out for one day. Go back five spaces.

7.   STUDENT: You have to go back to your locker but still get to your class on time. Move ahead one space.

TEACHER: There are no incidents or fighting while you are in the hall. Move ahead one space.

8.   STUDENT: You are given a compliment on your clothes by one of your friends. Move ahead two spaces.

TEACHER: The principal tells you he is pleased with your professional appearance. Move ahead two spaces.

9.   STUDENT: The teacher stops you in the hall to tell you that your work is really fine. Move ahead three spaces.

TEACHER: The principal tells you that school will be dismissed early. Move ahead one space.

10. STUDENT: You are able to con the secretary in the office into giving you a tardy pass. Move ahead two spaces.

    TEACHER: You find that there is no teachers' meeting after school and that you can go right home. Move ahead two spaces.

11. STUDENT: You get caught shooting spitballs in assembly. Move back three spaces.

    TEACHER: You have to break up a fight in the cafeteria. Move back three spaces.

12. STUDENT: You and a friend are able to get into class without a tardy pass. Move ahead one space.

    TEACHER: Your car won't start but you get to school on time with another teacher. Move ahead one space.

13. STUDENT: You were able to talk to your friends about the party on Friday night and still get to class on time. Move ahead one space.

    TEACHER: You were able to smoke in the teachers' room without a hassle, then you get back to class. Move ahead two spaces.

14. STUDENT: Someone pushes you on the stairs. You threaten their anatomy and get away with it. Move ahead two spaces.

    TEACHER: Your students want you to sponsor a new club they are starting. Move ahead two spaces.

15. STUDENT: You go to the lunch room and for a change they have good food. Move ahead one space.

    TEACHER: You have lunchroom duty and are able to get through the period without trouble. Move ahead one space.

16. STUDENT: Someone starts throwing food in the cafeteria. You don't get hit. Move ahead two spaces.

    TEACHER: You hear that there was a food riot at second lunch, and are thankful you weren't on lunch duty. Move ahead two spaces.

17. STUDENT: You are able to avoid the school "borrower" who wants a loan for lunch money. Move ahead one space.

    TEACHER: The principal passes you in the hall and compliments you on your fine teaching job. Move ahead one space.

18. STUDENT: While strolling through the hall you see a new "chick" or "cool" dude so fine that you almost freak out. Move ahead one space.

    TEACHER: Your supervisor stops you in the hall to tell you that he won't be able to visit you today. Move ahead one space.

19. STUDENT: You were able to catch a smoke in the bathroom without getting caught. Move ahead two spaces.

    TEACHER: You were able to mark all the test papers during your free period so you can go to a movie tonight. Move ahead one space.

20. STUDENT: You were caught walking through the hall while the Pledge of Allegiance was playing over the P.A. Move back two spaces.

    TEACHER: The board of education is withholding your check for some unknown reason. Move back four spaces.

21. STUDENT: You are caught wandering through the halls during a class without a pass. Move back three spaces.

    TEACHER: You forget to set your alarm clock and oversleep. The principal calls you out for being late again. Move back two spaces.

22. STUDENT: You forget your lunch money and con your teacher into giving you some money. Move ahead two spaces.

    TEACHER: The principal puts you down for talking to another teacher while on hall duty. Move back one space.

23. STUDENT: You find out that a person that you've been wanting to go out with really likes you. Move ahead three spaces.

    TEACHER: You are able to spend your free period in the teachers' room without getting into any argument. Move ahead three spaces.

24. STUDENT: Your teacher praises you for your excellent behavior on the class trip. Move ahead three spaces.

    TEACHER: You get through your class trip without any hassles. The kids are good, the buses don't break down, etc. Move ahead three spaces.

Guidance

1. STUDENT: You have been called to Guidance because of your truancy record. You are nearly expelled as a punishment?! Pay the principal one discipline credit.

   TEACHER: Why haven't you turned in your Frack form 150? Pay the principal two discipline credits.

2. STUDENT: You are called to Guidance because of tardiness and have to wait two periods to see the counselor. Miss one turn and pay the principal five discipline credits.

   TEACHER: Your last 49 attendance reports are obviously a figment of your imagination. Pay the principal four discipline credits.

3. STUDENT: You have been called in to see if you want to participate in an accelerated program. Collect two discipline credits from the principal.

   TEACHER: You are given only top sections to teach. Collect two discipline credits from the principal.

4. STUDENT: Guidance wants you to go to the learning disabilities classroom. Miss one turn.

   TEACHER: Guidance office wants to know why your student records aren't up-to-date. Pay the principal three discipline credits.

5. STUDENT: If your grades don't improve you will have to repeat the grade. Pay the principal three discipline credits.

   TEACHER: Why haven't your Phflug forms 245 been turned in yet? Pay the principal three discipline credits.

6. STUDENT: Your records indicate that you are eligible to be promoted to a higher track. Collect ten discipline credits from the principal.

   TEACHER: An assignment to a curriculum writing team has come through. Collect three discipline credits from the principal.

7. STUDENT: Congratulations. A teacher poll has shown you to be the biggest goody-goody in school. Collect five discipline credits from the principal.

TEACHER: You are now on the Guidance list and may be promoted. Collect five discipline credits from the principal.

8. STUDENT: Guidance wants to put you in a lower track. You aren't smart enough to be in an academic section. Pay five discipline credits to the principal.

   TEACHER: Why haven't you recorded those statewide test scores on the students' records? Pay two discipline credits to the principal.

9. STUDENT: Your record card indicates that you made the honor role. Collect five discipline credits from the principal.

   TEACHER: Guidance compliments you because your records are so perfect. Collect two discipline credits from the principal.

School Grounds

Student: **ROLL ONE DIE**
1—Somebody rips off your lunch money.
2 to 5—You get to and from school without a hassle.
6—Congratulations! You've met a cute boy/girl.

Teacher: **ROLL ONE DIE**
1—Your class runs out of school to a game. The principal chews you out, but doesn't penalize you.
2 to 5—You take a walk in the sun after lunch.
6—A former student thanks you for help.

Bathroom

Student: **ROLL ONE DIE**
1—You are caught smoking and are suspended one day. Pay the principal five discipline credits.
2 to 5—In and out with no hassles. No points.
6—You are able to have a smoke and not get caught. Collect two discipline credits from the principal.

Teacher: **ROLL ONE DIE**
1—You see a student smoking and turn him/her in.
2 to 5—You are on bathroom coverage but encounter no problems.
6—You get relieved from bathroom coverage and have a free period. Collect five discipline credits from the principal.

Cafeteria

Student: ROLL ONE DIE

 1—You are in a fight and have to spend two periods in front office. Miss one turn in the game.

 2 to 5—You are able to eat without a problem.

 6—You find a dollar under your foot when you sit down to eat. Move ahead one space.

Teacher: ROLL ONE DIE

 1—You had to stop a fight and your glasses were broken. Move back three spaces.

 2 to 5—You talk happily with students.

 6—Another teacher gives you a useful idea for your next day's lesson. Move ahead one space.

Bibliography

Alschuler, A. S. *Developing Achievement Motivation in Adolescents.* Englewood Cliffs, N. J.: Educational Technology Inc., 1973.

Alschuler, A. S. "The Discipline Game: Playing Without Losers." *Learning Magazine,* August-September 1974, pp. 80–86.

Alschuler, A. and B. Flinchum, "Raising Minimum Competencies," *Phi Delta Kappan,* May 1979, pp. 678–679.

Alschuler, A. S., D. Tabor, and J. McIntyre. *Teaching Achievement Motivation.* Middletown, CT: Education Ventures Inc., 1970.

Alschuler, A. S. "Toward a Self-Renewing School." *Journal of Applied Behavioral Sciences,* Vol. 8(5):577–600, 1972.

Alschuler, A. S., S. Atkins, R. B. Irons, R. McMullen, N. Wolpow Santiago. "Social Literacy: a school discipline game without losers." *Phi Delta Kappan,* April 1977, pp. 606–609.

Alschuler, A. S. "School Discipline through Social Literacy." In *Education for Values,* D. C. McClelland, (Ed.), Irvington Press, N. Y., 1980.

Andelin, H. *Fascinating Womanhood.* Santa Barbara, CA: Pacific Press, 1963.

Bailey, J. "Consciousness-Raising Groups for Women: Implications of Paulo Freire's Theory of Critical Consciousness for Psychotherapy and Education." Unpublished Doctoral Dissertation, University of Massachusetts, 1976.

Bayh, B. "Our Nations Schools—A Report Card: 'A' in School Violence and Vandalism." (Preliminary Report of the Sub-Committee to Investigate Juvenile Delinquency). U.S. Government Printing Office, Washington, DC, 1975.

Bayh, B. *Challenge for the third century: education in a safe environment.* U.S. Government Printing Office, Washington, DC, 1977.

Bayh, B. "Seeking Solutions to School Violence and Vandalism." *Phi Delta Kappan,* Vol. 59(5):299–301, January 1978.

Berne, E. *Games People Play.* New York: Grove Press, 1964.

Block, A. "Combat Neurosis in Inner-City Schools." Los Angeles, CA, Block Medical Clinic, 1830 W. Olympic Blvd., Los Angeles, CA, 90006. (Undated manuscript)

Block, J. H. and R. M. Elmore. "Conscription: the Students' Perspective." Paper presented at the American Educational Research Association Annual Convention, 1977.

Brayfield, L. "Social Literary Education for Women Educators: Will it Facilitate Them Entry into Public School Administration?" Unpublished Doctoral Dissertation, University of Massachusetts, 1977.

Children's Defense Fund. *Children Out of School in America.* Cambridge, MA: Washington Research Project Inc., 1974.

Children's Defense Fund. *School Suspensions: Are They Helping Children?* Cambridge, MA: Washington Research Project Inc., 1975.

DeCecco, J. P. and A. K. Richards. *Growing Pains: The Uses of School Conflict.* New York: Aberdeen Press, 1974.

Duke, D. L. "How Administrators View the Crises in School Discipline." *Phi Delta Kappan,* pp. 325–330, January 1978.

Empey, L. T. *Explaining Delinquency: Test and Reformulation of a Sociological Theory.* Lexington, MA: D. C. Heath, 1971.

Ernest, K. *Games Students Play.* Millbrae, CA: Celestrial Arts, 231 Adrian Road, Millbrae, CA, 94030, 1972.

"An Evaluative Study of the Social Literacy Program. Laboratory for Psychometric and Evaluative Research. University of Massachusetts, August 1977.

Fishel, A. and J. Potker. "Performance of Women Principals: A Review of Behavioral and Attitudinal Studies." *Journal of NAWDAC,* Vol. 38(3):110–117, 1975.

Freire, P. *Pedagogy of the Oppressed.* New York: Herder and Herder, 1972.

Freire, P. *Cultural Action for Freedom.* Cambridge, MA: Harvard Educational Review Monograph, Series #1, 1970.

Freire, P. *Education for Critical Consciousness.* New York: Seabury Press, 1973.

Freire, P. *Paulo Freire.* Washington, DC: LADOC Keyhole Series, (Undated).

Friedman, M. and R. Rosenman. *Type A Behavior and Your Heart.* New York: Alfred A. Knopf, 1974.

Frymier, J. R., R. E. Bills, J. Russell and C. Finch. "A Study of Oppressive Practices in Schools." Paper presented at the American Educational Research Association in Chicago, April 15, 1974.

Gallup, G. H. "Gallup Opinion Index." Report #66, 1970.

Gallup, G. H. "Ninth Annual Gallup Poll of the Public's Attitudes Towards Public Schools." *Phi Delta Kappan,* Vol. 59(1):33–47, September 1972.

Ginzberg, E. *The Manpower Connection: Education and Work.* New York: Columbia University Press, 1966.

Grantham, M. L. and C. S. Harris. "A Faculty Trains Itself to Improve Student Discipline." *Phi Delta Kappan,* pp. 661–663, June 1976.

Haney, C. and P. G. Zimbardo. "Social Roles, Role Playing and Education: On the High School as Prison." *Behavioral and Social Science Teacher,* Vol. 1:24–25, 1973.

Harris, L. "What People Think About Their High School." *Life Magazine,* Vol. 66(19):22–24, 1969.

Hemphill, J., D. Griffiths and N. Frederickson. *Administrative Performance and Personality: A Study of the Principal in a Simulated Elementary School.* New York: Columbia Teachers College, 1962.

Holmes, T. H. and R. H. Rahe. "The Social Readjustment Rating Scale." *Journal of Psychosomatic Research,* Vol. II, 1967.

Irons, R. B. "Person-blame Vs. System-blame Explanations of School Discipline Conflicts." Unpublished doctoral dissertation of University of Massachusetts, 1975.

Jackson, R. *Life in the Classroom.* New York: Holt Rinehart & Winston, 1968.

Kouin, J. *Discipline and Group Management in Classroom.* New York: Holt, Rinehart & Winston, 1970.

Malcolm X. *The Autobiography of Malcolm X.* New York: Ballantine Books, 1964.

Maslach, C., Johnson, S. "Burned out cops and their families." *Psychology Today,* May 1979, pp. 58–62.

Maslach, C. "Burned Out." *Human Behavior.* pp. 16–22, September 1976.

National Institute of Education. *Violent Schools—Safe Schools: The Safe School Study Report to the Congress.* U. S. Government Printing Office, Washington, DC, 20402, 1978.

Reform of Secondary Education: a report of the national committee on the reform of secondary education. McGraw-Hill Book Co., NY, 1973.

Rhea, B. "Institutional Paternalism in High Schools." *Urban Review,* 2:13–15, 1968.

Roberts, J. M. and B. Sutton-Smith. "Child Training and Game Involvement." *Ethnology,* Vol. 1(2):166–185, 1962.

Segal, E. M. and E. W. Stacey. "Rule-Governed Behavior as a Psychological Process." *American Psychologist,* Vol. 30(5):541–552, 1975.

Smith, W. A. and A. S. Alschuler. "How to Measure Conscientizacao: The C-Code." Available from the authors, 456 Hills South, University of Massachusetts, Amherst, MA, 01003, 1976 ($5.00).

Smith, W. A. "Conscientizacao, An Operational Definition." Unpublished Doctoral Dissertation, University of Massachusetts, 1975.

Swent, B., Smelch, W. "Stress at the desk and how to cope creatively." Oregon School Study Council, 124 College of Education, University of Oregon, Eugene, OR, 97403, 1978.

Sylvester, R. "Stress." *Instructor Magazine,* pp. 72–76, March 1977.

Walding, Faith. "Waiting." *Ms. Magazine,* December 1973.

Index

Achievement tests, 9, 36, 54, 126–128
Activism, 72, 93
Administrators, 23–24, 35, 39, 53–54, 73, 89, 135, 168–169
(*See also* Principals)
Agency for International Development, 4, 10
Alcorn, Alison M., 121*n*.
Alinsky, Saul, 40
Allen, Shawn, 121*n*.
Alschuler, Alfred, 16*n*., 23*n*., 27*n*., 30*n*., 44*n*., 87, 126*n*., 127*n*., 167*n*.
Alternatives, 112–114, 116, 118, 125, 128, 151, 155, 170
Andelin, Helen, 87
Arson, 53
Art classes, 121–122, 125
Association for Supervision and Curriculum, 49
Atkins, Solomon, 23*n*., 177*n*.
Attention, students', 26–28, 38
Authority, 150–151

Barriga, Patricio, 3–5, 10
Basic skills (*see* Problem-solving skills)
Battle fatigue, 132–135
Bayh, Birch, 52–53, 59, 160–161
Beatings, 54, 133
Bell, Lee, 92–93, 98, 165
Berne, E., 30*n*.
Bertram, Bert, 134*n*.
Betkouski, Marianne, 127*n*.
Bills, R. E., 49–50
Blacks, 34–35, 91–92, 101, 127
(*See also* Desegregation)
Blaming, 55–58, 60, 111
Block, Alfred, 53, 133
Block, James, 51*n*.
Bolden, Bernadine, 127*n*.
Boycotting, 29, 51–52
Brayfield, Clotean, 90, 165
Brazil, 10–11, 17–18
Burn-out, 132, 134–135

California, 52, 77, 124–125, 140–141, 160

Campesinos, 4, 6–9, 12, 19–20

Central conflicts (*see* Conflicts)

Cerins, Raymond, 152–153, 165

Chains of command, 75

Children's Defense Fund, 34, 56

Chile, 18–19, 154, 165

Classroom management (*see* Democracy in classroom management)

Classroom problem-solving skills, 147–155

Classroom rules, 36, 40, 42, 50, 69–70, 86–87, 104–105, 112–113, 149–151

Clawson, Thomas, 127*n.*

Commitment, 74–76

Community involvement, 9, 13, 15, 162–164

Competition, 7

Complaints, 144–145

Conflicts, 13–15, 18–19, 21, 23, 48
  analysis of, 27, 38, 85–88, 96, 99–105, 111–114, 147
  not reporting, 54, 93
  patterns of, 108–111, 115, 147, 162–163
  resolving, 38–45, 63–70, 85–88, 96, 114–118, 147, 169, 177
  search for and naming of central, 24–26, 76–81, 85–88, 96, 99–105, 108–111, 147, 154
  tactics of collusion, 53–59
  (*See also* Liberation from conflict)

Connecticut, 42, 90, 92, 111–113, 152, 157, 160–165

Consciousness raising, 83–96, 155

Critical-transforming stage, educational reform, 13, 15–16, 18, 20–21, 68, 85–88, 94–96, 147, 151, 155, 164–165

Curriculum:
  and Freire's method, 17–20
  games as part of, 6–10, 70
  "new," 155

questions about, 10

students' attitudes toward, 25, 50

traditional inputs of, 13, 128, 129

Curtis, John, 134*n.*

Dacus, James, 23*n.,* 177*n.*

Daniels, Lorraine, 127*n.*

Deady, John, 24

DeCecco, J. P., 50

Democracy in classroom management, 44–45, 50–51, 54, 60, 81, 89, 108, 111, 114–116, 118, 144, 147, 151, 153, 155

Depression, 132–133

Desegregation, 23–24, 34–35, 37, 42, 65, 107, 127
  (*See also* Blacks)

Detention, 54

Development, human, 12, 19, 45, 63

Dewey, John, 155

Dialogue:
  and lecturing, 73
  use of, 63–70, 93, 154

DiChiara, Joe, 112–114, 165

Discipline:
  positive, 11
  teachers with most discipline problems, 35, 37–38
  traditional, 9, 44
  (*See also* Conflicts)

Discipline Game, 70, 151, 177–204

Dissertations, 79–80

Domination, 64–65, 67, 69, 78
  (*See also* Oppression)

Drug abuse, 26, 49, 73, 133

Duke, D. L., 52

Ecuador, 3–21, 70, 165

Elmore, Robert, 51*n.*

Empey, L. T., 30*n.*

Erb, Charles, 121*n.*

Ernst, K., 30*n.*

Ethnic relations, 101–103
  (*See also* Blacks; Desegregation)
Existential meaning, 73, 114
Exploitation, objective, 12
Expulsion, 54, 59
Extortion, 54

Faith, 68, 165
Fears, 14
Feminism, 87, 89–90
Fights, 54, 133
Finch, C., 49–50
Fishel, A., 90
Flichum, Betty, 126*n.*, 127
Florida, 126–129
"Forgotten object" game, 30
Formal school rules, 26, 40, 42, 50, 57,
  59, 86–87, 98, 99, 109, 114, 162–
  163
Frederiksen, N., 90
Freire, Paulo, 10–20, 27, 42, 44, 49, 55,
  59–60, 63–64, 67–68, 71–72, 76,
  78, 81, 83, 84*n.*, 86–87, 92–94,
  153–155, 165
Frenzy, 132–133, 135
Friedman, M., 132*n.*
Frustration, 131–132
Frymier, J. R., 49–50
Functional literacy, 4, 9–10, 17, 21

Games:
  Discipline Game, 70, 151, 177–204
  Hacienda Game, 6–10, 20, 70
  as negative part of learning, 28–38,
    51–53
  as positive part of learning, 6–10, 70
Gangs, street, 157–165
Generative words and themes, 19, 21,
  76–78
Ghetto Brothers, 157–164
Ginzberg, E., 89
Goals, socially literate:
  liberation from conflict, 23–45

love as basis for problem solving,
  3–21
rebellion and peace as alternatives,
  47–60
Greek, Jimmy, 127*n.*
Griffiths, J. D., 90
Gustuson, Stephen E., 121*n.*

Habana-Hafner, Sally, 23*n.*
Hacendadas, 4–8, 12, 14, 19
  (*See also* Ecuador)
Hacienda Game, 6–10, 20, 70
Hammond, Rodney, 104–105
Haney, C., 51
Hartford (Conn.), 42, 92, 111–113,
  152, 157, 160–165
Hemphill, J. D., 90
Holmes, T. H., 136
Hope, 68
Hoxeng, Jim, 4, 7, 10, 20
Human development, 12, 19, 45, 63
"Humanistic" (descriptive term), 78,
  81
"Humanness," 94
Humility, 68, 76

Informal rules, 98, 100–101, 108, 111,
  145
Instructional materials, 27–28, 128
Intern teachers, 121–122, 125
Interruptions, 110, 145
Irons, R. Bruce, 23*n.*, 64*n.*, 65

Jackson, R., 50
Jacksonville (Fla.), 126–129
Johnson, S., 134
Juvenile delinquency, 56

Keenan, Donna, 127*n.*
Kiernam, Owen B., 52
Kounin, Jacob, 28*n.*

Lapid, Ginger, 77, 103*n.*
Lateness, 29, 52, 59
Learning time, 27–28, 51, 97, 110, 128
Lecturing, 73, 107
Liberation from conflict, 23–45, 97–105, 165
 ethnic relations and, 101–103
 feminism and, 87, 89–90
Life tests, 9
Literacy:
 functional, 4, 9–10, 17, 21
 with numbers, 4, 21, 127, 129
 social (*see* Social Literacy)
Loomis, Lou, 147–151, 153, 165
Los Angeles (Calif.), 160
Love, 11–13, 15, 21, 23, 36, 49, 60, 63–64, 67, 85, 115, 165

McIntyre, J., 167*n.*
McMullen, Ronald, 23*n.*
Magical-conforming stage, educational reform, 13–14, 16–17, 55, 85–88, 93
Mainstreaming, 41, 121–129
Malcolm X, 91–92
Maslach, C., 134, 144
Masochism, 64–65
Mason, Gary, 140*n.*
Massachusetts, 23, 41, 111–112, 152, 165
Merwin, William, 127*n.*
Methods, socially literate:
 consciousness raising, 83–96
 guides for survival and liberation, 97–105
 mainstreaming, 121–129
 nuclear problem solving, 107–119
 overcoming stress, 131–146
 problem solving in the classroom, 147–155
 problem solving in a street gang, 157–165
 use of dialogue, 63–70
 use of words, 71–81

"Milling" game, 31–33, 110–111
"Missing object" game, 30
Motivation, 9–10
Mutually Agreed-upon Learning Time (MALT), 27–29

Naive-reforming stage, educational reform, 13–17, 59, 85–88, 90–93
National Institute of Education, 51, 53, 59
Neurzer, Laurie Rose, 121*n.*
"New" curriculum, 155
New York, 52
Norms, 38, 109
Nuclear problem solving, 107–119, 126, 144, 147, 151
Numeracy, 4, 21, 127, 129

Objective exploitation, 12
Office of Education, U.S., 42, 158
Oppression, 11–15, 19, 21, 27, 38, 54, 58–60, 83–84, 97
 developing consciousness of, 84–87, 92, 153
 of students, 44, 49–51, 99, 150
 (*See also* Domination)
Oregon, 141

Paraprofessionals, 84–86
Parents, 54, 60, 89
"Passing out" game, 30
"Pet" students, 27, 33
Police, 54, 59
Positive discipline, 11
Potker, J., 90
Principals, 36–38, 40, 47–48, 53, 55, 90, 178*n.*
 (*See also* Administrators)
Problem-posing education, 153–155, 158
Problem-solving skills:
 in the classroom, 147–155

effects of socially literate, 43–45
Freire's method of, 4, 10, 13–21, 85
nuclear, 107–119, 126, 144, 147, 151
in a street gang, 157–165
Public address (P.A.) systems, 41, 73, 145
Puerto Ricans, 101, 158–165
Punishments, 12, 29–30, 34–36, 58, 69, 73

Questions:
about curriculum, 10
right to ask, 6–9, 15
techniques for questioning, 128

Racism, 34
(*See also* Blacks; Desegregation; Ethnic relations)
Rahe, R. H., 136
Rebel students, 27, 33, 36, 51, 54–57, 60
Recordkeeping, 74, 108, 118–119, 148
Referrals, 33–34, 40, 44, 58, 107, 127, 129
Reinforcement, 12, 29–30, 105
Rewards, 12, 29–30, 105
Rhea, B., 51
Richards, A. K., 50
Roberts, J. M., 30n.
Robinson, Andrew, 127
Roles and role playing, 7, 9, 20, 34, 38, 40–42, 45, 59, 86–87, 103–104, 108, 111–113, 115, 145, 164
of teachers, 10, 14, 47
Rosenman, R., 132n.
Rules:
classroom, 36, 40, 42, 50, 69–70, 86–87, 104–105, 112–113, 149–151
informal, 98, 100–101, 108, 111, 145
school (formal), 26, 40, 42, 50, 57, 59, 86–87, 98, 99, 109, 114, 162–163
"war game," 32–34, 38
Russell, J., 49–50

Sadism, 64–65
Sang, Herbert, 126–127
Santa Barbara (Calif.), 77, 124–125, 140–141
Santiago-Wolpow, Nellie, 23n., 138n., 177n.
Sarcasm, 67
Sartorius, Tara, 121–122, 124, 165
Schmohl, Suzanne, 121n.
School boards, 54, 76
School violence, 13, 26, 35, 47–49, 52–56, 59, 157
Schools, physical security of, 59
"Secret message" game, 30
Segal, E. M., 30n.
Self-affirmation, 12–13, 21, 85
Self-deprecation, 91
Self-discipline, 27
Senate, U.S., 52, 160
Sex roles, 103–104
(*See also* Women)
Sexism, 41
Shea, John, 24
Singletary, Rochelle, 92–93, 165
Skills (*see* Problem-solving skills)
Skipping class, 52
Smelch, Walter, 141
Smith, William, 16n., 87
Social Literacy, 21, 36, 38–45, 76, 81, 108, 115, 151, 165, 168, 170, 177
goals (*see* Goals, socially literate)
methods (*see* Methods, socially literate)
Social Literacy groups, 40–41, 90, 92–96, 97–98, 108, 111, 117, 123–124, 138–139, 141, 144, 147, 151, 158, 161, 167–176
Social Literacy Institute, 158
Socratic method, 73
Soldwedel, Bette, 127n.
Special education, 41, 121–129
Sponagle, Elizabeth, 121n.
Springfield (Mass.), 23–27, 34–35, 40, 42, 111–112, 152, 165
Stacey, E. W., 30n.

Stoddard, Ann, 127*n.*
Stopsky, Fred, 138*n.*
Street gangs, 157–165
Stress, 131–146, 149
Students:
  attention of, 26–28, 38
  attitude toward curriculum, 25, 50
  backgrounds of, 32–33
  behavior of, 30*n.,* 32–33, 36, 109,
    148–150
  blaming, 55–58, 60, 111
  involved in making rules, 105, 112,
    149–151
  not reporting conflicts, 54
  oppression of, 44, 49–51, 99, 150
  "pets," 27, 33
  rebels, 27, 33, 36, 51, 54–57, 60
  relationship with teachers, 10, 12–
    13, 17, 20, 28–38, 44, 48, 70, 109
  and stress, 135, 140–141
  suspensions of, 26–27, 34–35, 37–
    38, 52, 54, 56, 59
  tactics of, 29, 51–52
  and violations of rules, 26
  violent, 51, 157
  wanting to learn, 98
Substitute teachers, 97–98
Survival, 97–105
Suspensions, 26–27, 34–35, 37–38, 52,
  54, 56, 59
Sutton-Smith, B., 30*n.*
Swent, Boyd, 141
Sylvester, R., 53
"System, the," 90–92, 108, 115–116,
  151

Tabor, D., 167*n.*
Tardiness, 29, 52, 59
"Target shooting" game, 30
Tasiguano, Enrique, 4, 6–10, 12, 14,
  19–20, 158, 165
Teachers:
  collective action by, 39–41, 44–45,
    151

intern, 121–122, 125
with most discipline problems, 35,
  37–38
not reporting conflicts, 54, 93
in pairs, 44, 108, 118
relationship with students, 10, 12–
  13, 17, 20, 28–38, 44, 48, 70, 108
role of, 10, 14, 47
and socially literate problem solving, 40–44
and special education, 121–125
and stress, 131–146
substitute, 97–98
suggested assumptions by, 39
tactics of, 29–30, 40–41
violence inflicted on, 52–53, 133,
  157
women as, 89
Team teaching, 44
Television, 54
Tests:
  achievement, 9, 36, 54, 126–128
  life, 9
Theft, 53–54, 133
Themes, generative, 19, 21, 76–78
Threadcraft, Milton, 127
Tillman, Ann, 127*n.*
Torres, Calixto, 157–165
Traditional curriculum, 13, 128, 129
Traditional discipline, 9, 44
Transforming the world, 71–73, 75,
  93, 97, 147, 151, 164–165
Truancy, 52, 54, 59
Trust, 68
Truth and "true words," 71–81, 154

United Nations (U.N.), 4
U.S. Office of Education, 42, 158
U.S. Senate, 52, 160
University of Massachusetts, School of
  Education, 6, 16*n.,* 23, 27*n.,* 77–
  78, 90
University of North Florida, School of
  Education, 127–128

Van Vlack, Milt, 110, 165
Van Wart, Robert, 42*n.*
Vandalism, 26, 35, 49, 52–54, 56, 59,
   133
Verbalism, 72, 93
Vietnam War, 54–55
Violence:
   cycles of, 55–56, 157
   inflicted on teachers, 52–53, 133,
      157
   school, 13, 26, 35, 47–49, 52–56, 59,
      157
   and street gangs, 157–165
   students who cause, 51, 157
   on television, 54
Vocabulary, 19, 77

"War games," 28–38, 51–53

Watergate scandal, 54, 74
Weapons, 53, 133
Weighted Student Unit (WSU), 123–
   125
Women, 87, 89–90
   (*See also* Sex roles; Sexism)
Words, use of, 71–81
   generative, 19, 21, 76–78
   "true," 71–81, 154
Workshops, 41, 43, 90, 98

Young, Wynn, 111–112, 114, 165

Zarate, Lea, 121*n.*
Zide, Michele Moran, 23*n.*
Zimbardo, P. G., 51

About the Author

ALFRED S. ALSCHULER is professor of education at the University of Massachusetts. Since receiving his doctorate in clinical psychology at Harvard University, he has taught at several major universities, including the University of California at Santa Barbara and the State University of New York at Albany. Dr. Alschuler has conducted over 100 workshops on school discipline in 19 states and 4 foreign countries. Descriptions of his work have appeared in several major educational journals, and recently he received an honorary doctorate of humane letters from John F. Kennedy University for his efforts toward reducing classroom violence.

DATE DUE
REMINDER

JAN 04 '96

OCT 23 '96

NOV 2 3 2001

Please do not remove
this date due slip.